GO INSIDE THE MIND OF A DETECTIVE PURSUING THE MOST DANGEROUS CRIMINAL ON THE STREETS— A SERIAL KILLER . . .

On August 26, 1997, two bodies were found in separate places in Spokane, Washington. In the following months, another eight bodies were discovered—all drug addicts and prostitutes who had worked Spokane's red-light district.

The police wouldn't even consider the idea of a "serial killer." No one—not the media or the town's political leadership—spoke up. Because the victims came from the wrong side of town, "respectable" Spokane didn't seem to care that a brutal psychopath lived among them and that as many as eighteen women died by his hand.

Until Mark Fuhrman took on the case, working parallel with the Spokane Task Force. But it was only after the serial killer began to play with the police—planting bodies for attention and escalating the murders—did an intense effort go forward, resulting in the arrest of a brutal killer.

Also by Mark Fuhrman

MURDER IN BRENTWOOD
MURDER IN GREENWICH

MARK FUHRMAN

MURDER IN SPOKANE

AVON BOOKS
An Imprint of HarperCollinsPublishers

AVON BOOKS
An Imprint of HarperCollins*Publishers*
10 East 53rd Street
New York, New York 10022-5299

First Avon Books paperback printing: May 2002
First Cliff Street Books hardcover printing: June 2001

Avon Trademark Reg. U.S. Pat. Off. and in Other Countries, Marca
Registrada, Hecho en U.S.A.
HarperCollins ® is a registered trademark of HarperCollins Publishers
Inc.

Printed in the U.S.A.

10 9 8 7 6 5 4 3 2 1

CONTENTS

ACKNOWLEDGMENTS

The author would like to thank the following people, without whom this book would not be possible:

Stephen Weeks—A close friend and business partner. Steve helped me investigate and write this book, as he did the two previous. Now he's going to help with my new consulting business.

Mike Fitzsimmons—He was a great mentor, detective partner, and friend. Mike was on the serial killer case from the beginning and with me every step of the way. He also gave me the opportunity and the support I needed to make a career in radio.

Nina Rosenstand—A loyal listener and friend. Nina's help was essential to this book. Her organizational skills and attention to detail are second to none—she proves that a professor doesn't have to be absentminded. I look forward to Nina's calls each week.

MURDER IN
SPOKANE

CHAPTER 1

A Killer in My Backyard

You never forget what a dead body smells like. The stink of decomposing flesh. That retching, putrid stench that seems to penetrate right through your skin. That sticks to your clothing and clings to the hairs in your nose. That stays with you long after the body is bagged up and taken to the coroner's. Even after you've gone home and changed your clothes and taken a shower and sprinkled yourself with cologne, the stench still lingers.

That afternoon, I smelled it again. At first, I thought it was just my imagination, but the smell wouldn't go away.

I was stuck in traffic on my way to do a radio show in Spokane, Washington. Mike Fitzsimmons had asked me to be guest host on his program at KXLY 920 AM. He wanted to talk about a serial killer preying on prostitutes in Spokane.

On August 26, 1997, two prostitutes had been found shot to death in separate locations. Both the bodies were severely decomposed. One of them, Jennifer Joseph, was found in a hayfield. I remembered the heat that accompanied hay season, and imagined what that crime scene must have smelled like. I could see and hear the swarming flies. The farmers who found her were probably not unaccustomed to violent death, but they were no doubt sickened by seeing it take human form.

What were the chances that two different women would be shot and dumped and found on the same day? In a city like Los Angeles, where there are three homicides a day, it might just be a coincidence. Spokane was too small for co-incidences like that one. No, Spokane had a serial killer, and he was probably just getting started. Then I caught myself thinking that it wasn't just their problem, it was mine. The serial killer was practically in my backyard.

There's something about the Pacific Northwest that seems to breed serial killers. John Douglas, the famous FBI profiler, once called the region "America's killing fields." Cities like Seattle, Portland, and Vancouver offer a serial killer a victim pool to select from and give him a crowd to hide in. People are more friendly and trusting here. The surrounding wilderness makes it easy to hide bodies and almost impossible to find them. The weather—weeks on end of dreary rain punctuated by rare, brilliant days— probably has something to do with it. Or the fact that this is where the frontier ends, and America literally runs out of room.

Spokane is a little different. It's three hundred miles from the Pacific Ocean. Local boosters call it the Capital of the Inland Empire. The terrain is a mix of high plains and mountains. The weather is drier, hotter in the summer and colder in the winter, without the long, depressing rains. The city itself is much smaller than Seattle or even Portland. And there is something about Spokane—it isn't in-nocence, more like spoiled provinciality. A lot of the problems of big-city life hadn't reached the citizens of Spokane yet, or so they thought.

Well, now they had a serial killer.

I wondered how long the Spokane serial killer had been working. I wondered what he did to his victims, whether he was slick and sophisticated, or crude and frenzied. I wondered how many victims he had already killed. How many had not even been found. Women killed and dumped and rotting somewhere deep in the wilderness.

It's just a ninety-mile drive to Spokane from my home in Sandpoint, Idaho. In this part of the country, that's an easy commute. Sometimes it can take several hours, depending on the weather and the road conditions. This was September, one of the hottest days of the year. The sky was clear and the roads were dry, but the traffic was backed up for at least a mile.

The line of cars extended as far as I could see. After twenty years in Los Angeles, I retire, move up to northern Idaho, and find myself in another traffic jam. Go figure. At least the landscape was more scenic than, say, Sepulveda Boulevard. I looked out at Cocallala Lake and watched a fisherman trolling slowly by.

In the distance I heard a siren. Looking in the rearview mirror, I saw the lights of a paramedic truck. It passed in the other lane, siren wailing. Then the familiar whomp-whomp-whomp of helicopter blades cutting through the air. An Air-Med chopper passed overhead.

Must be a pretty bad accident, I thought. I rolled down the window to see if I could get a better look ahead.

That's when the smell really hit me. It was thick, choking, and unmistakable. The stench of rotting flesh. And it wasn't my imagination. I had to see what it was.

I got out of my truck and walked along the opposite side of the road. The smell grew stronger. Just a few yards into the tree line I found the victim. It was just a deer fawn that had been struck by a car and limped off onto the right-of-way to die. The fawn had been there for a couple days; her internal organs lay open, rotting and covered with insects. Between the heat and the bugs and the predators, it wouldn't take long until there was little more than a skeleton. Death is just nature's way of taking us back.

Having worked as a homicide detective, I tend to look at death from a detached perspective. Other people seeing a mangled, decomposing deer carcass might be sickened or fascinated. I was trying to figure out where the fawn was hit, which injury was fatal, how long it had been there.

Before I could even come to preliminary conclusions, I heard engines start and car doors close. The traffic was beginning to move up ahead. I ran back to my truck and started it up. As I passed the car accident, I saw that a BMW had crossed the center line and crashed head-on into a truck. From the look of the Beemer, the accident had been fatal. The helicopter would just be picking up the bodies.

As I pulled onto I-90 and hit cruising speed, I tried to concentrate on the radio show. A book I was reading, *Sexual Homicide* by the FBI's Robert Ressler and John Douglas, lay on the passenger seat. When I had stopped for gas that morning at Payless, Arnie asked me, "Read any good books lately?" I showed him *Sexual Homicide*.

"Not exactly beach reading, is it?" Arnie said.

Not exactly. Most people like their morbid curiosity satisfied by a tidy little story. Something they can handle, where the crimes are committed against people they don't know and the killer is caught in the end and justice triumphs over evil once again. I knew real life wasn't like that.

Four years ago, I had stood over the remains of what had once been two living, breathing human beings. The world became fascinated by their deaths, and that fascination threw everything out of whack. For all the countless hours of television coverage and commentary, the acres and acres of newsprint spent on the Simpson case, I wish that people had been able to see what I saw.

About 4:30 in the morning of June 12, 1994, the sun began to rise on the Bundy crime scene. I could see Ron

Goldman's blood spattered all over the foliage. The earth was soaked dark with his blood, as if somebody had dumped a gallon of syrup on the ground. The walkway was a thick stream of blood, smeared with footprints and paw prints. I had to be careful stepping over Nicole's body. She was crumpled and bloodless, stiffening with rigor mortis. She was wearing a short, black cocktail dress; her bare feet were clean. Her fists were clenched, her fingers bloody with defensive wounds. She had known death was coming, and she fought it, and she suffered.

Death is unforgiving. It shows no consideration for the young or the beautiful. Bodies cast aside in city alleys or dumped on country roads take the same course. The indignity of murder does not end in death itself. The victim suffers further degradation by the weather, insects, and animal predators.

You never see that on television. You never see how a murder victim's bladder and sphincter open uncontrollably. You never see, or smell, the other puddles of body fluids that spill and splatter when the corpse is moved. You never smell the sweet scent of coagulated blood. You never hear the irritating buzz of hovering flies. You never feel the tear of rotting flesh falling away from bone as police officers help the deputy coroner load decomposed remains into a body bag. You never see the blood and tissue splattering on their shoes. You never see the maggots that fall from the corpse.

There's nothing glamorous about being a homicide detective. You may wear a suit and tie, but that's about the only thing you have in common with other professionals. The hours are brutal—long and erratic. The work conditions can literally kill you. Depression is almost a refreshing state of mind in contrast to the brutal reality of your job. Murder—it isn't sexy, it isn't cool. It's just ugly and cruel and wasteful. Someone's got to clean up after it. And once you do something like this for a living, it can get hold of you and never let go.

Each homicide is a puzzle. Some are easy to put together. Others are nearly impossible. But every single homicide can be solved, if only you ask the right questions. After you've investigated homicides for a living, it's tough to do anything else. Besides, you owe it to society to exercise your talents as they can best be used. What could be more useful than helping solve a serial killer case?

The textbook definition of a serial killer is a sexual psychopath who kills three people or more with a cooling-off period in between. The cooling-off periods can range from days to weeks to years. The serial killer has a deeply ingrained psychic need to kill. He is aware of his criminality and conscious of his actions. He might not remember every single detail, but he is certainly aware of what he has done. He has no remorse.

That pathological need in the serial killer is sexual in nature. The serial killer derives sexual pleasure from what he does to his victims either before or after death (torture, necrophilia) or the very act of killing itself. For this reason, serial killers are often referred to as sexual psychopaths.

The serial killer is as evil as evil there is. He can appear to be as normal as your next-door neighbor. He is often highly intelligent with above-average social skills. His acts are premeditated, organized. He plans and fantasizes before he commits his crimes, and he does everything he can to hide his identity or any connection with the victim. Often, the only evidence he leaves at the crime scene is evidence he wants the police to see. He doesn't want to get caught. He enjoys killing, and he wants to keep doing it.

With each capture and kill, the serial murderer gets better at what he does, honing his skills as he goes along, learning what he likes and what he doesn't. He often keeps souvenirs or trophies of his victims, so he can relive the event again. Some will revisit grave sites and have sex with their dead victims, or masturbate over their rotting bodies, remembering what they did to their victims and bringing the fantasy, at least, back to life.

As the serial killer becomes more proficient, he also becomes more active. The thrill doesn't last as long as it used to. His cooling-off periods become shorter and shorter. He has to kill more frequently. Meanwhile, the police have mounted a massive investigation, into which he often will try to insert himself. We find that many serial killers are fascinated with law enforcement. Some of them have worked as emergency personnel or security guards. These interests make it easier for them to blend into a crime scene or a cop bar. Many detectives have interviewed the killer at the scene, only they didn't know it. Others have engaged the killer in conversation at a bar or some other public place, where he has learned a lot more about the investigation than the investigators know about him. In most serial killer cases, the suspect has been in the task force's database almost from the beginning.

Serial killers have always been with us, but beginning in the 1960s and 1970s, we started seeing a lot more of them. Whether that's because there were more serial killers, or we finally began to notice them, I'm not sure. In a series of high-profile cases like Son of Sam, Ted Bundy, and John Wayne Gacy, the public became aware of the heinous crimes committed by serial sexual psychopaths.

The Bundy case was a real shock for many people, particularly once Ted Bundy was apprehended and identified as the killer. People couldn't believe that someone so bright, articulate, good-looking, and sophisticated could be responsible for the deaths of more than twenty-five young women. The Bundy case also demonstrated how hard it is to catch a serial murderer. And it got me thinking that there were probably a whole lot more Ted Bundys out there, who had just never gotten caught.

How can any law enforcement agency capture a killer who is as intelligent as Bundy, particularly when he chooses victims who have no connection to him, and he leaves virtually no evidence? Indeed, many of Bundy's victims haven't been found to this day. Given all these conditions, it's a wonder that any serial killer is ever caught.

They usually aren't. More often than not, serial killer investigations end in failure. The few times they do succeed, it's usually by accident. Very, very few serial murders are solved as the result of good old-fashioned shoe-leather detective work. Instead, what usually happens is that the killer makes a mistake, gets sloppy and careless, or the violence escalates and he loses control.

I wondered if the Spokane serial killer would ever be caught. Or if he would just move on and kill elsewhere. I wondered how he would rate on the ghoul meter. Whether he might rank up there with some of the most famous serial killers or be just another vicious psycho.

Soon the city of Spokane came into view. There's no skyline, just the drab industrial outskirts of a small city— junkyards, railroad tracks, a bunch of dingy warehouses. I pulled off at the Sprague exit and drove down the strip, where the murdered women had been working.

Spokane is the biggest city between Minneapolis and Seattle. It is the place where residents of smaller towns and cities often come for things they can't find at home, including prostitutes. The red-light district is a stretch of Sprague Avenue on the east end of town. To the north are the city's railyards, where transients camp out on their way into or out of town. The Union Gospel Mission is nearby. To the south is Interstate 90, a major thoroughfare for the Pacific Northwest.

Sprague Avenue was once the pride of Spokane, the

city's Miracle Mile and most traveled road. Once the interstate was built and businesses began sprawling outside city limits, Sprague fell on hard times.

The city's vice district was originally in the seedy riverfront neighborhood right downtown. As Spokane prepared to host the 1974 world's fair, the town leaders decided that the downtown area had to be cleaned up for the visitors. Through a combination of urban development and police pressure, the prostitutes and vagrants who once inhabited downtown were pushed out to East Sprague.

Now Sprague Avenue is a collection of liquor stores, pawnshops, and hourly rate motels. There's the local Hell's Angels chapter. The Outlaw Diner. The Hitching Post Bar. Zip's Hamburgers. A couple of XXX video stores. A strip club. Kmart. A "family restaurant" that seems strangely out of place.

This was the serial killer's hunting grounds. Where the girls were. Driving down the street, hidden behind my sunglasses, I looked closely at the few people hanging out on street corners. Even on this hot September afternoon, a couple of prostitutes were out working in their shorts and tank tops. A drug dealer standing on the corner outside the grocery store. A couple more prostitutes pretending to wait for a bus. The usual assortment of losers and washouts and lost souls.

Once you've been a cop, you never look at people the same. You've learned to distinguish the dangerous from the merely pathetic, the leaders from the sheep. You read their clothes, their hair, most of all their eyes. Even at fifty feet, I could smell them. Body odor. Unwashed clothes. Bad breath from cigarettes and greasy food and rotting teeth. I could hear their voices, telling lies that they don't even expect you to believe. Running some con. Hoping to find some way to another cold forty-ounce, help get them through the day.

Yeah, police work is real sexy.

And the killer was here, somewhere. I wondered if he was in one of the cars in front of me, trolling for a new victim, or just cruising East Sprague. I wondered if the girls at the bus stop knew someone was hunting them. I wondered if they had already talked to him, if he was one of their regular tricks.

Every city has its Sprague Strip. Los Angeles had a bunch of them. It's the place where all the dirty little secrets come out of hiding. Crime, drugs, gambling, porno, prostitution. I could have been at Third and Main in LA eighteen years ago when I walked a foot beat on Skid Row. The only thing different was that here on East Sprague, there wasn't a single police officer to be found. No patrol cars. No foot cops. Not even a meter maid.

I wondered if they had cops working undercover, or at least video surveillance. Something. Because this is where everything was happening. It's where the cops should have been.

I didn't know anything about Spokane back then. I figured they were on the job, that I just didn't see them.

CHAPTER 2

On The Air

It all started with a phone call from Mike Fitzsimmons, a local radio talk show host. Mike had an idea he wanted to bounce off me. So we made plans to meet at Shari's Restaurant on Northwest Boulevard in Spokane. That morning I arrived early, a habit I can't seem to break. Sitting at my table facing the front door, I waited for him.

I had been on Mike's show on KXLY 920 AM several times before, but they were all phone-ins from home. Even though I had never met Mike face to face, I already knew him well. On the radio, Mike has a deep, rolling voice. He is very articulate and talks with a bit of a folksy twang.

I recognized Mike as soon as he walked in. He looked just as I had pictured him. A big man, average in appearance, exceedingly normal. Someone whom people would describe as wholesome more than handsome. Genuine more than nice. Honest more than slick. A workaholic family man and devout Catholic.

He already knew what I looked like. As we shook hands, I was struck by his warmth and his confidence. Here was somebody who knew who he was. He was friendly, but there was a strength behind his good nature.

Mike quickly got down to business. He told me how

much he enjoyed having me as a guest and asked if I would be interested in cohosting a series of radio shows.

I was definitely interested as long as Mike could accommodate my work and family schedule. He said that he would.

"And if these guest spots work out," Mike smiled, as if he already knew that they would, "how would you like to cohost a weekly show with me?"

By then, I had already received several offers for regular radio and television appearances, but this was the one media job I could work into the new life I was building for my family up in Idaho. I preferred radio to television, since it gave you more time to go in depth and you don't have to wear makeup. Although I had made friends in the media during my book tour, I really liked and trusted Mike Fitzsimmons.

Our shows would focus on crime and related issues. I felt much more comfortable discussing something in my field of expertise, instead of commenting on politics, where my opinion was no more informed than anyone else's. I wanted to put the knowledge I gained during my twenty years of law enforcement—and the hard lessons I learned during the Simpson trial about high-profile crime, the media, power and money—to use in a media outlet that would allow me to focus on what I knew best. I wanted to be able to make a difference, continuing my new career as a nonfiction author and a radio host.

KXLY News Radio 920 is a 5,000-watt AM talk-news station located in downtown Spokane. The ABC television affiliate and four FM radio stations are located in the broadcast complex.

Although I had grown up in Washington State, I was not very familiar with Spokane, but since the Inland Northwest was now my new home, I was eager to get involved. Mike called Spokane "a really big small town." The city population is just under 190,000, while the metro area numbers about 300,000. Residents often brag that Spokane is a nice place to raise a family. Crime rates and the cost of living are both low. Although the development is sprawling outside city limits, the surrounding areas are still relatively undeveloped, with some beautiful wilderness nearby.

The overall crime levels are low, and the homicide clearance rates are above the national average (homicide cases are considered cleared when there is evidence identifying a suspect, whether or not that suspect is successfully prosecuted). One crime category stuck out. A series of at least ten prostitute homicides dating back to 1984 remained unsolved. Three of these homicides occurred in 1990 and were attributed to a serial killer, who had never been apprehended. The two bodies dumped in late August 1997 seemed to indicate that either that killer was back, or another serial killer was preying on Spokane prostitutes.

Mike wanted to take a close look at the unsolved prostitute homicides. He had been frustrated by what he saw as public apathy toward these murders. He knew that if the victims had been more affluent or of a higher social standing, the police would have tried harder and probably succeeded in solving the cases. Since they were prostitutes, few people really cared. Mike believed that if more information was made available to the public, more pressure would be brought to bear upon local law enforcement and politicians. He hoped that pressure would help to get the cases solved.

In the fall of 1997, I was in the middle of writing *Murder in Greenwich*. The investigation I conducted with Stephen Weeks showed me what an experienced homicide detective can do working as an author, without a badge or a gun. Even though the Moxley case had been investigated by countless police officers, detectives, private investigators, and journalists, none of them had been able to solve the case.

The Moxley case also got me thinking about all the other unsolved homicides, the ones that didn't involve pretty blond teenagers and Kennedy cousins. From my work on cold case files as an LAPD detective, I knew that there were many different reasons why homicides go unsolved—insufficient evidence, intimidated witnesses, lack of resources, the detectives being pulled away on other work, and so on. The one reason I wouldn't accept, and was unfortunately evident in many of the unsolved cases I reviewed, was indifference on the part of the investigating detectives.

Apathy is unacceptable. If you're going to be a homicide detective, you have to be committed to solving every case, not just the ones that are easy or glamorous. The homicide detective has to answer for the deceased, and each murder victim deserves justice. All homicide cases—no matter if the victim is a street prostitute or a White House lawyer—should be treated with the same level of thoroughness and commitment.

While I was writing a book about a singular homicide in Greenwich, Connecticut, from nearly a quarter century ago, a series of grisly murders were being committed virtually in my backyard. Yet these murders were not attracting the attention of even the local media. Whenever a body was found, the local newspapers and television news programs would cover the story, but there was no follow-up and no investigation.

I've learned a great deal about the news media in the last five years, good and bad. When working the way they should, the news media do two things: they keep officials honest, and they provide useful information to the public.

As a detective, I had often used the media to disseminate information I thought might help smoke out a suspect or generate useful clues. I hoped that local law enforcement would be able to use my radio show the same way.

I worked as a cop for twenty years. This gives me a perspective that few journalists have. Not only do I have expertise in processing crime scenes, gathering clues, analyzing evidence, interviewing witnesses, interrogating suspects, attending autopsies, writing search warrants and arrest affidavits, and the thousand other responsibilities that come with being a detective, I also have the values and mind-set of a cop. I share the sense of duty, commitment, and loyalty that all good cops have. I'm still a cop at heart.

Starting out as a journalist, I wanted to do things differently. Over the years, and particularly during the Simpson case, I had seen how crime reporters got it wrong, either intentionally or unintentionally. Some reporters were the victims of spin. Others knew that they were being used by their sources. As long as it got them a good story, they didn't care. Very few of them understood the true nature of a homicide investigation. Some of them were ignorant or lazy or both. Others just didn't like cops. And there were some who, despite all their best intentions, simply didn't get it.

As the public grows increasingly interested in high-profile murder cases, the role of the media becomes more complex and more problematic. Lately, too many cases have gone sideways because of high-intensity media coverage. I felt, as an experienced homicide detective with a public platform, I could help the good guys. I wanted to work closely with law enforcement—sitting on information that they needed to keep secret, disseminating facts that might provide a break in the case. I assumed that my experience, my loyalty to the job, and all I had endured during the Simpson case would make it easier for law enforcement to work with me.

During the investigation of the Moxley case, local law

enforcement did all they could to frustrate my efforts to get to the truth. Once I had discovered a pattern of police incompetence and cover-ups, I understood why they were so reluctant to work with me. The Greenwich police had seriously bungled the Moxley investigation, and they knew it. They didn't want to be embarrassed by some big-city detective coming in and showing them how easy a case it actually was. It was an easy case; any experienced and determined homicide detective could have solved the Moxley murder within a week.

Thinking that the problems I ran into in Greenwich were just a localized response, I wanted a case in which I could work closely with law enforcement and maybe help them solve a case. I thought that everybody in Spokane would want these murders to be solved, but the apathy concerning these cases was pervasive. One day, my wife was on an airplane returning from a trip back East. Sitting next to her was a young woman from Spokane. They started talking, and my wife brought up the serial killer.

"Who cares?" the young woman said. "He's just killing prostitutes."

My wife was speechless. And so was I when she told me about it. I couldn't understand the attitude of that young woman. And I hoped the police didn't share it.

During a public meeting held at the height of the serial killer case, Carol Taylor, a resident of East Sprague, according to the *Spokane Spokesman-Review*, complained: "You can go out in the daytime and you can see the drug runners back and forth on the street. Why aren't they being picked up? . . .

"The prostitutes are having sex in our front yards," Carol Taylor said. She further stated that she didn't care how it happened, she just wanted the prostitutes off her street. "I feel sorry for these prostitutes being killed. But at least something is being done about it."

When a serial killer is out there, no matter who he's choosing for victims, the police have to rise to the challenge. Ever since I was a young patrolman, I dreamed of being part of a serial killer investigation. It's the greatest challenge of police work. Not only are the investigative difficulties immense, and sometimes overwhelming, but the responsibility of answering for the dead victims and stopping the serial murderer before he kills again are challenges that any dedicated cop should rise to meet.

Working a serial killer case is like the World Series of homicide investigation. It's the greatest measure of true investigative skill and imagination. The serial killer and the detective assigned to catch him are brought together by circumstance, the luck of a duty rotation, the fact that the detective was home when the phone rang, that he was the first one at the crime scene. However he gets the assignment, once the game is on, the detective has to give it his all. The serial killer and the homicide detective, whose job it is to catch him, develop a relationship, not unlike the hunter and his prey. Sometimes it's hard to figure out who's hunting whom.

Police officers on the whole are decent people, with families and hobbies, and all the attributes of normal life. Unfortunately, that's the very reason so many find it difficult to get into the mind of a killer. They're repulsed by his actions. They feel that he's sick—and they're right. But their reaction is beside the point. Too many law enforcement officers won't go beyond the boundaries of their own normality to enter the world of the abnormal, where they often have to work.

At the crime scene, you have to get into the killer's head, imagine what he's doing, and how he's doing it. A crime scene is telling you something, if only you listen to the evidence that is there. And every crime scene has evidence, if you know what to look for. Whenever a crime is committed, the suspect leaves evidence at the scene, and he takes evidence from the scene with him. No matter how meticulous and cunning a criminal is, he's going to leave clues. The smarter the suspect, the fewer the clues. But they're always there.

The challenge of interpreting the crime scene of a serial murder is greater not only because of the lack of connection between the suspect and victim and the apparent lack of evidence left by the suspect, but also because of what is done there. The detective has to make some sense of bizarre, sadistic acts that are incomprehensible to most people. When you see a beautiful young woman with her breasts mutilated and foreign objects jammed into her vagina, how do you make sense of that? It's the detective's job not to understand the violence in terms of motive, but to re-create the movements and actions of the suspect. This isn't possible without an act of imagination that is as frightening as it is necessary. The detective has to place him- or herself in the killer's shoes and walk through the scene, trying to figure out how and when he committed these acts of horrible brutality.

The detective has to think the unthinkable—to see the crime scene and the victim as the killer did. That's what I tried to do from the beginning.

Armed with only the information that was already public record (evidence described in news reports, press releases, and death certificates), Mike's insider knowledge of the city and its players, and my experience as a homicide detective, we went out and worked the prostitute murders as if they were our case. Mike was the journalist, I was the cop. Over the course of our investigation, that changed. Mike became a detective, and I became a journalist.

Mike was the perfect guide and mentor. He's a veteran Spokane newsman, having worked in the local media for thirty years. He went to Gonzaga Law School, but instead of practicing law, he started working for a local news station. The legal profession might have lost an honest man, but the city of Spokane gained one hell of a journalist.

"You know why you didn't become a lawyer?" I asked Mike one day over lunch.

"Why?"

"Because your parents were married."

He responded with a hearty laugh.

Mike is as normal as they come. He married his college sweetheart and raised three great kids. He is stable, dedicated, and moral. In many ways, he resembles a typical father from a 1950s sitcom.

The more I got to know Mike, the more I realized how that stereotype fell short. You'd never see Ozzie Nelson or Robert Young rooting around at the scene of a recent homicide. He had a toughness that his easy manner often hid.

Soon Mike and I started spending Thursday afternoons on the air, talking *All About Crime*.

CHAPTER 3

The 1990 Murders

Yolanda Sapp, age 26. Body found February 22, 1990, dumped on an embankment along the Spokane River near 4100 East Upriver Drive. Cause of death: gunshot wounds to upper body.

Nickie Lowe, age 34. Body found March 25, 1990, draped over a guardrail under the Greene Street Bridge on 3100 East Upriver Drive near the Spokane River. Cause of death: gunshot wound to upper body.

Kathy Brisbois, age 38. Body found May 15, 1990, near the Spokane River south of Trent Avenue (East 12300 block). Cause of death: gunshot wounds to upper body.

One Thursday morning in the fall of 1997, Mike and I drove out to the earliest crime scenes from the three prostitute murders in 1990.

The first scene we visited was 4100 East Upriver Drive, where Yolanda Sapp had been found at 8:25 A.M. on February 22, 1990. Her naked body was lying on the embankment above the Spokane River. A wool army blanket was found nearby. None of her clothes or personal items were found at the crime scene. There were no shell casings or evidence of a struggle.

Sapp was an African American born on January 10, 1964, in Tacoma. She was a high school dropout who had worked as a nurse's aide. Her parents, Neville and Anna Sapp, still lived in Tacoma at the time of her death.

For three years prior to her murder, Sapp had been living at the Spokane Street Motel. Linda Rose, the motel manager, had previously thrown Sapp out of the motel for bringing men back to her room. Sapp had been arrested eleven times for theft, drug possession, prostitution, and disorderly conduct. On the street, she was known as "Marilyn."

She had been shot by a small-caliber firearm more than once in the anterior left chest. During the autopsy, coroner Dr. Graham McConnell estimated that Sapp died within minutes of being shot.

Sapp was last reported seen alive on February 20, 1990, in the East Sprague neighborhood. Her body was stiff with rigor mortis when the police arrived at the crime scene, indicating that she had been dead less than thirty-five hours. There was no evidence that she had been sexually assaulted and no defensive wounds, which meant that the attack could have come as a surprise.

According to the coroner, Sapp had been shot at another location and then dumped by the river. The army blanket found next to her body was soaked in blood. Apparently, she had been wrapped in the blanket when the killer transported her to the dump site. She was probably dumped there sometime after dark the night before she was found.

Two nights before her body was discovered, Sapp had gone out. The next day, her boyfriend was looking for her. Linda Rose, who ran the Spokane Street Motel, where Sapp lived with her boyfriend, called the police to report her missing the morning her body was found. She had been missing for two nights. The killer might have abducted her and kept her for a full day before dumping her the night prior to her discovery.

Sapp's clothing was eventually discovered in a Dumpster behind Trudeau's Marina at 304 East Sprague Avenue. Green carpet fibers had been found on her body. The same fibers were also found embedded in her clothing. These fibers were traced to carpeting in boats at Trudeau's Marina, where prostitutes often turned tricks after the marina closed.

Mike briefed me on all the details on the Sapp case as I examined the dump site. Upriver Drive overlooks the Spokane River, with homes along the north side and a vacant riverbank along the south. It was a steep embankment, covered with grass and underbrush, which would have been dead and leafless in late February, when Sapp's body was found. About seventy-five feet down was the river's edge.

To me, it appeared that the suspect had been driving eastbound, out of town. He picked Sapp up in the East Sprague neighborhood, at or near Trudeau's. They had sex somewhere nearby, and he probably killed her there, throwing her clothes in the Dumpster before driving off to dispose of her body. I figured he would have a vehicle large enough for him to have sex with her inside it, then to transport her body without being noticed—in other words, a van, a pickup truck with a camper top, a semi with a sleeper berth, or a delivery truck. This was a commonplace observation; how else could the suspect have transported and dumped his victim?

Standing there above the embankment where the killer had dumped Sapp's body, I tried to take what we knew of the crime and re-create it in my mind. The art of detective work is just that, an art, and often requires using your imagination to get as close as you can into the killer's head. By reading the evidence and then taking it a step further, imagining how the suspect and the victim left that evidence there, and what else they did without leaving any trace, the crime scene will give you at least a rudimentary picture of what happened. It's not an occult power like a psychic profiler, it's just using your imagination to make sense of the facts that you know.

He's driving eastbound, the body's in the van, wrapped up in an army blanket. He pulls over on the right side of the road, gets out of the car, looks up and down the street—there's no traffic. He opens up the vehicle door and drags the body out. His actions are shielded by the vehicle.

Her body is inert, awkward. She's heavier than he thought. Maybe he's never handled a dead body before. He drags her over to the embankment and pushes her over. She rolls halfway down the hill, falls out of the blanket on the way, but stops before she reaches the river.

Shit! He wanted to dump her in the river, to get rid of any hair or fiber evidence. Maybe he was hoping that the river current would take her away, and her body would never be found. Now what's he going to do?

There she is, lying on the embankment, in plain sight of anyone who walks by. At least it's dark, she probably won't be found until morning. The headlights of a distant car shine behind him. He better get out of here.

He takes one last look at the body before getting back into the van. As he drives off, he's sweating, even though it's cold out. He's scared, exhilarated, wondering if he'll get caught, wondering when he can kill again.

"Well, what do you think?"

Mike's question took me out of my trance. As I described my impressions from this crime scene, I could see that Mike had already come to some similar conclusions. Mike had the intelligence and the instincts to be a good detective. Now I could see that he had the imagination as well.

We got back in the car and drove to the next site, which was also on Upriver Drive, about a mile back toward town.

Nickie Lowe was discovered draped over a guardrail along Upriver beneath the Greene Street Bridge overpass at 6:00 A.M. the morning of March 25. Except for her bare feet, Lowe was fully clothed, with her clothing pushed around her body.

Lowe was a thirty-four-year-old Spokane prostitute, a heroin addict involved in the local drug trade. Born on June 20, 1955, in Idaho, Lowe was a high school dropout with no stated occupation. Her parents, Edmond Lowe and Diane Matney, lived in Spokane. According to Lowe's mother, Nickie knew Yolanda Sapp. Matney told the *Spokesman-Review* that her daughter had talked about Yolanda after her body was found.

She had been shot once in the chest, and the bullet perforated the abdominal aorta. A .22-caliber bullet was recovered during the autopsy. She had been shot in another location, and her body was dumped along Upriver Drive. She had been dead less than six hours when her body was found.

Lowe had last been reported seen around 10:00 the night before, when her pimp had dropped her off near Sprague and Altamont to meet a john. They had plans to meet back at a tavern on East Sprague later that night. Five hours later, when Lowe didn't show up, her pimp contacted Nickie's mother, Diane Matney, who called the police.

"He probably picks her up on Sprague," Mike said, looking back across the bridge toward town. "Drives north on Freya and Greene, crosses the bridge here, doubles back to the underpass, and then stops and dumps her."

As Mike filled me in on the details, I walked around the scene. This area was less exposed than the location where Sapp was found. He could have scouted this location when he had Sapp, but for some reason took Sapp farther along Upriver Drive. Maybe he saw this location on the drive back and remembered it. With Lowe in the vehicle, he parked beneath the overpass, probably thinking he had more time to conceal the body. But for some reason, he just left her there. Why?

He's driving north on Greene. It's after midnight, there's very little traffic. He crosses the bridge and circles around; he knows where he's going. He stops the van by the guardrail and gets out. This one still has her clothes on, so he didn't bother wrapping her in a blanket. As he pulls her out of the van, her clothes get moved around on her body. He drags her out of the van, leans her over the guardrail, and . . . Something happens. He sees another car coming. He hears a suspicious noise. He notices a light on in a nearby house. He's tired and just wants it all over with. Fuck it, he says, I'll just leave her here. As he drives off, he can see the shadow of her body slumped over the guardrail. It won't be long before she's found, but that doesn't matter, because he's already gone.

Once again, I told Mike, we have an inexpert, disorganized dumping. He could have wanted to stage the body, but the staging is not very elaborate, and it isn't similar to the other body dump. He probably just got lazy and left her there. The body could easily be seen by passing cars, which means that he's not afraid of her being found quickly, and he has no connection to her. He doesn't live in the immediate vicinity, and the dump site does not point toward him in any way. He wasn't trying to hide the body or delay discovery. He just wanted to get rid of her.

Mike told me there was no evidence of sexual assault. That didn't mean that the suspect couldn't have had consensual sex with his victims prior to killing them. It did mean that the medical examiner had probably not found, or possibly did not look for, foreign DNA by taking vaginal, anal, and oral swabs, which are standard procedures in most female homicides.

As soon as the autopsy on Nickie Lowe's body was completed, or perhaps even sooner, the police knew that her death was connected to Yolanda Sapp's. The proximity of the dump sites, the similarity in victimology, and, most important, the matching and distinct murder weapon—a .22-caliber handgun—clearly indicated that this was the work of the same suspect. They didn't want to admit that there might be a serial killer preying on local prostitutes.

"They didn't want to make the connection," Mike said. "Because then they'd have to admit they had a serial killer. But once a third body showed up, they had no choice."

We drove back across the river to the site where the third body, Kathy Brisbois, was found.

This site was a little different from Sapp and Lowe. It was several miles farther east along the Spokane River, on the other side of the river. The crime scene was located at a landing south of Trent Avenue where you can drive down to the river's edge. It was a graveled parking area not far from Plantes' Ferry Park, a popular swimming area in the summer, and a place where couples often parked at night. Though the parking lot was semisecluded, there were houses within sight, and the area was not remote enough to hide a body for long.

We pulled down close to the river and got out. Mike told me all about this case.

Kathy Brisbois was found at approximately 7:30 P.M. on May 15, 1990, by two high school students walking along the river. Her body was naked, laying facedown approximately twelve feet from the river. It appeared as though she had been thrown down the slight embankment after a struggle. The crime scene indicated that Brisbois put up a fight. She had been severely beaten and there were numerous defensive wounds. Brisbois was killed on the gravel road, her clothing strewn nearby. A blood and hair trail led from the road to the location where the body had been found.

Brisbois had contusions and lacerations on her head, consistent with assault by a blunt object. There were several unusual burn marks on her back. She had been shot three times in the upper body and head with a .22-caliber firearm. Official cause of death was cerebral pulpefaction and cardiac perforation. According to detectives, her chest wounds were inflicted while her clothes were off. Time of death was estimated at 7 P.M., approximately thirty minutes before her body was found. There was no evidence of sexual assault.

Kathy Brisbois was a thirty-eight-year-old prostitute and drug addict. Born on June 24, 1951, she had eight brothers and sisters. As a child, her nickname was "Wiggy." One-quarter Spokane Indian, she had been married twice and her three daughters were all in foster homes.

Brisbois attended Spokane's Lewis and Clark High School, but did not graduate. She married and had the first of her three children when she was nineteen. She was divorced and remarried, then moved to Ford, Washington, where she drove a dump truck for Western Nuclear, a mining operation on the Indian reservation.

In 1979, Western Nuclear shut down and Brisbois moved back to Spokane, where she became involved in drugs and prostitution. Brisbois was arrested several times for prostitution and once, in 1985, on drug charges. She had been through several drug rehab programs, and had just been released from a Seattle halfway house months prior to her death. At the time of her death, she was living at the Spokane Street Motel, where Yolanda Sapp also lived.

Shortly after her death, one of Brisbois's daughters had a child. She would have been a grandmother.

"After dumping Sapp and Lowe on the north bank of the river," Mike said, "he picks Brisbois up on Sprague, and then just drives east on Trent until he hits the water."

"Why did she go with him?" I asked. "Didn't she know what happened to Sapp and Lowe?"

"Yeah, in fact, she had contact with the police just before she died."

It turned out that two weeks prior to her death, Brisbois told detectives that she was scared for her life because of the recent murders, but that she was being careful. She stated that she did not get into any cars and would not go with anyone she didn't know.

"Maybe she knew him," I said. "Maybe he was a regular john. Maybe he's someone she knew from somewhere else. Like a drug connection."

"How about a cop?" Mike suggested.

"It's possible. Hell, anything is possible."

The Brisbois scene and the evidence that Mike described set this homicide apart from the two previous cases. The killer had been able to subdue and kill Sapp and Lowe fairly easily. With Brisbois, something went wrong. Sapp and Lowe were already dead by the time he got to the river. Brisbois was still alive.

Mike and I stood there at the landing for a long time, just soaking it all in. There was a house nearby, but it was far enough away that the inhabitants probably didn't hear the fight or even the gunshots.

He arrives at the landing with her. This is where they're going to do it. She's starting to take her clothes off when she realizes something's up. She's not going along with his plan. She fights back, breaks free, and runs out of the van. He chases her down, throws her to the ground, and starts beating her with the gun butt. She's a small woman, but tough. And she's fighting for her life.

He shoots her, but she doesn't stop fighting. He shoots her again. Finally, she slumps on the ground and he finishes her off with one to the head.

He wants to get her away from the van, so he drags her toward the river. Just get her out of sight and get the hell out of here. He leaves her lying facedown.

It's still daylight. Someone could have heard the shots. He's got to get out of there, even though he hasn't done what he wanted to. He goes back into the van and grabs her clothing, throws it on the ground near her body.

"She put up one hell of a fight," Mike said.

"Yeah, and it scared him," I replied.

"Maybe that's why he stopped killing," Mike said.

Serial killers often undergo cooling-off periods in which they stop killing. Some of these periods, in the early phases of a killer's career, are precipitated by an experience in which they are almost caught or are frightened, either by the prospect of apprehension or the realization of their own sickness.

In a prison interview with journalists Stephen Michaud and Hugh Aynesworth, Ted Bundy described his own reaction after one of his first kills. Although Bundy uses the third person, he is clearly speaking about himself.

"He stayed off the streets and vowed he'd never do it again and recognized the horror of what he had done and certainly was frightened by what he saw happening, it took him only three months to get over it. In the next incident, he was over it in a month."

As the serial killer cools off, the urge grows until it becomes uncontrollable. During these early killings, he has not yet developed an efficient modus operandi and so is easier to catch, since he will inadvertently leave more evidence at the scene. The more the suspect kills, the better he gets at it.

The 1990 suspect seemed to be going in reverse. The evidence at the Brisbois scene indicated that the killer had less control over her than he did over Sapp and Lowe. Instead of getting more efficient with his MO, he seemed to be getting sloppier. Or else he didn't figure on Brisbois being as tough as she was.

Serial killing is all about domination and control. The killer dominates and controls his victims, and once those victims start to mount, he begins dominating and controlling the police, the media, and the public. Here at the river landing his victim put up a fight and nearly got away. The killer lost control.

Although we don't know whether the suspect had killed before, the 1990 homicides appeared to be the work of a sexual psychopath who was inexperienced or inept in his MO. His pathology drove him to kill, but he hadn't learned how to do it efficiently.

One of the classic category distinctions of homicide suspects is organized/disorganized. The organized offender is someone who has planned out his crime and executes it as closely as possible to that plan. He thinks out his crime, chooses his victim. When he abducts his victim, he knows where he is going to take her, how he is going to kill her, and what he is going to do with her body once he's done with her. Everything is a well-oiled machine. Sometimes things don't go exactly as planned, but generally he is able to commit his crime with efficiency and a minimum of unforeseen difficulties.

The disorganized offender is someone who has not planned his crime. He is emotional, rushed, out of control, whether due to psychosis, fear, excitement, or inexperience. Nothing is planned. He selects his victim because an opportunity presents itself. Whatever he does is spur of the moment. His weapons are usually weapons of opportunity, whatever is available to hand.

O. J. Simpson was a disorganized offender. He probably didn't come to Nicole's house with the intention of killing her. He didn't expect Ron Goldman to show up. He was in a neighborhood where his face and vehicle were well known. He flew into a rage that quickly became homicidal, and the Swiss Army knife was a weapon at hand. He left hundreds of pieces of evidence, all pointing to him. He had no plan to dispose of the bodies, no plan to cover up the crime. He didn't even have an alibi that made any sense.

Most serial killers can be put into the organized offender category. They plan and prepare the murders, often involving elaborate fantasies both before and after their commission. Some of the evidence indicated that the 1990 killer was a disorganized offender. All three crime scenes were different. The Brisbois scene showed a real lack of control.

In this case, the distinction between organized and disorganized offender doesn't quite hold up. The suspect was organized enough to premeditate the killings, even if he didn't have a plan that he stuck to. He went out those nights ready to kill. He had no connection to his victims and apparently left very little evidence. Whatever degree of psychopathology he was experiencing, the fight with Brisbois, and probably to some degree the media attention given to the murders, caused him to stop killing for a while, at least in Spokane.

In general, the distinction between organized and disorganized offenders isn't always predictive of the criminal experience and emotional or mental state of the suspect. Detectives see only what the evidence at the crime scene tells them. The suspect could have been in a complete panic, but somehow he left very little evidence. Or he could be totally calm, executing his crime exactly as he had envisioned it during months of extensive preparation—but somehow it all goes sideways through no fault of his own. What looks like premeditation and flawless execution could just be happenstance. And what looks like chaos and disorder could be the result of a well-ordered criminal mind. You never know for certain, because all you're doing is reading the evidence. You can attempt to re-create how it all got there, but you can never be entirely sure what the suspect's intention or mind-set was. Even if you catch him and he confesses, you have no guarantee that he's telling you the truth.

To be able to solve homicides, a detective must take categories like organized/disorganized and decide to what degree they are helpful in determining the identity or characteristics of the suspect, and to what degree they are just psychological mumbo jumbo; when theories like this are useful tools of detection, and when they are a waste of time.

I explained this to Mike, and he got it. I could see him soaking up everything like a rookie detective.

Mike had assembled a notebook of newspaper clippings and other information he had uncovered. Mike's notebook told the story, not just of the 1990 killings, but also of the investigation that followed.

Soon after Brisbois's body was found, Spokane city police and the sheriff's department formed a joint task force. The city and county joined forces because Sapp and Lowe were found in the city, while Brisbois was found in the county. The city police acted as lead agency, probably because they had two bodies, and the prostitute district where the victims had been working was within city limits. The Spokane PD's Major Crimes Unit, headed by Lieutenant Jim Hill, led the investigation. As many as ten detectives were assigned to work the case with occasional help from other units.

The task force stated that there was no signature in the 1990 killings. Signature is a distinct method of torture, killing, or staging—arranging the body or crime scene—common to all victims. The MO, or modus operandi, is the method by which a serial killer, or any other suspect, commits a crime. A signature is the unique act that fulfills the serial killer's psychosexual fantasies. The task force did state that they were able to connect the three murders through ballistics.

The task force initially focused on the leads surrounding Brisbois's death. Customers at the nearby Blue Keg Tavern gave descriptions of vehicles they saw the night her body was found. Sheriff Larry Erickson said that Brisbois's body appeared to have been at the site for two or three days, but that seems unlikely.

Detectives also looked for suspects among recent releases from prison and psychiatric institutions. They examined records of men who had been arrested for soliciting prostitutes and searched for evidence in Dumpsters in the East Sprague neighborhood.

By forming a task force, local law enforcement was admitting that the three homicides were connected, and they had a serial killer working the streets of Spokane. The similarities between the three victims, their cause of death and manner of disposal, were all too obvious for the police not to link them publicly. In fact, they said that they had privately linked the Sapp and Lowe killings almost as soon as Lowe's body had been found.

The victimology of the three homicides presented several challenges to the task force. Prostitutes are easy prey for a serial killer. They have numerous daily contacts with strangers and have to get into cars or go to motel rooms or secluded areas with them in order to conduct their business. Prostitutes are often more reluctant to cooperate with law enforcement than other victim groups, especially when the police do not have a good rapport or working relationship with street hookers, which seems to have been the case in Spokane.

The Spokane PD did not have an active vice unit, so their street intelligence was severely limited. There was very little rapport with the prostitutes and other street people on Sprague.

The task force quickly appealed to more experienced investigators for help and guidance. They met with a detective from the Green River Task Force in Seattle, which was still investigating the deaths and disappearances of fortynine women (most of them prostitutes) in Seattle and Portland. Tom Jenson of the Green River Task Force spent two days with Spokane detectives before reporting that their investigation was "right on track."

In the Moxley case, an inexperienced Greenwich Police Department contacted expert homicide detectives from Detroit and Nassau County, New York, to review their investigation. Instead of actually learning from the more experienced detectives, the Greenwich cops just wanted their seal of approval. I wondered if the same thing had happened in Spokane.

Jim Hansen, a Spokane sheriff's detective who had worked on the Green River Task Force, was picked as one of the lead investigators of the 1990 homicides. Spokane police chief Terry Mangan was quick to deny any connection between the Spokane homicides and the Green River slayings.

"We seem to have more serial killers running about—highly mobile killers—than we thought we did," Mangan told the *Spokesman-Review*. "At any given time in the Pacific Northwest, we may have fifteen serial killers."

Mangan, who had been involved with the Hillside Strangler case while a cop at Bellingham, Washington, also promised that Spokane law enforcement would work closely with the FBI's Violent Criminal Apprehension Program (VICAP) to see if the Spokane homicides matched other killings around the country. A detective from the Spokane Task Force flew to the FBI campus at Quantico, Virginia, to discuss the case with the Bureau's Behavioral Sciences Unit. The purpose of the Quantico trip was to develop a profile of the suspect, leaning on the expertise of John Douglas, who at the time was the FBI's head profiler.

Back home, the task force focused on the Kathy Brisbois murder, since it seemed most evidence-rich. They didn't get anywhere. After months of investigation and no tangible results, the task force was quietly disbanded.

The killings had seemed to have had an effect, however temporary, on the sex trade along Sprague Avenue. Neighborhood residents and business owners noted a sharp drop-off in streetwalkers, and those prostitutes who were out working seemed to be more cautious, even if the brutal murders of three of their colleagues didn't scare them off the streets entirely. Soon it was back to business as usual. Local prostitutes, and the rest of Spokane, seemed to forget about these three murders.

Before our radio show went on, Mike and I had lunch at the Viking, a bar near the radio station. We discussed the case like a couple of working detectives, chewing sandwiches while talking about grisly details like decomposition, blood spatter, and lividity.

We knew nothing about the suspect, but there were several solid pieces of evidence that might lead us to his identity.

The task force detectives had stated that the killer used a .22-caliber handgun, a weapon that is easy to transport, conceal, and dispose of. It makes very little noise and often the slugs are so damaged that identification by rifling and other characteristics is impossible.

A .22 is a very unpredictable weapon. It can be very deadly, but sometimes the bullets can bounce around inside the body without hitting anything vital. A high-velocity small-caliber round can hit a bone and channel itself along the bone, starting out in the chest and exiting at the wrist.

Another problem with a .22 is that the killer has either to surprise or to control his victim enough to get a clear and close shot to either the head or vital organs. In the case of Brisbois, this obviously didn't happen. The suspect had to shoot her several times.

I was told by a former task force member that the gun used in those killings had "a loose barrel." That probably meant worn-out rifling, which would give you inconsistent ballistics. Maybe it wasn't the barrel, but the bullet. Different bullets have different tolerances. Some run tight through the barrel, others don't. There is a wide range in quality of .22-caliber ammunition—from Olympic match fire ammunition to the cheap stuff you can buy at Target. There are different loads and bullets and lengths, from .22 shorts to .22 mini mags. Still, the task force was able to match the three victims up ballistically. Maybe not to the point where it would stand up in court as evidence, but at least for their own purposes of investigation.

Even if the ballistic evidence wasn't perfect, we could conclude that the serial killer shot Sapp, Lowe, and Brisbois with the same weapon. The bullets retrieved from the victims have at least some similarities in lands, grooves, and twists. It was probably a revolver or derringer, a gun that doesn't eject shell casings when fired; otherwise shell casings would have been recovered, at least at the Brisbois scene, where the suspect didn't have time to retrieve them.

Without a gun, the ballistic evidence didn't go anywhere. In order to get closer to the suspect, you have to focus on evidence that would provide a connection between him and the victims. In this regard, the most interesting evidence was the green carpet fibers.

These teal green carpet fibers were identified as coming from glue-down carpeting commonly used in Sea-Ray boats. The carpet had been manufactured for only two years, but was widely used in boats and other applications. The fibers led detectives to Trudeau's Marina. They discovered that prostitutes would turn tricks in boats parked in Trudeau's lot. They also were taking carpet remnants and using them as blankets and seat cushions.

Here we had a connection that linked the victims but might not have anything to do with the killer, except for the fact that Sapp's clothes were found in Trudeau's Dumpster. Since the fiber evidence didn't come from the killer, it didn't lead directly to him. We could assume that the killer was contacting his victims, at least Sapp, at or near Trudeau's Marina. Sapp probably took off her clothes to turn the trick, and he might have shot her there, then driven her body out to Upriver Drive to dump it.

After lunch, Mike and I went to the station and did the radio show on the 1990 killings.

FITZSIMMONS: Mark Fuhrman, having been out to the crime scenes and read up on these cases, what do these homicides look like to you?

FUHRMAN: They were the work of an inexperienced killer, someone who had not yet developed an effective MO. But he had gotten a taste for killing, and however long his cooling-off period might have lasted, he would kill again.

FITZSIMMONS: Do you think it's the same guy who's killing some of these other prostitutes?

FUHRMAN: Either that, or Spokane has two serial killers.

CHAPTER 4

Heather Hernandez and Jennifer Joseph

Jennifer Joseph, age 16. Body found August 26, 1997, in a hayfield near Forker and Judkins Roads, northeast Spokane County. Cause of death: gunshot wound to chest.

Heather Hernandez, age 20. Body found August 26, 1997, in an overgrown lot behind the 1800 block of East Springfield, Spokane city. Cause of death: gunshot wound to head.

Our review of the unsolved prostitute homicides led us back to the original pair of homicides that made Mike first think that a serial killer was working in Spokane.

On August 26, 1997, a transient collecting aluminum cans in a lot behind 1800 East Springfield discovered a badly decomposed body among the weeds.

The body was eventually identified as Heather Hernandez, a twenty-year-old prostitute from Arizona. She had been shot once in the head. Bloodstains and drag marks indicated that she had been dragged from one corner of the parking lot to the grassy area where she was found.

Very little is known about Heather Hernandez. She was a transient prostitute who had been in the Spokane area for about a month, after working in California, Idaho, and Arizona. She was born on April 11, 1977, in Phoenix, Arizona. Phoenix remained her official residence. She was a high school graduate and, according to the death certificate, married to one Bladimir Hernandez.

Lynn Everson, a Spokane County social worker, knew Hernandez from the street and told the *Spokesman-Review:* "She was a thoughtful woman who had a good sense of humor."

The same day Hernandez's body turned up, two farmers were working on a hay-baling machine in a field in northeast Spokane County, near the intersection of Forker and Judkins Roads. They noticed something in the tall grass alongside the hayfield. It was a human body.

The body was so severely decomposed that detectives guessed it had been dumped at least a week prior to discovery. On September 2, the body was identified as Jennifer Joseph, a sixteen-year-old Amerasian prostitute from Tacoma. Jennifer Joseph was born October 6, 1980, in Hampton, Virginia. She was a high school dropout who never married. Her parents, John C. Joseph and Mi Hae Chong, were divorced. Joseph lived in Spanaway, Washington, near Tacoma. Chong lived in Hawaii. Joseph was a retired Army sergeant; Chong was Korean. They met while Joseph was on duty in South Korea.

Jennifer lived in Virginia, Denmark, South Korea, Massachusetts, Hawaii, and Spanaway, Washington. After her parents' divorce, she had a history of running away from home. She had been arrested for prostitution in San Francisco and Salem, Oregon. Apparently, she had started working as a prostitute when she was fifteen.

"She was raised as a military brat, like a lot of the rest of us," one woman who worked with Joseph as a prostitute told the *Spokesman-Review.* "She was used to meeting strangers and becoming friends with people real fast."

Joseph had been hospitalized in San Francisco for severe head injuries after jumping out of a moving car when a customer pulled a gun on her. She had moved to Spokane in July with her pimp.

The autopsy on Joseph was performed August 28, and revealed the cause of death to be a gunshot wound. Joseph's remains were cremated on September 4. The next day, John Joseph drove to Spokane to pick up his daughter's ashes. Police took a blood sample from him, apparently because he was a possible suspect. John Joseph was cleared of suspicion.

Another suspect was a pimp who ran Jennifer in San Francisco and Tacoma. He had reportedly told mutual friends that Jennifer was dead before her body had been discovered. The pimp was interviewed and given a polygraph. He was also cleared.

The blood sample taken from Jennifer Joseph's father told me that the police had recovered foreign DNA from his daughter's body. If detectives thought that John Joseph was a suspect, then they must have been considering the possibility that her homicide was not the work of a serial killer. I didn't understand why detectives would take DNA from Jennifer's father, but only give her pimp a polygraph. Whether Joseph's death was a singular homicide or connected to Hernandez, the pimp was a better suspect. I wondered what evidence would make detectives think that John Joseph was responsible for his daughter's murder.

By what little we knew about the suspects the detectives had considered, it looked as if they were treating the Joseph case as a singular homicide, not connected to either the 1990 serial killings or to the other unsolved homicides. They didn't even seem to link it to the Hernandez case.

To me, it appeared that the Joseph and Hernandez homicides were linked, at least to each other. The similarities between the two homicides were evident. Both bodies were found the same day, but in different locations from where they were killed. Both bodies were decomposed. Both were shot to death. Both women worked as prostitutes and had a history of drug abuse. Whether or not the Joseph and Hernandez homicides were the work of a serial killer, we didn't know for certain, but it looked like the same suspect.

The West LA Division of the LAPD is about the same size as Spokane, in terms of population and police force. If we had two homicides with these similarities, we would consider them connected until the evidence proved otherwise.

I doubted that there was an identifiable signature common to both victims. If there was, then the cops wouldn't have investigated the Joseph case as a singular homicide. Within a matter of days, any bullets, fragments, or casings that had been recovered would be examined. And there was a good possibility that the ballistics didn't match. Maybe identifiable missiles were not recovered from one or both bodies. Or else bullets were recovered, but they didn't match. Even if the ballistics are different, that doesn't mean the two homicides weren't connected. The same suspect could have used a different gun. Or there might have been a second suspect, also armed.

Heather Hernandez had been shot once in the head. If the murder weapon was a small-caliber handgun, and the bullet had entered or exited her skull, then the chances of identifiable ballistics were pretty slim, as the hard bone of the skull would probably damage the missile beyond recognition. If she had been shot through the soft tissue, like the temple or the eye socket, then a good bullet might have been retrieved. Joseph, by comparison, had been shot in the chest. There was a better chance that a good bullet was retrieved from her body.

Even without a pristine missile, investigators could at

least determine caliber and metal content of the bullets used. Even the weight of the bullet can help determine the possibility of a common weapon being used in both homicides, as most weapons would be loaded with similar ammunition.

We already knew that Sapp, Lowe, and Brisbois had been shot by the same .22-caliber handgun. If either Hernandez or Joseph (or both) were shot by a .22, that was a good indication that the 1990 suspect was responsible. Even if the ballistics didn't match, the MO did.

Mike and I went out to view the lot in the 1800 block of East Springfield, where Hernandez's body had been found. The area, notorious for transient traffic, was near the railroad tracks and a collection of small business warehouses, and not far from the East Sprague strip. The exact location was a right-of-way off the railroad tracks, not far from a traffic crossing, the kind of place where you'd expect to find a dead body. In fact, bodies had been found here on other occasions. Considered in isolation, it might appear that Hernandez was a singular homicide. With Joseph found the same day, we couldn't consider her in isolation.

The Jennifer Joseph dump site was markedly different—a hayfield in the rural area of northeast Spokane, not far from Mount Spokane Drive. Her body was lying in a ditch off the side of the road, surrounded by high scrub grass. Two other prostitutes had been found dumped nearby on separate prior occasions (Sherry Palmer in 1992 and Shannon Zielinski in 1996).

Both Joseph and Hernandez were severely decomposed. In high summer, bodies break down pretty quickly. Both women had come to Spokane from out of town, and didn't have family in the area. Neither one of them had been officially reported missing, although Joseph was last reported seen on August 16, 1997. Both Joseph and Hernandez had to have been killed about ten days to two weeks prior to discovery, in order to reach that stage of decomposition.

Where had they been between death and discovery? Was it possible that Joseph and Hernandez had lain in their respective locations for the period of time necessary to reach a state of severe decomposition?

Hernandez was dumped in an area heavy with transient traffic. The witness who discovered her body was collecting aluminum cans. Her body was described as severely decomposed; about a quarter to a third of her body mass was already gone. A detective who had seen her said that she had probably weighed 130 pounds at death, but was down to about 80 when she was found. The remains would be putrid, and anybody in the vicinity would smell the unmistakable odor of rotting flesh. I doubted that she would be able to lie there decomposing for more than a day without being discovered.

There were blood and drag marks from one corner of the parking lot to the place where Hernandez's body was eventually discovered. This led investigators to conclude that Hernandez had been shot at the location, and then dragged over to where she was found.

With this scenario, she would have had to lie there for at least a week, and no one saw or smelled her. That's unlikely. The stain detectives saw was probably not blood spatter from her fatal gunshot. Instead, it was probably a mix of postmortem body fluids. After death, various body fluids pool inside the body cavity. The resulting soup, though containing a great deal of blood and resembling blood, is not pure blood.

This is what could have happened. When the suspect took her body out of the car, he dropped it on the ground. Those accumulated fluids exited the body, causing what appeared to be a bloodstain, but in fact was more than that.

The stain and drag marks only make it more probable

that her body would have been discovered earlier, if she had been shot at the site and dumped there. Not only detectives have eyes. If the stain and drag marks had been there a week or so earlier, then transients would have seen them. It would not be unreasonable to suppose that at least one of them would follow the drag marks and find her body in the high grass of the nearby lot.

Heather Hernandez died from a single gunshot to the head from a small-caliber handgun. That wound would be fairly small and self-contained. Decomposition and animal depredation are most pronounced in areas of the body that are already compromised or exposed. Any additional wounds would speed up the process. Were there other wounds in addition to the gunshot to the head? If Heather Hernandez had been tortured or mutilated, then the decomposition process would have been sped up and her remains would have been more vulnerable to animal depredation. Animal predators are numerous in Spokane, particularly in that area.

My gut told me that Hernandez had been killed elsewhere and then dumped at the scene. I also figured that she had been tortured and/or mutilated. But where had her body been before she was dumped?

From the first time I heard about these two homicides, I thought it highly unlikely that the discovery of both bodies on the same day was just a coincidence. I felt that one, or both, of the bodies had been moved in order to facilitate discovery.

It was certainly possible that Jennifer Joseph had lain undiscovered for more than a week, but it was also possible that she had been held somewhere else for at least a couple days and then dumped.

Joseph's body was found by a couple of farmers out haying a field. It was late summer, time for the second cutting. I wondered if the farmers had had their haying equipment out in the field the day before. And I wondered if the killer had seen the equipment, knew that meant the field would be cut the next day, and moved her from some other location.

The 1990 suspect dumped his victims in areas where they would be found. The Joseph and Hernandez dump sites, like the 1990 scenes, were remote enough to allow the suspect to dump the bodies without detection, yet exposed enough to be discovered. This indicated to me that the suspect wanted the bodies to be found. Whether he planned for them to be found the same day, only he knew.

On September 3, 1997, a little more than a week after the Joseph and Hernandez bodies were discovered, an article in the *Spokesman-Review* seemed to indicate the police were considering the possibility that these two homicides were connected, not only to each other, but also to the 1990 cases, and perhaps some of the other unsolved homicides.

The story ran on the front page:

POLICE SEEK LINK IN PROSTITUTE MURDERS

RECENT DEATHS RENEW FEARS OF SERIAL KILLER IN SPOKANE

Two recent murders have resurrected fears that a serial killer may be stalking the streets of Spokane, preying on women who work as prostitutes.

Undersheriff Mike Aubrey said Tuesday that police and sheriff's detectives are working together to find a possible link between the deaths of Heather Hernandez and Jennifer Joseph. . . .

Investigators also are comparing their murders to similar unsolved homicides, and they are beginning to compile a criminal profile of someone who might commit the crimes, Aubrey said.

Since 1990, five other women have met similar

fates—shot to death and dumped, either along the Spokane River or in the woods and fields south of Mount Spokane.

"We're concerned," Aubrey said.

The article went on to state that police officers and outreach workers were warning prostitutes to be on the lookout for suspicious customers.

"I didn't hear nothing about this from cops," one prostitute told the newspaper. "But I heard somebody might be killing us. I'm scared."

While local prostitutes seemed to think that the killings were the work of one suspect, the police refused to connect the cases.

There is no strong evidence tying any of the murders to any of the others, Aubrey said, just vague similarities that have piqued the interest of detectives.

"We do not have a direct link between these two cases, but we're not discounting that there is a link, either," he said.

Aubrey also said that investigators were focusing on the Joseph and Hernandez cases because they were the freshest and most likely to produce witnesses.

"We're looking at pretty much everything right now," Aubrey told the newspaper.

In a sidebar that accompanied the September 3 article, detectives were described as "looking for links" between seven unsolved prostitute homicides in Spokane dating back to 1990. These cases were: Sapp, Lowe, and Brisbois; Sherry Palmer and Shannon Zielinski, whose bodies were found near Mount Spokane in 1992 and 1996, respectively; Joseph and Hernandez.

All the victims were prostitutes. Most of them were

drug addicts. All were shot by a small-caliber handgun. All were probably killed at one scene and dumped somewhere else. There were apparently no good suspects in any of the homicides when treated singularly. Two of the bodies were found on the same day. At least three were linked ballistically. And all of them remained unsolved.

These are more than just "vague similarities." The fact that the Spokane PD and the sheriff's department were working together on the cases was further indication that they were connected. There was no talk of a new task force at that time. Whatever information they might be sharing, these two jurisdictions were, at least officially, handling the cases separately. The Joseph case was being investigated by the Spokane Sheriff's Department, since her body was found in the county. The Hernandez case was being investigated by the Spokane PD, since she was found in the city.

Could that be why he dumped their bodies in separate locations? Was he manipulating the investigation already, trying to get both agencies involved?

This indicated a highly intelligent and organized killer. If it was the same suspect from 1990, then he had certainly gained experience and poise since nearly losing Kathy Brisbois.

Until proven otherwise, Mike and I connected Joseph and Hernandez to the 1990 serial killings. Now we needed to determine whether this suspect was responsible for even more deaths.

CHAPTER 5

Sherry Palmer, Shannon Zielinski, and JoAnn Flores

Mike and I looked at all the unsolved prostitute homicides in Spokane from 1984 to 1997, working only with information readily available to the public through newspaper articles, law enforcement press releases, and death certificates.

The victimology of these homicides indicated that if they hadn't been connected, at least some of them probably would have been solved. Prostitutes live a dangerous and highly mobile lifestyle. They can go missing for a long time and never be reported as such. They are easily victimized, but the circumstances and/or the explanation for their deaths are usually easy to identify. They live on the streets. Whatever hassles they get into with another prostitute or a pimp or a john or a drug dealer, there are usually witnesses. If any of these homicides involved other suspects, the police would be eager to disconnect them from the serial killer cases. Even if they couldn't actually solve these singular homicides, at least they'd be able to keep their number of serial homicides down.

Between 1984 and 1987 there were four unsolved homicides.

Debbi Finnern, age 30. Body found June 22, 1984, in the 1800 block of East Front. Cause of death: stabbing.

Ruby Jean Doss, age 27. Body found January 30, 1986, in a field near Fiske and Ferry. Cause of death: strangulation and blow to head.

Mary Ann Turner, age 30. Body found November 4, 1986, next to a garage at 100 South Ivory. Cause of death: strangulation.

Kathleen DeHart, age 37. Body found July 5, 1987, in the basement of an apartment at 911 South Hatch. Cause of death: strangulation.

These homicides didn't look like the work of a serial killer. Each was committed by bodily force. Unless they were committed by a different suspect, whose preferred method of death was strangulation, I had no reason to think they were connected.

Still, I wondered why these homicides hadn't been solved. (But I guess that's another book.)

There was one homicide that occurred shortly after the Joseph and Hernandez cases, but got very little notice in the press.

Teresa-Lyn Asmussen, age 22. Body found October 17, 1997, floating in the Spokane River near the Post Street Dam. Possibly dumped on Upriver Drive. Cause of death: blunt trauma to head.

It did not appear that Asmussen was connected to the other victims. The cause of death was different. There were no instances of blunt force trauma in any of the victims we had already connected, except for the nonfatal wounds that Brisbois suffered. By now the serial killer had developed at

least the coup de grâce of his MO—a small-caliber gunshot wound.

The other thing that made me think Asmussen was not
a victim of the serial killer was the lack of reaction by either
the police or the press. Two months after the frenzy of activity and attention following the Joseph and Hernandez
homicides, another young prostitute is found dead, floating in the river. These are enough connections for Spokane
to sit up and take notice. Yet nobody talked about Asmussen. This told me that there was either a good suspect
in the case, who they couldn't find enough evidence to arrest, or that there was some evidentiary connection lacking
in this case—other than the cause of death—which had
been present in the previous homicides.

According to the death certificate, an autopsy had never
been conducted on Asmussen. I gave a copy of the death
certificate to KXLY investigative reporter Tom Grant, who
found out that an autopsy had in fact been conducted, but
the death certificate had been filled out wrong. Reading the
Asmussen autopsy, I concluded that she most probably
died of blunt force trauma, and it didn't appear that she
was drowned. Absent of any other evidence, she didn't
seem to be connected to the other victims.

A man who knew Teresa Asmussen called in to the radio
show one Thursday. He ran a soup kitchen downtown, and
she had come in on several occasions for a meal. Because of
her lifestyle, the caller assumed that Asmussen had been a
victim of the serial killer, even though she had never been
officially linked to any of the other homicides. As this book
goes to press, her murder remains unsolved.

Sherry Palmer, age 19. Body found May 12, 1992, near Bill Gulch
Road near Mount Spokane Drive. Cause of death: multiple gunshot
wounds. Plastic bag on head.

Sherry Palmer was last seen at 11 P.M. on May 1, 1992, leaving Al's Motel on North Division Street, where she had been living for at least three days.

She was reported missing on May 5. Her partially nude body was discovered on May 12 in a wooded gulch near Mount Spokane (a few miles from where Jennifer Joseph was found). Palmer had been shot several times in the chest. There was a plastic bag wrapped around her head.

Shortly before her death, Sherry Palmer appeared on a KXLY television news program during a series about the street life of prostitutes. "It's just like a game . . . like Russian roulette," she told the KXLY reporter. "Every car you get into, you don't know if you're going to get hurt."

I don't think that Palmer's death was connected to her appearance on television. If her pimp, or some other criminal associate, wanted to retaliate for what she said on the program, I doubt they would have dumped her body near Mount Spokane, with a plastic bag wrapped around her head. The plastic bag and rural dump site indicated premeditation and an organized suspect—in other words, not a street hassle or bad trick.

The plastic bag was an interesting piece of evidence, which had not been reported before in any of the other cases. Mike and I wondered whether there had been plastic bags on any of the previous victims, but the police had been able to keep that information out of the media. Palmer might have been a victim of the 1990 killer, who had decided, for whatever reason, to put a plastic bag on her head. Or she could have been the victim of another serial killer, a copycat or someone from another area, whose MO or signature was a plastic bag over the head.

Mike and I wondered how, when, and why Sherry Palmer's head was wrapped in a plastic bag. Was it part of the suspect's MO, or his signature? If the bag was put on her head after she was shot, then it could be part of his MO, done to facilitate transport of her body. Or it could be a signature—possibly an attempt to depersonalize the victim and blot out her identity. If there was any way to prove that the suspect had sex with her dead body, and her head was covered with the plastic bag, then we had a very unique signature, not to mention a very sick suspect.

All suspects have MOs. Only serial killers have signatures. This made us think Palmer was the work of a serial killer, either the suspect from 1990 or someone else.

Even if the ballistics in the Palmer homicide didn't match the 1990 cases, even if the caliber didn't match, it still could be the same killer. Suspects often change guns. They discard weapons for a variety of reasons: The police are about to stop them; they don't want to be linked up through ballistics; their weapon is taken in an unrelated arrest or by a co-suspect; they lose their weapon. An organized offender would be very much aware of the fact that ballistics can be matched up, and might use a different weapon if he doesn't want his homicides connected. Or he might keep using the same weapon, if he wants investigators to connect his victims ballistically.

When Palmer's body was found, the 1990 task force had already been disbanded. Police told Palmer's mother, Teresa Ayres, that they didn't believe her daughter's murder was connected to the 1990 cases.

Mike and I thought Sherry Palmer was connected, even if the police didn't.

Palmer had some very clear links to the 1990 homicides: victimology, method of death, and dumping of the body. Only two years had elapsed since Kathy Brisbois was killed. In the intervening time, the suspect could have been in a cooling-off period. He could have been incarcerated for another crime. He could have moved away and come back. He could have been killing somewhere else.

Donna Lynn Harris, age 40. Body found April 7, 1996, along railroad tracks near Trent and Fiske. Cause of death: multiple stab wounds, including a slashed throat.

Because Harris was killed with a knife, without any other connective evidence or unique signature, we assumed that she was not a victim of the serial killer. She was a prostitute who had spent her life in Billings, Montana, and had just recently moved to Spokane. This homicide was probably a street beef, committed either by a local suspect or someone who knew her from Montana.

Shannon Zielinski, age 39. Body found June 14, 1996, near Holcomb Road and Mount Spokane Drive. Body was badly decomposed. Could have been killed up to four weeks before discovery. Cause of death: gunshot wound to head.

Zielinski was a native of Washington State whose last reported address was Melrose Place in Los Angeles. The time, date, and location of her death were undetermined by the autopsy, conducted by Dr. George Lindholm on June 17, 1996. Her body was cremated three days later.

Here was another body dumped in the same area where Sherry Palmer (and later Jennifer Joseph) was found. Another gunshot death. While news reports did not state whether Zielinski had a plastic bag on her head, it wouldn't have surprised me that the police were now withholding that information, particularly after it had been reported in the Palmer case.

When Palmer was found, the plastic bag didn't mean anything. It might even be used to disconnect Palmer from the other homicides, if no plastic bags were found on those bodies. But what if Zielinski had turned up with a plastic bag on her head? Suddenly there is a very strong connection between Palmer and Zielinski, which might even indicate a separate killer from the 1990 suspect. Or that the 1990 killer was back with a new wrinkle in his MO, and had now killed at least five victims.

JoAnn Flores, age 31. Body found November 7, 1996, in an alley in the 200 block of West Riverside. Cause of death: not disclosed.

When JoAnn Flores was found dead, the Spokane PD would not release the cause of death. That fact was available on the death certificate, which is a public document, easily obtained through the Washington State Department of Health.

When Mike and I got the Flores death certificate, it stated the cause of death as midbrain disruption as a consequence of a very close gunshot wound to the head. In other words, the same MO as the 1990 homicides, and those we thought were probably connected (Joseph, Hernandez, Palmer, Zielinski).

The fact that the police didn't want the method of death to be public knowledge made us think there was evidence, possibly a plastic bag or matching ballistics, that connected Flores with the other homicides. Otherwise, what reason did they have not to disclose the cause of death? Before getting the death certificate, I had asked Spokane County sheriff Mark Sterk and Corporal Dave Reagan specifically for this information, but they both refused to provide it. Were they withholding that information because it would connect Flores to the serial killer?

Of course, there were some differences between Flores and the other killings. Flores's body was found in an alley downtown. That didn't fit either the 1990 dumpings or Palmer and Zielinski. If Palmer and Zielinski were the work of the same suspect as the 1990 cases, it appeared that he was moving farther out of town. Flores would be an anomaly, moving right downtown, but that didn't mean she wasn't connected. Something could have gone wrong. Maybe she didn't want to go with the killer. Maybe he just didn't like her. Maybe he got scared. I didn't feel that the differing location from the other homicides necessarily excluded Flores.

At this point, the only evidence indicating that Flores was connected came from the police themselves. If Flores wasn't connected, then they had no reason to try and keep the cause of death from us. So we figured that until we learned anything else, we would consider Flores to be possibly connected.

Roseann Pleasant, age 34. Last reported seen alive September 29, 1992. Body never found.

Roseann Pleasant was a local prostitute who was also involved with drugs. She was last seen on September 29, 1992. She had been visiting her daughter Valiree at Mission Park in Spokane. Her estranged common-law husband, Brad Jackson, reported that he gave Roseann a ride to West Spokane, dropping her off on the corner of Nora and Ash, and that was the last anyone saw of her. Jackson was a suspect in Pleasant's disappearance, but police had also told members of her family that she was possibly a victim of a serial killer.

Roseann Pleasant was a friend of Sherry Palmer's. Could she have been killed by the same person who murdered Palmer, only her body was never discovered? Or was her estranged common-law husband, Brad Jackson, responsible? When we first looked at the case, Mike and I didn't know that Brad Jackson would be the suspect in a later homicide, but the disappearance of Roseann Pleasant looked as if it could possibly be connected to the serial killer.

* * *

After examining these ten unsolved prostitute homicides, Mike and I had at least three cases that might be connected: Palmer, Zielinski, and Flores. The others might possibly be connected, but at the time we had no reason to think they were.

The Joseph and Hernandez bodies shook Spokane law enforcement into action, and garnered some media attention, however short-lived. The other victims who could have been connected—Sherry Palmer, Shannon Zielinski, JoAnn Flores—got very little press and were virtually ignored. Now the victim count had risen to as many as ten.

The police were paying close attention to the media. Of course, the killer was as well. Would he try to make a bigger splash, and perhaps get his work back on the front page?

CHAPTER 6

Darla Sue Scott

Darla Sue Scott, age 29. Body found November 5, 1997, partially buried near the Hangman Valley Golf Course. Cause of death: gunshot wound to head. White plastic bag over head.

In the early fall of 1997, we knew that the three 1990 homicides were connected. And if any of the other five killings (Palmer, Zielinski, Flores, Joseph, and Hernandez) were connected to each other, but not to the 1990 cases, then Spokane had at least two serial killers.

"What is it with this city?" I asked Mike. "Do they need a serial killer traffic cop?"

It was a joke, but it wasn't funny. At least eight women had been murdered, and nothing was being done about it. Spokane went on with its business, getting ready for winter and gearing up for the holidays, ignorant of the fact that East Sprague had become a killing field.

And it was only getting worse.

At approximately 9:00 on the morning of November 5, 1997, Harold Lebsock was walking his Rottweiler through the woods adjacent to the Hangman Valley Golf Course south of Spokane. Lebsock had been taking his dog through that area for the past couple of days, and the dog kept running off the trail and sniffing something near a creek. That morning, Lebsock got curious and followed his dog.

He soon came upon the near-skeletal remains of a woman buried in a shallow grave. The body was partially clothed. There was a white plastic bag over her head.

Lebsock went home and called the police. When they arrived, police cordoned off the wooded area adjacent to Hangman Valley Road and began processing the crime scene. They sifted through the grave for evidence. While sheriff's deputies described the body as badly decomposed, they said they weren't sure how long the body had been at that location. It had been pulled partially out of the grave, which detectives said suggested that animal predators had been at the body.

Later that day, volunteers combed the wooded area around the grave site, looking for evidence. The area was heavily traveled, popular with joggers, walkers, and children riding bicycles. But the body had apparently lain there for weeks.

Since the remains were so badly decomposed, the sheriff's department had to consult a forensic anthropologist for help in retrieving it from the grave site. Lieutenant John Simmons told the *Spokesman-Review* that detectives had called the anthropologist for a "few pointers."

The evening the body was discovered, the man who owned the property noticed all the police activity on his land and went over to see what was going on. He approached the crime scene with his hands in his pockets, and one of the detectives screamed at him, "Get your hands out of your pockets!" The man obliged, then asked the police what was going on. They told him not to worry about it. The man explained that he owned the property. They told him to go away. The man stated that he would be home if they had any questions. The police never came to his house to question him, even though he was probably home the night the body had been dumped, and might possibly have seen something, even if he didn't know its significance.

The body had been found in the morning. By the end of the day, police and criminalists had not finished processing the crime scene. Instead of bringing out light trucks and finishing the scene by artificial lights, they decided to secure the body and leave the crime scene until the next morning. So they erected a tent over the body and left it guarded by personnel. The next day, they returned to finish processing the crime scene.

When I heard this, I was dumbstruck. I had never heard of a crime scene being left overnight while the detectives and criminalists went home. Was this the way the Spokane County Sheriff's Department normally handled homicide scenes? I hoped that there were other circumstances of which I was not aware that made it necessary to leave the scene. Still, I couldn't think of what they might be.

When the body was recovered from the crime scene the next day, it was determined that the victim was a white female, about five feet six inches tall. The autopsy, conducted on November 11 by Dr. George Lindholm, determined that she had died as a result of cerebral pulpification from a gunshot wound to the head. Time or date of death was unknown.

Using dental records, detectives identified the body on November 13 as Darla Sue Scott, a twenty-nine-year-old local prostitute and drug addict. Scott's remains were cremated by a local funeral home on November 18.

Darla Sue Scott was born on September 16, 1968, in Milwaukie, Oregon. She was a high school dropout who had never married. Her last known address was in Spokane, where she had lived for twenty-nine years. Her parents, Dale Douglas and Barbara Ann Scott, lived in Yakima, Washington. Darla Sue Scott had a criminal record that included numerous arrests on drug and prostitution charges.

In 1995 Scott was pregnant. She requested methadone treatment from the Spokane County Health District. After her baby was born, Scott went back to drugs and prostitution. The baby was taken into foster care.

Darla Sue Scott fit the victim profile and the MO. Unless this was the work of a very, very smart copycat killer, she was connected to at least some of the previous homicides.

While the police reported that Lebsock's dog had partially unearthed Scott's body, that didn't mean that the killer had fully buried her in order to keep her concealed. He could have left her half-buried, revisiting the site, having sex with her dead body, or masturbating over her while reliving his sadistic fantasies. After a while, he might have grown tired of her and left her body in its original grave site. Or he could have partially unburied her, in hopes that she would eventually be discovered. Another possibility was that she had been buried in another location, and he had exhumed her and partially buried her at the Hangman Valley site.

The location itself told me that the suspect knew the area and was comfortable moving around in it. The trail off the golf course was remote enough to afford him some privacy, but also public enough that if he was seen, he would have a reasonable excuse to be there—if anyone even noticed him. This indicated that the suspect would be able to blend into this neighborhood. He might live nearby, or in a similar upper-middle-class neighborhood. Or he could work in the area as a utility worker, deliveryman, repairman, or someone in the construction trades—anything that would allow him to drive around the neighborhood in a truck or van, or even be seen parked in the same location at different times, and not arouse suspicion. He could have some connection to the golf course, either as a regular golfer or as maintenance personnel. There were many different possibilities, but what was important was the apparent ease with which he moved through the area. Residents like the man who owned the property on which Darla Sue Scott was found could possibly have seen him several times and not thought anything about it.

The road leading to the woods where Scott was discovered was a cruising spot for couples and young people drinking beer. If someone saw a car parked near those woods, they probably wouldn't pay much attention.

Hangman Valley is on the opposite end of the county from the Jennifer Joseph dump site and Mount Spokane, where Sherry Palmer and Shannon Zielinski were found. If this was the same killer, then he was highly mobile, familiar with the greater Spokane area, and probably scouting out his dump sites.

To Mike and me, the most significant piece of evidence was the plastic bag. This apparently connected at least Sherry Palmer and Darla Sue Scott. The Scott suspect was either a copycat, or he had killed Palmer as well. That placed him killing in Spokane as early as 1992, only two years following Kathy Brisbois.

In addition to being a possible nexus between at least two of the homicides, the plastic bag was a powerful bit of evidence. Properly analyzed and understood, it could offer a unique perspective on at least the Scott and Palmer homicides. Mike and I had countless discussions about the plastic bag and what it signified. We talked about it at the station, over lunch at the Viking, on our way to and from crime scenes, and on the air. Neither one of us had a firm opinion on what it meant, but we were constantly testing theories.

Before the plastic bag could offer us any insight into the

killings, Mike and I had to establish why it was there. The main question was whether the plastic bag was signature or MO.

We went back and forth on the question, taking different sides and playing devil's advocate with each other, exploring the various possible explanations for a plastic bag being wrapped around the victim's head.

These explanations ranged from the mundane to the bizarre. If the plastic bag was a signature, the killer could be using it to dehumanize his victims, deprive them of their identity and personhood. This would indicate a very disturbed individual, with a violent hatred of women, possibly dating back to a troubled relationship with his mother, and probably involving extensive and escalating use of pornography, some of it quite violent in nature. He might also feel particular anger toward prostitutes, indicating guilt and confusion over his own use of them. Though I did not believe that he was a messianic serial killer, who felt he was cleaning the streets of wickedness, there was a strong possibility that he felt very conflicted about his own sexual desires and the way in which he gratified them.

That was one of the bizarre explanations, assuming the plastic bag was his signature. A more mundane answer was that the plastic bag was part of the MO. The suspect was shooting his victims in the head, then wrapping them in plastic bags to keep blood and tissue from seeping out during the period in which he held or transported their bodies. If he was keeping their corpses for some time, then the bag could serve a dual purpose of MO and signature. Considered strictly as MO, the bags could simply have been a way to keep his victims from bleeding inside of his house or vehicle. We knew that Darla Sue Scott, Yolanda Sapp, and Nickie Lowe were not killed where they were found. We figured that many of the other victims had also been killed at one location and then dumped elsewhere. This would require the suspect to drive them to the dump sites. The plastic bags would facilitate this transportation.

Even considered simply as MO, the plastic bag was intriguing. It indicated a highly organized, intelligent, and experienced killer. He was learning as he went along. Perhaps an earlier victim had bled inside his vehicle, so he began bagging his victims' heads.

This also indicated that the suspect was a psychopath, not an out-of-control psychotic. He was aware of his criminality, in control of his actions, and did not want to get caught. He took extra precautions not to leave evidence. This made him even more of a challenge to the detectives trying to catch him.

Mike and I tried to keep an open mind concerning the purpose of the plastic bag. We didn't want to tie ourselves to one theory, particularly since we knew so little at this point. We wanted to understand what the killer was doing, not as part of an intellectual exercise, but in order to help catch him. Knowing what purpose the plastic bag served would help us determine what the serial killer was doing with his victims, and quite possibly who he was.

Ever since the signature/MO distinction was first developed by John Douglas and Robert Ressler of the FBI, there has been a great deal of study and debate on the subject. The theory has helped detectives distinguish between serial sexual psychopaths and common criminals. Too often, the theory has been taken into the less useful realm of attempting to understand the motives of these psychopaths.

Law enforcement professionals, mental health experts, journalists, and academics have spent their careers examining the psychological makeup of serial murderers in an attempt to understand what drives them to kill. If they ever do come up with a theory that might explain this, that's fine. But I doubt it will happen. I've always found human nature too perverse and mysterious to fit into the precise formulations of scientific models.

I'm a detective, not a psychologist or profiler. I'm interested only in using the signature to connect victims in order to catch the suspect. I also know that sometimes the signature can vary between victims. What was Ted Bundy's signature? Was it the act of killing itself? Or was it necrophilia? Dismemberment? Beheading his victims and taking them home and putting makeup on their faces?

Signature is rarely a consistent single act. While the Green River Killer placed three pyramid-shaped rocks in some of his victims' vaginas, there were many other victims who didn't have this unique evidence. Did that mean another suspect was responsible? How would anyone, aside from the killer himself, ever know?

Signature is motive. Understanding a serial killer's motive—as if I ever could—is not going to help me identify the suspect. A detective doesn't need to understand why the suspect kills. The detective needs to know how he kills in order to catch him.

Motive is the one thing you don't have to prove in a criminal trial. It might be important for the criminal profiler or psychologist who is trying to understand how the mind of the serial killer works, and help law enforcement identify him or predict his next moves. For a working detective, trying to figure out motive is a waste of time. It's one thing to try to get into the serial killer's head and to re-create his movements and actions at the crime scene. It's something else entirely to try to understand why he's doing it.

I worked robbery for years. In robbery the motive is very clear. The suspect wants money. The victim has it. Most robbers kill only when they feel they have to—when somebody stands between them and getting away with their crime.

Murder never makes sense. People kill because of jealousy, anger, greed. Your marriage breaks up, your business partner rips you off, you catch your girlfriend in bed with your next-door neighbor—are these good reasons to kill somebody? Even a revenge killing or murder for hire might have a motive that is rational to the suspect, but still incomprehensible to the rest of us.

Detectives often trap themselves into thinking that if they understand the motive, they'll understand the murder and be able to fit everything into a neat little theory that will lead them to the killer. This is a fruitless pursuit that will only frustrate and distract a homicide detective, leading him or her further away from a solution.

Listen to the evidence. Let the evidence say what it is going to say. If you don't understand the motive—and in many cases I would be worried if I did—don't worry about it. If the motive is obvious, that's fine. But don't waste any time, effort, or energy trying to figure out a killer's motive. Particularly in the case of serial murder, in which the desire for violent sexual gratification is deeply rooted in the twisted psyche of the killer.

How can we possibly understand why Jeffrey Dahmer wanted to erect a shrine of skulls in his bedroom? Why did Angelo Buono and Kenneth Bianchi torture their victims with vise grips? Why did Ed Gein dance around his Wisconsin farmhouse wearing the skin of corpses he had dug up from a local graveyard?

Sexual psychopaths are, by definition, irrational. A working detective has no hope of understanding what even experts who devote their lives to the study of criminal psychology can't figure out. The motives of normal humans are mysterious enough—how can we possibly expect to understand the motives of sexual psychopaths?

The questions a detective should be asking at a serial killer crime scene are What happened here? What does the evidence say about the movements and actions of the suspect? Even the most intelligent and experienced killer will leave clues—if the detective is observant enough to recognize them. The answers are all there, if only you ask the right questions.

So what did the plastic bag mean? After hours of discussion and debate, the best that Mike and I could do was conclude that the plastic bag meant that Palmer and Scott were probably connected. That might not sound like much, but it was more than the police would admit.

Once Darla Sue Scott's body was discovered, I figured that her body would be quickly linked to the other unsolved prostitute homicides, and Spokane would form a task force to investigate the cases.

That didn't happen. In fact, nothing happened. Except that more prostitutes turned up missing.

Nine days after Scott's body was found, the sheriff's office issued a press release which stated they were looking for three missing women "who are persons of interest possibly connected to the four recent homicides of local prostitutes."

I didn't understand what this meant. Was the sheriff's department reporting these women missing? Were they considered suspects or possible victims? The sheriff's department was unwilling to state the obvious. After at least four prostitute homicides in a matter of months, three more women who fit the victim profile were missing and now feared dead.

The three women were Lonna Marie Hughes, Shawn Johnson, and Laurie Ann Wason. Hughes had been reported missing on October 27, Johnson on October 29, and Wason on November 3. They had all been reported missing prior to the discovery of Scott's body. Why weren't we hearing about them until now?

Granted, the lifestyle of these women made it difficult

to determine when, or even if, they were missing. Prostitutes don't have the same routines and responsibilities that you and I do. They are often not in close touch with family, and what friends they have would probably not find it odd if they weren't seen for a few days. Street prostitutes usually don't have a fixed place of abode. They live day to day. If they make enough money for a night in a cheap motel, then that's where they sleep. If they don't make the money, they try to find an overnight trick, or go to a drug house, where they can trade sex for shelter.

It is not uncommon for a prostitute who is also a drug addict (as most of these women were) to go off on a binge for several days. They can also run into a john who takes them somewhere. In Spokane there are many transient prostitutes who work the circuit, traveling between different western cities, depending on conditions like the weather and local police.

These are not the kind of women who would initiate contact with law enforcement, so even once they are reported missing, they might not come forward. Many of them have outstanding warrants or other criminal beefs.

All of this presents challenges for police trying to locate such women, or even establish if they are missing in the first place. That's what Spokane was up against.

Darla Sue Scott hadn't been reported missing. And there was a good chance that if Scott hadn't been found, then Hughes, Johnson, and Wason wouldn't have been reported missing, either.

Of the three missing women, Lonna Marie Hughes was located almost immediately. She was still in Spokane and was interviewed by the detectives assigned to the Scott homicide.

Johnson and Wason remained missing, and there was no sign of either one of them. In a November 18 *Spokesman-Review* article, Johnson's mother, Margaret

Dettman, pleaded for her daughter to call home. The same article stated that "police and sheriff's detectives asked the community Friday for help in finding the women, saying they may have information that could aid an investigation into the recent murders of several prostitutes."

What information were the cops looking for—whether these women were alive? Prostitutes were missing. Prostitutes were turning up dead. Why not just say it?

Whatever level of investigation the sheriff's department was conducting at this point, whether it was just the singular homicide of Darla Sue Scott and the singular homicide of Jennifer Joseph (while the city handled Heather Hernandez), I didn't understand why they wouldn't refer to Johnson and Wason as possible victims. If anything, trying to massage, control, or suppress information about missing prostitutes only gave the serial killer a head start. Apparently, he had already abducted three women (Scott, Johnson, Wason) before the community even realized he was snatching prostitutes off the street.

If both law enforcement agencies involved in these cases were stubbornly refusing to link any of the unsolved prostitute homicides, at least the media was beginning to see the connections.

The *Spokesman-Review* reported that nine unsolved prostitute homicides were possibly linked. These nine were Sapp, Lowe, Brisbois, Palmer, Zielinski, Scott, Joseph, Hernandez, and Teresa-Lyn Asmussen. Of the nine dead prostitutes, at least three of them had been connected by ballistics. Two others were connected with plastic bags.

In 1990 a task force had been formed after only three victims. In 1997 they had three times that many, and still no task force had been announced.

Now there were three more missing women. Were they dead, or had they just run off somewhere? The killer knew, and I had a feeling we'd find out pretty soon.

CHAPTER 7

Shawn Johnson

Shawn Johnson, age 36. Body found December 18, 1997, in the 11400 block of South Hangman Valley Road near sewage treatment station, approximately one mile away from where Darla Sue Scott was found. Cause of death: gunshot wound to head. Plastic bag over head.

If the Spokane authorities had hoped that the prostitute homicides weren't connected, those hopes were dashed with the next body find.

At 1:15 P.M. on Thursday, December 18, 1997, the partially decomposed body of a white female was discovered by maintenance workers at a water treatment plant off Hangman Valley Road. They found the body at the bottom of an embankment approximately twenty-five feet from the road. The body was fully clothed in blue jeans and a top. It was covered with leaves and brush. (We later found out that there was a white plastic bag wrapped around its head.) The victim had been killed in another location and then dumped over the edge of the embankment, rolling down the hill until she came to a rest in a clump of cottonwood trees.

Eventually, the body was identified as Shawn Johnson, a thirty-six-year-old resident of Deer Park, Washington. Johnson was born on March 17, 1961, in Palmer, Arkansas. She was a high school dropout, and had been married and divorced. She had worked as a cashier in a grocery store. Her parents, Eldred Johnson and Margaret Dettman, lived in Oak Harbor, Washington.

Johnson was five feet six inches tall, 150 pounds, with brown hair and hazel eyes. She had a rose tattoo on her ankle. Her last known address was in Deer Park, Washington.

While Johnson had never been arrested for prostitution, she was a known prostitute, often working on East Sprague. She had a history of arrests for drug and driving offenses and trafficking in stolen property. She was last seen by her family in mid-October, attending a wedding in Deer Park. Johnson had been reported missing October 29.

Sometime after her body was found, Johnson's family erected a small white cross at the dump site on Hangman Valley Road. The cross was made of old, painted wood, with her name, birth date, and the date her body was found inscribed on the cross. They also left a small stuffed animal in her memory.

Shawn Johnson's autopsy, conducted by Dr. George Lindholm, could not determine when she was killed. The cause of death was cerebral tissue disruption as a result of a gunshot wound to the head. Her body was cremated on New Year's Eve, 1997.

Johnson's body was about a mile north of where Darla Sue Scott had been found about six weeks earlier. The day her remains were discovered, the sheriff's department stated that investigators had not even determined the gender of the victim. The body was described as "decomposing," and was said to have lain at the bottom of the embankment for at least two days.

After giving out these and other details, police said they

would not discuss any particulars of this latest homicide. Lieutenant John Simmons, who headed the sheriff's Crimes Against Persons Unit, told reporters, "There's a couple of distinctive things about the scene that likely only the killer would know. We don't want that made public right now."

When I read that comment in the newspaper, the first thing I thought of was a plastic bag. Although I didn't know it at the time, I had a feeling that this latest victim was bagged, too. And the police didn't want to discuss this piece of evidence, not because it was a holdback—a piece of evidence only the killer would know about—but because then they would have to link up this victim with Scott and Palmer. Eventually, Mike and I were able to confirm, through our source on the task force, that Johnson had a plastic bag on her head.

It is routine to hold back one or even several specific pieces of information that only the killer would know. This may become useful in the future, as an interrogation tool against the real suspect, or to disprove false confessions from other suspects. People often come into a police station and confess to crimes they didn't commit, particularly high-profile murders. Information that is held back from public disclosure can help disprove these bogus confessions.

Even beyond holdback information, the police have reasons, and the right, to keep information out of the public realm. But once that information does come out, they are well advised to confirm accurate information, or deny inaccurate information. The Spokane Sheriff's Department, and later the Spokane PD, had a tendency to not answer any questions from reporters, but then to release some information that clearly should have been kept confidential. Once that sensitive information was out, they would neither confirm nor deny its accuracy. This was not only a disservice to the public, it also made them look as if they were trying to hide something.

The plastic bag is one example of this egregious policy. It had already been published in the newspapers that Sherry Palmer had a plastic bag on her head. It was widely known, though neither confirmed nor denied by the police, that Darla Sue Scott also had a plastic bag on her head. Same with Shawn Johnson.

Obviously, the plastic bag was an important piece of evidence. But why was it necessary for the police to try to keep it a secret? Their efforts to suppress this information only made the plastic bag seem more important. To me, it was an evidentiary item that was impossible to suppress. All the bodies were being found by civilians. They would probably notice the plastic bag, and there was no way to keep them from talking to their family, friends, neighbors, or the press. This was a piece of information that the police simply couldn't control.

And it wasn't the only one. When Shawn Johnson's body was found, police stated that they were looking for four more missing women. Once again, they stated that these women "may have information about the unsolved prostitute homicides." I didn't understand what possible benefit they got from refusing to call these women possible victims. Not only didn't they call them possible victims, but now they wouldn't even name the additional missing women.

How could you investigate a missing person case without mentioning the missing person's name? How could you possibly expect to keep the name a secret if you are using it during the course of your investigation?

This was the second announcement of missing women. The first was on November 14, when the sheriff's department stated that they were looking for Hughes, Johnson, and Wason. Since Johnson was now dead, and Hughes had been found alive, this indicated that in addition to Laurie Ann Wason, who was still presumed missing, there were at least three more missing women, although the police would not give out their names—until they were found. When Lois Jean Spicer was located by police shortly after Johnson's body was found, she was announced to have been one of the missing women. That meant there were two more missing and unidentified women, in addition to Wason.

Once again, it appeared that the police felt they had to control this information, even if it went against all standard police procedure, or even common sense, in missing person cases. Were they doing it to protect the case or to protect themselves?

It seemed that the Spokane police were afraid to admit, at least publicly, that they had a serial killer on their hands. I wondered what they were saying among themselves. Were they afraid of the challenges that a string of serial murders posed?

I worked robbery for years. And robbery is a lot like serial killing. Robbers are organized, intelligent, aggressive, and violent. They are usually not incapacitated by drugs or physical weakness. They are career criminals who keep committing the same crime in the same manner, doing their best not to get caught. And they need a live victim.

Think of it this way: Robbers are serial bandits. Their MO is almost like a signature. A professional robber will usually not deviate from his pattern. He'll use the same weapon, the same approach, the same words. He'll choose the same time, location, and victims. Of course, robbers don't have the mystique, or the mythology, that serial killers do, which is one reason why they're easier to catch. The process that a robbery detective uses to analyze the evidence, connect up the crimes, and pursue the suspect is quite similar.

I chased robbers by learning how they committed their crimes, and by trying to predict when and where they might strike again. I made sure my own officers knew everything that I did and told the public what to look out for. Since robbers are committing a series of crimes, the detective should focus on one case that provides the best evidence and the most information about the suspect. I always looked at it this way—solve one, solve them all.

It's the same thing with serial killing. Unfortunately, we are intimidated by the serial killer, because he kills for reasons we can't comprehend and generates much more attention, not only from the police department, but from the public as well. There is much more pressure and attention in a serial murder case than a series of jewelry store robberies.

Too often, detectives working a serial murder case think they have to do everything different. They seem to forget everything they knew when they venture into this new territory, and years of experience are overlooked. As the bodies pile up, the evidence mounts, and the pressure builds, the detectives lose confidence in their own abilities, and consider the case a burden rather than a challenge.

The serial killer is a cunning psychopath. He might even be more intelligent than you are. But he still leaves evidence. In fact, because he commits his crimes in a series, he leaves much more evidence. Some of that evidence will be consistent among the various crime scenes. Some of it will be different. By looking at the similarities, much the same as in robbery, you will see what the killer likes to do, where he is comfortable, where he is not. By looking at the differences, one case will stand out. This case will have all the evidence and leads necessary to capture the suspect.

With the body of Shawn Johnson, the serial killer was connecting up his own crimes. He was also developing a unique and identifiable MO. His victims were all female prostitutes and/or drug addicts. They were abducted, shot with a small-caliber handgun, and dumped in a rural area. At least one body was exhumed and dumped in another location. In two cases, there were plastic bags around the victim's head. In all cases, there was probably some form of sex act, whether it was consensual, rape, or necrophilia. I made this assumption because the victims were all involved in prostitution; they were all found naked or partially clothed; and serial murder usually involves a sex act.

There were at least four opportunities for the suspect to be observed during the commission of his crime: when he first made contact with his victims; when he dumped them; when he was exhuming them; or when he was visiting their graves.

Somebody saw something, although it might have seemed innocent at the time. Just as I would inform the public about a robbery suspect's MO, the Spokane police needed to make public what they knew about this killer so that witnesses of his actions would be able to know that they might have been watching a killer.

Serial killers and robbers are creatures of habit. They have zones of safety in which they prefer to operate. They return to the same place repeatedly. The Spokane serial killer was probably contacting his victims along East Sprague. He would keep going back there until it got too hot. The police needed to be on East Sprague, because that's where the victims were, and where their suspect would return.

The Shawn Johnson dump site was a crime scene that held a great deal of evidence, not only about the Johnson homicide itself, but also about the other serial murders. If the police looked at the Johnson case, or any of the others, as a singular homicide, and tried to solve it that way, they had a good chance at success.

Shortly after Johnson's body was found, Mike and I took a

drive out Hangman Valley to view the areas where Scott and Johnson had been found. Along the way, Mike gave me a travelogue of the region. Hangman Valley is a wide, open creek bed winding south-southeast out of town. Along the hills that frame the valley is some prime residential real estate. What's interesting about these homes, Mike pointed out, was that many of them had a direct line of sight to where the bodies of Darla Sue Scott and Shawn Johnson were buried.

"It's a relatively new neighborhood, mostly professionals who commute into the city," Mike said. "Real high-rent district."

"How much does a house around here cost?" I asked.

"Oh, anywhere between three hundred grand and a million," Mike said. "Out of our league."

"Yeah, I'd say."

We pulled over at the water treatment plant, a small facility right off Hangman Valley Road. Adjacent to the facility was a parking lot, and beyond that Hangman Creek. At the beginning of the driveway, the embankment was only a couple feet from the road's edge, widening as it followed south and turned into the parking lot. At the bottom was the clump of dogwood trees where Johnson's body had been found. Here the embankment was about twenty-five feet high and very steep.

Since the body was found resting against the trees at the bottom of the embankment, it appeared that the killer had pulled off on the street above, and dumped her from there.

Mike and I parked on the edge of the road and sidestepped down the embankment. The body had been rolled down the hill, coming to a rest against the dogwood trees at the bottom. A steep embankment, a body of water—this dump site bore some resemblance to the Sapp and Lowe crime scenes.

Just like those victims, it appeared that the suspect

wanted Shawn Johnson to be found, if not immediately then eventually. The sewage treatment plant was visited regularly, both by utility workers and by cruising couples and beer-drinking kids. The suspect must have known that it would not take long for this body to be found. In fact, he was probably counting on it.

Mike and I had already discussed the possibility that the killer had wanted Darla Sue Scott found. The Johnson site was a little more obvious.

"So why did he dump her here?" I asked, and knew that Mike was thinking the same thing.

"It's just a mile from Scott's shallow grave. Similar MO. Same method of death. Probably the same gun," Mike said, already picking up the lingo of a homicide detective. "Why did he bury one, and dump the other?"

I didn't know. So I walked closer to the clump of trees and stood there a minute, soaking in the scene.

There's something about her. She looks just like the last one. They could be sisters. Perhaps, in a way, they were. She's been dead more than a month. He's already buried her some-where. But she hasn't been found. So he digs her up, taking some of the leaves and brush from the first burial site along with her decomposed body.

He's driving south down Hangman Valley. He knows the area, because he's been there before to bury Darla Sue Scott. He came back several times to revisit her grave.

He pulls off on the side of the road and dumps her body down the embankment. This time he wants the body to be found. He knows that the workers will come to check on the plant sometime tomorrow. Or maybe some teenagers drink-ing beer in the parking lot will find her. Either way, it shouldn't be long before this one is discovered. Now Spokane will have to pay attention.

I explained to Mike how I saw it. He was thinking right along with me.

"Could he have been on his way to the golf course, and then he saw that it's closed and he had to dump her off here?"

"It's possible." I thought about it. "Or maybe somebody spooked him. Maybe he saw a patrol car or a nosy neighbor and he decided he didn't have time to take her to the golf course."

"Or maybe the golf course was closed. It is December, after all," Mike said with a smile.

"Hey, I'm not a golfer," I said.

"No, that's your buddy, what's his name, the football player . . ."

"Don't say it."

"There's a couple different ways in and out," Mike said, pointing out the roads that snaked along both sides of Hangman Valley. "There's side roads that lead into private property. But the thing about this area is not just its accessibility, but its relative seclusion. There's very little traffic here. Maybe in the morning when people go to work. Or in the evening when they come home. Or when the golf course is open, you'll see a few cars. But right now, look around you. How many cars have we seen since we've been here?"

"Maybe two or three," I said, looking up and down the valley. "And you can hear them coming from a long way off."

"Why did he pick this location?"

"Because he knows it. He feels comfortable here. Maybe he lives here. Maybe he has some reason to come out here," I said. "Maybe he works for a utility company—a telephone lineman, a cable installer."

"Maybe he's a rural postal delivery person."

"A postal worker? They've never been known to kill anybody."

"Yeah," Mike said with a sly grin on his face. "You're right about that one."

Mike began mapping the killer's route out of the valley.

"As he drove off, he didn't have to turn around," Mike explained, "since the road circles back around and starts heading north on the other side of the creek."

"With all these houses around," I said, looking at the expensive homes that ringed the valley heights, "somebody might have seen something."

We figured that the houses had been canvassed when Johnson's body was found, and that if any witnesses had seen anything, like a vehicle or a suspect, the police would have released this information in order to stimulate more clues.

So Mike and I focused on the crime scene.

When the body was first discovered, Lieutenant John Simmons had told the press, "We're going to pick up cigarette butts. We're going to pick up beer cans. Anything that looks like it was left by a person, we'll either pick up or photograph."

When Mike and I searched it just a few days later, the parking lot was still strewn with cigarette butts, beer cans, used condoms, scraps of fabric, and other trash. All these items were possible evidence. Much of it had obviously been there for weeks. Maybe the police had retrieved a lot of evidence from the crime scene, but they also left a great deal. One of those beer cans or cigarette butts could have the killer's fingerprints. Even after Shawn Johnson's body had been discovered and removed from the site, he might have come back, just for the memories. Or maybe for some other reason.

"You think there's another body out there?" Mike asked, looking across Hangman Valley.

"You're thinking the same thing I am," I replied. "Maybe there's more bodies. And Johnson's body is just a marker. Is the killer communicating with the police? Telling them there's more bodies?"

"How many more?"

That I didn't know.

The police seemed to think there were additional bodies, since they returned to Hangman Valley to search for them. It was like looking for a needle in a haystack, especially if the killer was burying his victims in the woods. The cops needed to have a direction in their search, some indication of what the killer was doing. Maybe he had already given them the clue, but they missed it. Maybe Shawn Johnson was the clue. But what exactly did it mean?

If Joseph and Hernandez were the work of the same suspect who killed Shawn Johnson and Darla Sue Scott, was he killing and dumping them in pairs? Or were there more bodies out in Hangman Valley? Where was Laurie Ann Wason? Who were the other missing women? Were they already dead? If they were dead, when and where would they show up?

We took our questions to the airwaves. We connected the Scott and Johnson homicides and began a dialogue of murder, discussing the ABC's of homicide investigation, the regular and not so glamorous process of trying to connect the victims to a common denominator, and with luck a possible suspect. I described the many avenues that must be considered, and eliminated, as well as the hot tips and clues.

As we got more involved in the serial killer case, I watched Mike's natural curiosity take over. He was excited, dedicated, and hungry for knowledge. I knew Mike would have made a great detective and partner.

FITZSIMMONS: We'll pass on any information that is germane to these murders to the authorities, and I know that some of them are listening anyway. If you live in the

vicinity of one of the crime scenes and you noticed anything during or prior to the day these bodies were discovered, please call the station. You just might know
more than you think . . .

On those early shows, I was very supportive of the local
cops, even if what little I knew about their investigation did
not inspire confidence. Their attempts to control information seemed not only doomed to failure, but also indicated
that they were afraid of something. I just wasn't sure what
it was.

I kept those suspicions to myself. I figured the Spokane
Sheriff's Department and the city police were, like most
cops, dedicated and competent. Of course they wanted to
solve this case. The last thing I wanted to do was second-
guess them. I had been there myself, and knew how frustrating and unhelpful criticism from the media could be.

I also wondered whether they had the tools that the
challenges of this kind of investigation required. I wasn't
convinced they had the resources or the support necessary
to catch a serial killer, especially when they wouldn't even
admit they had a serial killer.

With the discovery of Shawn Johnson's body, and all the
obvious connective evidence, Spokane's politicians, police,
and public could no longer deny that they had a serial
killer working in their city. Now, I wondered—and the
killer was probably wondering himself—what are they going to do about it?

CHAPTER 8

The Task Force

It was early morning, just a couple days before Christmas. I was out feeding the animals, and everybody else was still asleep, so when Mike called, he left a message on my machine.

"Hey Fuhrman, did you read the newspaper yet? Call me."

I hadn't read the newspaper that morning, because I never read it, because I didn't like to read it. Sometimes I'd buy a copy of the *Spokesman-Review* to start a fire in the stove or line the parakeet's cage, but I never actually read it. Now that I was a journalist, I was supposed to read the newspaper. Mike had been bugging me, but I just didn't want to do it. Besides, I knew that if there was anything in there that I should read, he'd call and tell me, which is exactly what happened.

So I drove down to Arnie's gas station. He gave me his copy of the newspaper, so I didn't actually have to buy one.

"Are the boys in Spokane gonna catch that psycho killer?" Arnie asked.

"I sure hope so."

"Well, if they need help from the posse, tell them we're ready to ride."

"Okay, Arnie."

I drove back home to read the newspaper over breakfast.

TASK FORCE TACKLES MURDERS

FOUR DETECTIVES WILL CONCENTRATE ON RECENT PROSTITUTE MURDERS

Spokesman-Review December 23, 1997

A four-detective task force began working full-time Monday on a string of unsolved homicides involving women who worked as prostitutes, Spokane authorities said.

A four-detective task force? I nearly coughed up my Grape-Nuts. Four detectives aren't a task force. Four detectives are two detective teams, the same personnel who were already investigating the Joseph and Hernandez homicides since August. Since Joseph was found in the county and Hernandez in the city, four Spokane PD and sheriff's department detectives were already assigned to that case. That meant that the deaths of Scott and Johnson would be handled by the same detectives already investigating the Joseph case.

I kept reading as assistant city police chief Roger Bragdon described the task force.

On Monday, the sheriff's office and police department each assigned two detectives full-time to the task force, Bragdon said. The group will receive support from other investigators as needed.

I couldn't believe what I was reading. Nobody had been working full-time on these homicides until just a couple of days ago. What had they been doing for four months?

The task force will scrutinize the deaths of five women found dead in the Spokane area this year, as well as the unsolved homicides of seven other prostitutes dating to the mid-1980s.

So the task force would be looking at Johnson, Scott, Joseph, Hernandez, and ... Who was the fifth victim in 1997? Could that be Asmussen?

"We're going to be looking at all the prostitute homicides we've had, including ones we've solved, just trying to find any inkling about what might be going on," Bragdon said.

I didn't know that the Spokane police had solved any prostitute homicides. Whenever Mike and I asked about possible solved cases, they wouldn't give us any information, which made us conclude that they hadn't solved any.

For the past two months, the four detectives now assigned full-time to the task force have been laying the groundwork for an intense investigation, Bragdon said.

They researched serial killings, reviewed the files on the latest cases, and assembled special computers and software they will use to track clues, all while reporting to their unit supervisors and pursuing other cases.

On Monday, authorities established a joint command and freed up the four detectives to work solely on the prostitute murders, Bragdon said.

During the time that they were "laying the groundwork for an intense investigation" at least two more women had died. What other cases had the detectives been working on?

Burglaries? Car thefts? Purse snatchings? What could possibly be more important than a serial killer investigation?

Well, I figured at least they would finally admit that Spokane had a serial killer. And I figured wrong.

Still, local authorities hesitate to call the string of murders the work of a serial killer.

"The first thing our people have to do is prove or disprove the serial aspects of this case," Bragdon said. "We haven't been able to prove anything yet. Of course, any thinking person can see that there are an awful lot of coincidences to some of them."

If they were willing to call their two detective teams a task force, why wouldn't they admit these killings were connected? What were they afraid of? If they had been my cases, I would rather look at the homicides as connected until proven otherwise. For all the difficulties and challenges that a serial murder case presents, if you solve one homicide, you solve them all.

But Spokane law enforcement apparently thought otherwise.

"If a serial killer is at work in Spokane, detectives will have to work long and hard to stop him," Bragdon said. The infamous Green River killings in Western Washington, where nearly 50 women were murdered, remain unsolved.

"We realize that if we start making connections (among the killings), we're in for the long haul," Bragdon said. "We're looking at a mammoth task that's going to be very, very frustrating."

Bragdon was actually being honest about their reluctance to even admit Spokane had a serial killer. They didn't want it to be true, because they didn't want the responsibility of having to catch him. Bragdon was a leader in local law enforcement. The fact that he felt so reluctant about pursuing a serial killer was bad enough, but to make comments in the press, where not just the citizens, but his own personnel, would read them, was poor leadership. It was like a football coach telling a sportswriter on the eve of a big game, "Well, we really don't want to play against these guys, because they scare the hell out of us and we don't stand a chance."

It seemed that Bragdon was lowering expectations to such a point that nobody, not even the police themselves, would expect the task force to be successful. Is that any way to initiate a serial killer investigation?

After I read the article a couple more times, I called Mike.

"Four detectives isn't a task force," I said.

"I know," Mike replied.

"Why did they wait four months?"

"Because of the women who were killed," Mike said. "If this guy were killing nursery school teachers, there would have been a task force after the second body. But he's killing street prostitutes. And no one cares. It's a disgrace."

Mike went on to tell me about the Kevin Coe case. In the late 1970s, a serial rapist assaulted dozens of women in the upper-middle-class Spokane neighborhood of South Hill. For months, no one seemed to notice. Not the public, not the newspapers, not even the police. As the number of reported rapes doubled in one year, the city finally started paying attention. A task force was formed. Police decoys were deployed in hopes of catching the suspect in the act. South Hill and the rest of "respectable" Spokane were gripped with fear. Women armed themselves with Mace and derringers. Men wore T-shirts saying "I'm not the South Hill Rapist."

It turned out that the South Hill rapist was a son of Spokane society. At least forty-three rapes were connected to Kevin Coe, son of Gordon Coe, the assistant managing editor of the *Spokane Chronicle*. Kevin was arrested and brought to trial on seven counts of rape. During the trial, his mother tried to hire a hit man to murder the judge and the prosecutor. She was convicted during a separate trial. Kevin was convicted on three of the seven counts of rape, two of which were overturned on appeal. He is now serving out his sentence on the one remaining rape charge in Walla Walla Prison. He is due to be released in 2006.

As Mike saw it, the lessons of the Kevin Coe case were that Spokane was reluctant to admit it even had serious crime. Mike hoped that the Spokane cops had learned their lesson from the Coe case. But Kevin Coe had raped women of the middle class, schoolgirls, young professionals, and housewives. The serial killer was preying on prostitutes, at least for now.

"If this guy kills some legal secretary who's chipping heroin, or the wayward daughter of a high school principal," Mike said, "then they will turn this city upside down trying to find him."

On December 24, another article appeared in the *Spokesman-Review*. Now, at least, the police seemed to admit that they were trying to link up the homicides.

> The four detectives on the task force are looking for connections in the cases that might point to a serial killer.

By now, nearly a week after Shawn Johnson had been found and two days after her autopsy, the task force had ballistics evidence, if there was any. They knew whether there was foreign DNA on the bodies. They knew which victims had plastic bags on their heads, even if they were trying to keep this information out of the press. In other words, they knew which homicides were connected, and which, if any, weren't.

Despite our concerns about the lack of resources and Bragdon's public reluctance even to link any of the cases, Mike and I both hoped that the announcement of the task force would stir things up a little. When you form a task force, the case demands solution. Now we hoped that other police who were not part of the task force would help out. We hoped that the detectives in charge would be more aggressive in their investigation and that they would release more information, to inform the public and possibly to stimulate new leads. We also thought that the public would become more active themselves.

I remembered the fear that gripped Los Angeles during the Hillside Strangler killings. The first victims were prostitutes, and yet the entire city was terrified. Mike and I didn't want Spokane to become hysterical, but we did want citizens to be aware of the threat to their community. This awareness would not only pressure local law enforcement to catch the killer, but it could also generate tips from the public that might lead to his capture.

If they were investigating all the unsolved prostitute homicides from 1984 through 1997, the task force had at least twenty cases. That might seem overwhelming, but it also meant that there was a lot of evidence—if not in each individual case, then at least cumulatively.

By looking closely at all twenty cases, an experienced detective would begin to find connections that link the victims not only to each other, but maybe to a common suspect. First he has to organize his evidence and information in such a way that he can have a handle on what he already has and is able to keep up on new clues as they come in.

There are going to be connections in these cases. Some of those connections might not lead to a common suspect, since the victims had similar lifestyles, knew many of the same people, and probably knew each other. Still, you have to investigate these connections, to see if they do lead to a suspect.

The first, and most obvious, connection is victimology. The victims were all prostitutes and drug users who hung out on East Sprague. That's a good place to start. The other prostitutes and street people knew what was going on. Get your detectives down there on Sprague, working snitches, developing intelligence, seeing if there was anybody who saw something. Set up a surveillance. If you don't have the manpower, put up a video camera at a busy intersection.

Using the information you already have from the autopsies, crime scenes, and victimology, you create an evidence database. Get a civilian employee to input twenty-five or so key factors of the case: method of death; rape yes/no; forensic evidence; ballistics; and so on.

Make a flowchart for quick reference. Then the detectives start analyzing the information. The first thing you need to do is eliminate cases that don't seem connected. That frees you up to focus on the cases that definitely are. Spend more time and energy looking at the more recent cases, which are not only clearly connected, but also more evidence-rich. I'd look at Johnson, Scott, and Palmer for the link with the plastic bag. I'd also want to look real closely at Joseph and Hernandez. By the process of elimination that Mike and I had done in the Viking a few weeks previous, we knew that the 1984–1987 cases were probably not the work of the same suspect. That would help narrow things down a little.

Start with the most recent victim and work back. The

latest body was Shawn Johnson. Aside from the obvious, what are some other common denominators between Johnson and Scott, Joseph, Hernandez, and Palmer? How was the killer contacting his victims? Was he a john, or did he have some other way of gaining their trust?

The kind of organization needed to run an effective task force would take real leadership. From what I heard the police brass saying to the newspapers, I wasn't too confident that Spokane had the necessary leadership.

And what about the personnel? Were the four detectives assigned these cases the best and most experienced homicide investigators, or was it just the luck of the draw? Or, worse, were they on the task force because of political or bureaucratic considerations? That would be the kiss of death, to have somebody on the task force, particularly one of that size, who clearly didn't belong on a homicide team. You want experienced, dedicated detectives with imagination and passion. Cops who will do what they're supposed to, come up with ideas, and have enough leadership to assert themselves.

Even if the personnel were experienced, talented, and dedicated, they needed the freedom and authority to do their jobs without interference from administration. The rest of the department (in this case, both the Spokane PD and the sheriff's office) had to be involved. That would mean communication between the task force and everybody out on the streets—detectives, patrol officers, traffic cops. And other agencies—neighboring police and sheriff's departments, the Washington State Patrol, the FBI—would also have to be brought on board.

Most important, the task force needed support, and not just in terms of money, logistics, and equipment. They needed to feel they had the full support of their administration, political leaders, and the community. There was no indication that the Spokane Task Force was getting anything close to the support they needed to get the job done. And Bragdon's comments seemed to indicate that this task force was a perfunctory effort at best, doomed to failure.

While I was in the LAPD, I had been involved in two serial killer task forces, the Hillside Strangler and the Night Stalker. Both those cases were solved, and my involvement was peripheral. It gave me a taste of the excitement, the challenge, and the responsibility of trying to catch the most elusive of prey—the serial killer.

As a young patrol officer just starting out, I used to dream about being a homicide detective. In the same way my son dreams of playing in the World Series, I would dream of being part of a serial killer task force.

Of course, it's all about being in the right place at the right time, or the wrong place at the wrong time, depending on how you look at it. Just like my involvement in the Simpson case. Assignments are often just the luck of the draw.

Little did I know that very early on in my police career I would have a chance to participate in two task forces.

In October 1977, the naked body of a Hollywood prostitute was discovered in Forest Lawn Cemetery. In a little more than a month, there were five more victims of the "Hillside Strangler." These women had all been abducted, tortured, raped by two men, strangled to death, and then dumped on hillsides in sexually staged positions.

The Hillside Strangler case was highly publicized. It was almost as if, in the wake of San Francisco's Zodiac Killer, Seattle's Ted Bundy, and New York's Son of Sam, the Los Angeles media wanted its own serial killer and welcomed the opportunity, responding with graphic and sensational coverage. Soon the city was terrified. As the Hillside Strangler kept killing, and began making women who weren't prostitutes his victims, the political pressure to catch the killer mounted until the LAPD was given carte blanche—catch the Hillside Strangler, no matter what it cost.

When the Hillside Strangler Task Force was put together, I was working on the first gang unit in Los Angeles. The unit, called CRASH (Community Resources Against Street Hoodlums), was federally funded in response to the growing gang violence in the city. We covered five divisions in the center of the city, identifying gang members, enforcing any law necessary to curb gang violence, and of course investigating gang homicides.

Word around the department was that the LAPD homicide detectives assigned to the Hillside Strangler case were in trouble. The task force had virtually unlimited resources, but they weren't any closer to catching the killer. Meanwhile, the media kept turning up the volume, and the pressure to solve the case continued to build.

At the height of the Hillside Strangler frenzy my partner Ted Severns and I were assigned to work a day watch, plainclothes intelligence detail. This was a routine function to develop information on gang movements, analyze graffiti, and groom snitches, among other tasks. What did happen one morning was not so routine.

Ted and I were told to report to LAPD headquarters at downtown Parker Center for a briefing. Our supervisor informed us that we were on loan for a few days to the Hillside Strangler Task Force.

The task force was so large that the briefing had to be held in the auditorium. There were close to two hundred people—vice cops, undercover dope cops, motor officers, Metro cops, uniforms, suits, brass. I had never seen so many cops together in one room, all working on the same case. It was unbelievable. During roll call, information was given faster than I could write. Composite drawings of two suspects were passed among us. Assignments were yelled out from the stage. Ted and I were sent to the heart of Hollywood Division. Our mission was simple: Look for men who matched the suspect's possible description.

Nothing prepares you for the realization that you are searching for a serial killer. Sure, Ted and I knew how to arrest bad guys, but this was much different. The chances of catching him were one in a million, but we had to go out there thinking that we could.

Since our standard issue four-door, dark-green, small hubcapped Plymouth was a bit too obviously a police vehicle, particularly on the streets of Hollywood, Ted and I decided to go on foot. We walked up and down the streets, checking out business establishments, scanning alleys, looking everywhere for a man who fit the composite's description. I don't know how long we had been looking when we both saw him at the same time. He matched the composite almost exactly, like a photograph of the suspect standing in front of us just a few yards away.

The man was wearing jeans, a long-sleeved shirt, and a lightweight jacket. Ted moved toward him as I casually positioned myself to his right rear. As Ted started speaking, the suspect's hands were in his pockets. To this day I don't know what made me do it, but suddenly I grabbed both of his hands from behind. I held on to his wrists as tightly as I could and felt his strength pulling against me. Then I started slowly pulling his hands from his pockets. As his hands became visible, Ted saw something.

"Gun!" Ted yelled.

The man had a .25 auto in his hand. I held his hands while Ted came over, and we wrestled the gun away from him. When we handcuffed the man, we thought we might just have caught the Hillside Strangler.

Ever since then, I've wondered why I reacted the way I did. I hadn't seen the gun, and I can't say that I had enough experience to develop a honed instinct for such confrontations. Maybe I did have a sixth sense. Or maybe I was just being overprotective of my partner, who had almost died two years prior in a street shooting. Since then I had been in countless situations like that, but this one always made me think, perhaps because of the nature of the killer we were trying to catch—a cunning, violent psychopath—that I was operating on another level of intuition, or maybe I was just being paranoid.

The incident occurred in front of a Hollywood bar the suspect had just left. Ted went into the bar and spoke to the bartender and patrons. He quickly learned that the suspect was furious at the Channel 7 evening news, ranting about the station substituting for the local anchor Christine Lund. The suspect told anybody who would listen that there were actually seven "Christine Lunds," and they constantly changed their hair and makeup to trick us.

Needless to say, Ted and I knew we had a live one, whether he was a serial killer or just another psycho. On our way to Rampart Station the suspect made direct threats to kill all of the Christine Lund "impostors" and described how he had been on his way to Channel 7 to do just that. At the station, we contacted the Hillside Strangler Task Force and gave them a full report. They responded by sending a detective team to interrogate the suspect.

While the Robbery-Homicide detectives conducted their interview, I phoned Channel 7. After a series of frustrating conversations in which I tried to convince people at the station that I was really the police and not just another crackpot, I finally got Christine Lund on the phone. I explained to her what Ted and I had just done and gave her some idea of what the suspect was saying about her. I made it very clear that this man was obsessed, even psychotic, and had been carrying a handgun when we apprehended him. I also told her about the threats that the suspect had made to the bar patrons and to my partner and me.

It soon became obvious that Christine Lund had been

through this before. She began referring to the suspect by name and then asked whether we had hurt him. She seemed much more concerned with his safety than her own.

I figured Lund didn't know how serious these threats actually were, so I stopped playing patty-cake with her and described what the suspect had said in as harsh terms as he himself had used. She started getting angry at me, saying that she knew the suspect, and he would never hurt her. She told me that he had come to Channel 7 on numerous occasions, which made me wonder whether he had been armed. As I kept trying to warn her, she just got more upset with me. Christine Lund was a sophisticated, big-city television news anchor who had no idea what kind of danger she was in.

As it turned out, the suspect wasn't the Hillside Strangler. Still, it was a good arrest that showed Ted and me something that perhaps neither one of us consciously realized at the time. Despite our youth and inexperience, we both believed that we could catch a suspect in a serial murder case. We were confident, eager, and proactive; but most important, we believed in ourselves.

Ted and I went back to working CRASH, and the task force started dwindling down. By early 1979, the task force was all but disbanded. There were only two detectives working the case. Then a report came from Bellingham, Washington, stating that two women had been found dead in a car near a house they had been hired to house-sit by a security guard named Ken Bianchi, whose name had surfaced in the Hillside Strangler investigation when the last Los Angeles victim had been registered with a modeling agency Bianchi had contacted.

Bianchi and his cousin Angelo Buono did, in fact, turn out to be responsible for the Hillside Strangler murders.

The lesson of the Hillside Strangler case, for me at least,

was that even with all the resources that the LAPD had at its disposal—an almost unlimited budget; pressure from the top brass; carte blanche from city hall; a media that, while it was engaging in a feeding frenzy, was also relatively cooperative with the police; and a community that was scared, angry, and active in trying to catch the killer—with all this, the LAPD and LA Sheriff's Department, the two leading homicide agencies in the country, could not catch the Hillside Strangler.

Bianchi was caught because he had a connection with his victims. Usually, serial killers are too smart, too controlled, to make such a mistake. If Bianchi hadn't killed two women he hired as house sitters, he and Buono might still be killing today.

Five years later, I had another brush with a serial murder case. In 1984, the Night Stalker was terrorizing Los Angeles and its suburbs. At that time I was working Investigative Analysis in Parker Center. Once again, the city was gripped with fear. News about the Night Stalker killings was in the paper every morning and on television every night. The Night Stalker was not smooth, consistent, or efficient. He was a brutal opportunist whose murders did not derive from some consistent psychic need, but rather as a by-product of his other crimes. He didn't go out to kill. He went out to break into houses and burgle them. If he came upon someone, he might kill them, or he might not. He did not have a signature. While he evidently enjoyed torturing, raping, and killing his victims, he did these things almost incidentally in the commission of his burglaries.

Still, the Night Stalker did prove very difficult to catch. As time went on, the suspect continued to elude arrest.

One day, a task force detective, Lieutenant Robelto, came into Investigative Analysis looking for me. My first reaction when I heard a lieutenant was looking for me was that I must be in trouble. Robelto came over to my desk and explained that he had heard of some charts and a layout I did for the 1984 Olympics and asked if I could help him out with a project. I was flattered and responded, "Sure, what do you need?"

Evidently the task force had compiled hundreds of pieces of evidence and information about the Night Stalker, but they needed to organize the material in some coherent fashion. They wanted to see the evidence before them, so they could analyze it and make connections. I knew exactly what Robelto was talking about.

"You guys need a flowchart," I said.

Robelto took me up to the Robbery-Homicide offices. A couple of the task force detectives joined Robelto and me. Soon the ideas and suggestions and requests started flying. I took notes and made sketches. I listened to evidence and particulars of MO, ballistics, and autopsies.

I returned to my desk with a mission to plan the flowchart categories, design, and function. I tried to hide my excitement, but don't think I succeeded. I was very proud to be asked to be a part of the task force and looked forward to meeting the challenge presented to me.

Meanwhile, little did I know that a suspect had been identified through fingerprints lifted from a getaway car used by the Night Stalker. Those prints had been matched with a suspect, whose photo was then circulated to the media.

As I went into work and sat down at my desk, planning my flowchart, Richard Ramirez tried to steal a car in broad daylight. People on the street recognized him as the Night Stalker suspect and swarmed around him, beating him bloody and holding him for the police.

Again, the suspect was caught, not by supersleuthing detective skills, but simple, basic police work and stupidity on the part of the suspect—and in this case, the task force using the media to get the suspect description out to an aware and active public.

Both the Hillside Strangler and Night Stalker cases show how difficult it is to catch a serial killer. More often than not, detectives don't catch serial killers; instead, the killers catch themselves. Careless, overconfident, careening out of control, these men made mistakes and the police simply recognized them as suspects once they were captured.

Bob Keppel was the lead investigator in the Ted Bundy task force. When I had Bob on the radio show in April 1998, he credited the media with helping to catch Bundy. Immediately following the disappearance of two young females from Lake Sammamish State Park on July 14, 1974, the task force made a suspect and vehicle description public through the media. That information stimulated clues that ultimately led to identifying Bundy as the killer of at least ten women in the Seattle area.

BOB KEPPEL: If it wasn't for the fact that the broadcast of the suspect description and details of what happened at Lake Sammamish State Park were out there, we never would have gotten any information about Ted Bundy. There were people who called in about Ted—the media coverage actually assisted us in collecting the right data.

FITZSIMMONS: So is it pretty critical that certain information be filtered through the media so that you can find information more quickly?

BOB KEPPEL: Yes, when you have a physical description of a suspect, like we had at Lake Sammamish, plus a vehicle description. There were hundreds of leads coming in, but we were still getting leads that applied to the right person.

FUHRMAN: In a lot of serial cases, that's the break—knowing where they're contacting the victims. Then you can start using normal police procedures, stakeouts, informants, whatever, to focus on a certain area. But you need the public to sometimes help you identify something that seems normal to them until somebody sees it on the TV.

Of course, Bundy was arrested in Utah when an attempted abduction went awry and one of his potential victims got away. He was convicted in Utah, escaped from two jails in Colorado, and was eventually arrested and convicted on murder and assault charges in Florida, where he was electrocuted in 1989.

Bundy never faced charges in Seattle, but Keppel's release of this information to the media and other law enforcement agencies no doubt saved the lives of women who never even knew they were in danger. Had Keppel not gone public with the clue that the suspect was named "Ted" and that he drove a tan Volkswagen, there is a very good chance he would have continued killing young women in Seattle for months, maybe longer. Keppel, an acknowledged serial killer expert, now works for the Washington State Attorney General's Office and was advising on the Spokane case. Were they listening to him?

The task force investigating the Atlanta child homicides in the early 1980s is one of the rare examples of a serial killer caught by commonsense police work. Maybe the Atlanta task force didn't know exactly what the child killer was doing. Maybe they didn't understand his motives. But they knew one thing: He was dumping bodies in a river. So they used a little Kentucky windage to figure out where the bodies were probably going in, and they surveilled it, and lo and behold they caught Wayne Williams dumping a body.

The Atlanta task force had the resources and the commitment to catch the killer. They had experienced personnel and almost unlimited resources. They reached out to other agencies, both local and national. They released a great deal of information about the homicides, in hopes of stimulating clues from the public. They tried to provoke the suspect into action. And most important, Atlanta had the political will to do whatever was necessary in order to solve the case.

I wondered if Spokane had what it took to catch a serial killer.

CHAPTER 9

Laurie Ann Wason and
Shawn McClenahan

Laurie Ann Wason, age 31. Body found December 26, 1997, buried in a vacant gravel pit near Fourteenth Avenue and Carnahan Road in southeast Spokane. Body in severe state of decomposition, clothed with no shoes or socks. White plastic bag over head. Cause of death: gunshot wound to head.

Shawn McClenahan, age 39. Body found December 26, 1997, buried beneath Laurie Wason's. Body in a state of advanced decomposition, fully clothed with no shoes. White plastic bag over head. Cause of death: gunshot wound to head.

"They've found another body."

It was the day after Christmas, 1997, and Mike was on the phone. He wouldn't have called unless it was important, and this was. Speaking with the measured excitement of a veteran newsman, Mike brought me up to speed. He was cool and calm, but the words came quickly and he was definitely pumping adrenaline. He told me that a jogger had been running through a vacant lot on the south side of town, near a new development, when he saw a body partially buried under leaves and debris. That was earlier this afternoon. Detectives and criminalists were still processing the crime scene, and the media was all over the place.

"Is the body a female?" I asked.

"They don't know."

"They don't know, or they won't say?"

"You're catching on, Fuhrman."

"Keep me updated."

"Don't worry, I will," Mike said. "By the way, Merry Christmas."

"Merry Christmas to you, too."

As I played with the kids, I tried not to think about the case. Over the years, I've learned to compartmentalize my life, to try not to bring my work home with me. Sometimes it has a habit of intruding. How does somebody find a body the day after Christmas? Was it a recent dump, like Johnson, or had the body been there for some time? Was this body meant to be found, like the others? Was it meant to be found yesterday, only no one stumbled onto it? A body is dumped only three days after the task force had been announced. Was the killer making a statement? What was he trying to say?

I tried to imagine who he was and what he was doing right now. Did he have a family? Was he with them? Or was he alone with all his trophies? Was he cruising Sprague? Did he have another girl with him?

The whole point of retirement was to spend more time with my family. Here it was the day after Christmas and I was thinking about some psycho. I put it out of my mind, until Mike called me again the next day.

"They found another body."

"You already told me that."

"No, they found another body at the same scene."

"What?"

"The killer dumped two bodies at the same scene."

During the next couple days, facts came trickling in about this bizarre and evidence-rich crime scene.

At 2:00 P.M. on December 26, Fred Dullanty was jogging through a vacant lot about twenty feet from Fourteenth Avenue and a quarter mile west of Carnahan Road, when he discovered a body partially buried under leaves and vegetation. The area where the body was found is an old gravel hill. Neighbors use it as a jogging and walking path, and also as a dumping ground for household debris.

Soon as many as fifty officers, crime scene personnel, and volunteers were at the scene. They closed down Fourteenth Avenue and secured the crime scene. Police tape kept out onlookers and officers diverted traffic away from the closed area.

After only a couple hours at the crime scene, detectives and criminalists decided to leave the body until morning. Investigators placed tarps over the body, and police guarded the scene overnight.

Why did they leave the crime scene overnight? What's more, how could they? How could the detectives go home and not worry about a snowstorm, or an ice storm, that would ruin their crime scene? How could they sleep, knowing that their work was unfinished? A police department is a twenty-four-hour organization. I wondered what the hours in Spokane were. What did they do when they found a body at night—just let it sit until morning?

I had been on enough crime scenes during the holidays to know how it goes. It was the day after Christmas, one of the shortest days of the year. Everybody wanted to go back to his or her home and family. But this wasn't the first time that Spokane cops had left a crime scene unprocessed. They did the same thing with Scott and Johnson.

The next day, more than thirty volunteers from the Spokane PD and the sheriff's office conducted a line search in the fields on both sides of Fourteenth Avenue. The search lasted for two hours, and police would not comment on whether any evidence was uncovered. As volun-

teers searched the surrounding area, detectives and criminalists finished processing the crime scene.

The family members of two women who had been reported missing came to the crime scene before the bodies
had been removed. Kathy Lloyd, sister of Shawn McClenahan, and Darcy Acevedo, sister of Laurie Wason, were both
standing by the crime scene.

As criminalists slowly lifted the first body from the
grave site, they noticed something buried beneath. It was
another body.

Now they had two bodies to deal with. Police refused to
let family members see either body as it was taken from the
grave site. The victims were not officially identified until
the autopsies were conducted three days later. The two
women were identified by fingerprints. They were Laurie
Ann Wason and Shawn McClenahan, the two women
whose families had shown up at the scene.

Wason had been missing since November 3. McClenahan was last seen December 17. Wason's body was removed
from the scene at 12:15 P.M. McClenahan's body was removed a half hour later.

McClenahan was the first to be autopsied. Her autopsy
was conducted on December 30, by Dr. George Lindholm.
Time and place of injury were not determined. Cause of
death was a contact gunshot wound to the head. Her body
was turned over to her family for cremation.

Shawn McClenahan was born on May 30, 1958, in Walla
Walla, Washington. She graduated from high school there
and went on to receive a phlebotomist's certification from
Spokane Community College. She worked at two local
hospitals, but had trouble keeping jobs. She was married
and had a twenty-one-year-old son.

McClenahan was a heroin addict who had been in and
out of jail and rehab facilities. She was arrested for prostitution in 1993. On November 6, 1997, she pleaded guilty to

forgery for passing a stolen check during a heroin binge. She was sentenced to thirty days of community service, placed on probation, and released.

McClenahan's family was well known in Spokane. Her father was the late Jim McClenahan, a sports entrepreneur and part owner of the Spokane Golden Hawks semipro football team.

Her body was clothed and was described as being in an "advanced state of decomposition." Her feet were bare. There was a white plastic bag over her head.

Nine months prior to her death, McClenahan had testified against Joseph Andrews, who was accused of shooting McClenahan's boyfriend, Larry Eaves. McClenahan testified that Andrews had threatened Eaves just a few days before Eaves was found shot to death in a car parked in west Spokane. After two juries deadlocked over murder charges, Andrews pled out to manslaughter charges. Shannon Zielinski was also a witness in the Andrews case. Could this have something to do with her homicide? I doubted it. Connections like the Andrews case are common among prostitutes and street people. I wouldn't be surprised if there were a lot more connections like that between the serial killer's victims.

Wason's autopsy was conducted the next day, also by Dr. Lindholm. Her time and place of injury could not be determined. Cause of death was cerebral pulpification as a consequence of a gunshot wound to the head. Wason was buried in Richland, Washington, on January 3, 1998.

Laurie Ann Wason was a thirty-one-year-old white female, a heroin addict, and a prostitute. She was born on January 22, 1966, in Portland, Oregon. Wason was five feet six inches tall, 105 pounds, with brown hair and hazel eyes. She had a rose tattoo on her left shoulder and was missing one of her upper teeth. Her last known address was in Spokane.

Wason once ran an adult-care home. She was a dog breeder whose picture once appeared in *Rottweiler Quarterly* with her dog Lucky. She was married and had a twelve-year-old son, who was being cared for by others.

Her parents, James and Clara Page, lived in Spokane. After Wason was reported missing, her family posted fliers all over Spokane, and spoke to local prostitutes, trying to find Laurie. Wason's sister, Darcy Acevedo, said that Laurie turned to prostitution in the summer of 1997 to support her heroin addiction, after having stayed clean for six years.

The autopsy determined that Wason died from a gunshot wound to the head. Her body was described as being in a "severe state of decomposition." She was clothed in a black sweater and black jeans. Her shoes and socks were missing. There was a white plastic bag over her head.

By now, several of the victims had been found with no shoes and socks. This led me to speculate that the killer had some kind of foot fetish, or that he was keeping the shoes and socks as trophies. Serial killers often cherish possessions of their victims, in order to fantasize about and relive the acts they committed upon them.

Following the autopsies, the task force stated that both Laurie Wason and Shawn McClenahan had died of gunshot wounds, but they wouldn't say where they had been shot, how many times, or what kind or caliber of firearm was used. Spokane Sheriff's Department captain Doug Silver, who had been designated as one of the task force's spokesmen, stated that they didn't know yet whether the women had been sexually assaulted, because the test results had not come back yet. When those tests did come back, the results were never released.

The task force clearly did not like talking about two bodies being stacked together in the same grave site. We were able to determine that though Wason was killed prior to McClenahan, her body was on top. This stacking of victims in reverse order of killing might have meant that the killer was trying to tell the task force something.

What could the killer be saying?

With the discovery of two bodies dumped together, and several women missing at the same time, Mike and I were beginning to think that the killer was abducting women off the street in some manner other than picking them up as a trick. If he had been a regular john along Sprague, then we would have heard a vehicle or suspect description by someone who saw one of the victims get into a car.

Shawn McClenahan was last seen by her family on December 15, when she visited her father in a Spokane nursing home. Two days later, she was seen leaving her brother-in-law's house in a blue van. Another woman was accompanying her.

Who was this other woman? Could she have been an accomplice of the serial killer? Could she be another victim? I hoped that the task force tracked down this clue first, and found both the woman and the owner of the van.

By dumping two bodies stacked on top of each other, in reverse order of time of death, the killer was telling us something about what he was doing with them, either intentionally or by mistake. Mike and I speculated that he was abducting them and possibly keeping them alive for some period of time—maybe days or weeks, maybe just hours. Then he was killing and burying them. Once he decided that he wanted the bodies found, he would exhume the remains and dump them in a manner and a location in which they would be discovered.

We also thought that the stacking of two victims was an indication that he could be holding two or more victims alive at the same time.

This is bizarre, but it's not unknown behavior for a serial killer. On July 14, 1974, Ted Bundy abducted and killed two women from a crowded public park at Lake Sammamish, Washington. He later admitted taking both victims to a remote area and having one watch while he assaulted and killed the other. Then he assaulted and killed the second victim.

The Spokane suspect obviously had no problem handling dead and decomposing bodies. Was there an element of necrophilia? Did he have more of an obsession with these victims in death than in life? If he had more than one victim in his control at the same time, were they alive or dead?

Whether or not Wason and McClenahan had been kept captive together alive, they were certainly together in death. This grave site was obviously meant to be discovered. The suspect had left Laurie Wason's hand sticking out from beneath the pile of debris. Shawn McClenahan was beneath her, even though she had been killed after Wason. This was a clear indication, at least, that the killer had buried Wason at another location, exhumed her, and then dumped her on top of McClenahan at the Fourteenth and Carnahan site.

That much we knew. Now the question was—how long had each victim been buried there?

It was possible that McClenahan had been buried at Fourteenth and Carnahan shortly after her death (anytime after December 17), and had lain undiscovered in that vacant lot for nine days. Or she could have been killed and buried elsewhere, then dumped at the Fourteenth and Carnahan location sometime shortly before December 26.

Wason could have been buried elsewhere with McClenahan, or at another location. She had been missing since November 3, and could have been dead since then, but she was definitely not at the Fourteenth and Carnahan location until after McClenahan was buried there. McClenahan had been missing only since December 17. She must have been killed shortly after she was abducted, otherwise there wouldn't have been much decomposition at all.

Knowing that Shawn Johnson had probably been exhumed before being dumped at Hangman Valley Road, we knew the killer was comfortable handling dead, and even decomposing, bodies. It was highly likely that he had also exhumed Laurie Wason, and perhaps Shawn McClenahan, to dump them at the Fourteenth and Carnahan scene. From there, it's not that much of a leap to assume that the killer wanted these two bodies found, and staged the crime scene in such a manner that he was certain they would be.

Imagine you're the detective who first arrived at this crime scene. You see a hand sticking out from beneath a pile of debris and vegetation. The first conclusion you can make was that the victim wasn't still alive and trying to crawl out of the grave. The next conclusion you can make is that this crime scene was staged by the suspect. Why else would the suspect leave a victim's hand sticking out in plain sight? Why would he even dump a body in an area as public as this one, unless he wanted it to be found?

Given all these considerations, the first thing that the task force detectives should have thought was that their suspect was in the area, and probably watching them. There was a group of several onlookers from the neighborhood. The suspect was either there, or in the group of volunteers assembled to search the area the next day. But I would bet that he was there, watching the show.

As soon as they noticed the body of Shawn McClenahan beneath Laurie Wason, detectives should have realized that their suspect was probably within sight. Many serial killers have inserted themselves into the investigation that is trying to catch them. What better place to be than with all the other lookie-loos at Fourteenth and Carnahan the moment that second body was found? The police should have photographed all the onlookers at the scene, and taken the license plate numbers of all the vehicles parked nearby.

They should have done this at every crime scene where there were onlookers and parked cars.

The day Wason and McClenahan were recovered from the site, Lieutenant Gerry Fojtik of the sheriff's department said, "It's obvious that the bodies weren't freshly dumped."

Task force spokesman Doug Silver had stated that detectives didn't know whether the two bodies had been dumped at the same time, but that they hoped lab tests would determine times of death and when the bodies had been dumped. When those lab tests did come back, Silver never made them public.

Spokane County undersheriff Mike Aubrey stated that the bodies had been there "in excess of forty-eight hours."

Let's assume Aubry's statement is based on hard evidence. Forty-eight hours from December 26 was Christmas Eve. Had the killer dumped Wason and McClenahan to be found on Christmas Day?

I doubt that either body had been at that location for more than two days. Both bodies were in the process of decomposition, although that of Wason was probably more advanced. This was December in Spokane, and even though the winter had been relatively mild, it would freeze nearly every night. A body stops decomposing around thirty-nine degrees. This means that the only periods during which the bodies would decompose would be in the day, after they had warmed up from the overnight frost, and before the sun went down and the temperature dropped again. The less sunlight they were exposed to, the cooler their bodies would remain. This all indicated a slow decomposition process. The plastic bags over each victim's head, at least in the winter weather, would preserve their features from decomposition and animal depredation. That's exactly what Kathy Lloyd noticed when she viewed her sister Shawn McClenahan's body at a local funeral home.

"She looked like she had just died," Lloyd told me.

The police told Lloyd that her sister had been shot in the back of the head, but she was not hurt anywhere else. The funeral director asked if she wanted to view the rest of the body, but Lloyd refused.

Decomposition will occur more rapidly in areas of the body where the skin has been compromised. If Shawn McClenahan was mutilated, her face, hands, and feet could have been fixed up by the funeral home.

Even if the bodies at Fourteenth and Carnahan were not rapidly decomposing, they would emit a very strong odor. If they had been buried at Fourteenth and Carnahan, one of the many humans or animals traveling through that lot would have smelled something. It didn't appear that either Wason or McClenahan had been disturbed by dogs, or other animal predators, even though this area is filled with dog droppings and evidence of other animals. Compare this to Darla Sue Scott, who was found in early November; she was severely decomposed and showed signs of animal depredation.

There were three possible scenarios.

One, McClenahan had been dumped at Fourteenth and Carnahan shortly after her death. Wason was buried elsewhere. On or about Christmas Eve, the killer disinterred Wason and dumped her body on top of McClenahan, staging the crime scene with Wason's hand sticking out of the covering debris so that the bodies would be found.

Two, both bodies had been buried in a different location, either separately or together. The killer disinters them both, and dumps Wason on top of McClenahan, knowing that he killed Wason first. This is a clue to the task force that he's placing these bodies so that they know the bodies were not in that location from the beginning.

Three, both bodies had been buried elsewhere. On or about Christmas Eve, they were moved to Fourteenth and

Carnahan. It was only happenstance that Wason ended up on top of McClenahan.

No matter which way you cut it, Wason was not originally at that location. And I would argue that McClenahan was not there longer than a day or two, otherwise her decomposing body would have attracted animal predators and pets, much the same as Darla Sue Scott's had at Hangman Valley Golf Course.

Fourteenth and Carnahan was a staged crime scene. Those bodies were left there for a purpose. The killer was giving the task force a message. I just wondered whether the task force understood what he was trying to tell them.

A serial killer's pathology involves fantasy of domination and control, not just over his victims, but over the public, and the police who are trying to catch him.

I believe the suspect wanted credit and he wanted respect. The task force still wasn't officially connecting any of the victims. And they would never use the term "serial killer" to describe the suspect. On the radio show, I urged them not to underestimate him.

FUHRMAN: You better respect this guy's intelligence, because you're trying to catch him, and you haven't done it yet, so he's one step ahead of you. You also have to think that maybe this guy could possibly be toying with you, changing his MO just in order to mess with your head.

If the suspect had dumped Wason's and McClenahan's bodies in order to get the police to pay more attention to him, the task force seemed to get the message.

A Spokane PD press release issued December 27, 1997, stated: "The cooperative unit was developed several months ago to look into the possibility that killings of several street women this year might be the work of a single killer."

Were they trying to say that the task force had been formed after Joseph and Hernandez? If it had been formed back then, why didn't they say anything to the media? And why didn't they take the four detectives off their other cases?

It was obvious that the Spokane PD and the sheriff's department wanted to make it appear that they had been on the case prior to the time when they actually started seriously investigating it. With this release, issued the day after Wason and McClenahan turned up in a field off Fourteenth and Carnahan, the task force finally, and with great reluctance, acknowledged what everyone else had long accepted as fact: There was a serial killer working in Spokane. Only the task force wouldn't actually use the words "serial killer," preferring to use the term "single killer." As if it made any difference.

If the suspect had dropped Wason and McClenahan in order to get the task force to acknowledge the connections between at least some of these homicides, and admit that there was a serial killer, single killer, lone gunman, or whatever you wanted to call him—then he succeeded. If he wanted to strike fear into the heart of the Spokane community, even dumping two bodies on the edge of a suburban development wasn't going to do that. As long as his victims came from East Sprague, and not upscale South Hill, the citizens of Spokane would continue to go about their business relatively unconcerned that a sexual psychopath was killing women in their city.

Immediately following the Fourteenth and Carnahan body finds, I expected at least some level of public emotion, whether it was hysteria, outrage, or simply curiosity. The bodies were examined. The crime scene was cleaned up. There were a couple of newspaper articles, and some stories on the local TV news. The biggest story in Spokane over those holidays was the Washington State Cougars playing in the Rose Bowl, not a serial killer murdering women.

On December 29, Mike and I met at the radio station and drove to Fourteenth and Carnahan. It was a brand-new housing development in the middle of a fairly rural area at the southeast edge of town. Tract houses abutted a vacant five acres, with shrubs and trees rising from the ground. It looked as if the vacant lot itself would be developed in the near future.

A middle-class neighborhood at the edge of a growing city, it could have been anywhere in the suburban Pacific Northwest, a stark contrast to the gritty reality of prostitution and murder.

The day was bone cold, overcast with low, dark clouds. Somehow the weather seemed appropriate for our visit. The vacant lot where the bodies had been found was a raw, wasted place. Black plastic bags of garbage were indiscriminately scattered about, along with beer cans and old tires. It was a neighborhood eyesore. The terrain was unnatural; everything had been dug up, poked around in, and moved about by man, pockmarking what would otherwise have been a pleasant landscape. It almost seemed as if a great battle had been fought here a long time ago, with the earth first churned up and then grown over with weeds, shrubs, and wild grass.

Mike and I got out of the car and oriented ourselves to the location. From watching the television footage of the crime scene being processed, we had a pretty good idea where the bodies had been found.

I looked around us, at the housing development just a few hundred feet to the west, all the tract homes done up in Christmas decorations, cars in the driveways, lights on in the living rooms. To the east, traffic was humming down Carnahan Avenue, a major north-south thoroughfare into and out of town.

For some reason, the killer felt comfortable and confident here. Even more so than in Hangman Valley. Here he took a big chance, dumping not just one but two bodies. Why here? What was it about this place?

Mike and I walked into the vacant lot and started looking around. There were very few trees, and some obvious footpaths that looked regularly traveled. I imagined that this was a playground for the kids who lived up in the tract homes. Not much to look at, to be sure, but a fun place to go exploring, or play cowboys and Indians. From all the droppings we saw, several neighbors walked their dogs here, probably every day. There were also beer cans and cigarette butts, evidence that local residents came here to do whatever they weren't allowed to do at home.

I pointed out a used condom and said, "So much for *Leave It to Beaver.*"

"You gonna collect that for evidence?" Mike asked.

"No, I'll leave it for the criminalist."

I hadn't worked as a cop in more than three years, but when I walked out to the grave site, I felt it all come back to me. My senses were heightened. Everything around me could be a possible clue. Even though the crime scene had already been processed and cleaned up, there was still evidence here.

I scrutinized the tiniest details, passing up nothing as insignificant. Although the day was cold, I no longer felt the discomfort. I was too focused on seeing the scene as he did.

He drives up from Carnahan, turns onto Fourteenth. It's late Christmas Eve, early Christmas morning. The houses are dark. Everybody's asleep. He's scouted out this location before. He wants to say something with this dump. He wants Spokane to sit up and take notice. He wants to give them a Christmas they won't forget.

Both bodies are in the van. It's cold and he's afraid of being seen. He had his spot picked out, but once he parks the van, he realizes he can't find it. He takes the first body out, drags it over to a ditch and throws it in.

The second body is lighter. She has been dead a longer time, and she was a smaller woman when she was alive. He liked this one, that's why he kept her around. But now she has to go.

He throws her on top of the first body, and then covers them both with foliage and debris. He is careful to leave the hand of the top woman sticking out so someone is sure to see it. He wants them both found tomorrow.

He comes back to the van, winded from all the exertion, breathing in the frigid air. Before he gets in, he looks back up at the houses, all done up in Christmas lights, people sleeping peacefully inside.

He imagines how the body will be found. First the neighborhood, then the entire city will be shocked that murder could be right at their doorstep. The task force will finally pay him some attention and respect.

Maybe they'll give him a nickname. He'll become famous, even in anonymity. And the game will suddenly get a whole lot more interesting.

Merry Christmas, Spokane.

Christmas morning he wakes up, excited like a little kid. He watches the news, listens to his police scanner. Nothing. No one has found his girls yet.

The next day they turn up. As the police and media arrive, he cruises back and forth, waiting for some civilians to blend in with. He stands there at the edge of the crime scene. He jokes with the cops. He volunteers for the search party. On his way out, he commiserates with the victims' families, telling them he's sorry for their loss.

And the whole time he's laughing inside.

Where was he now? I asked myself, looking around at the houses in the development, and the other residences on the hillside across Carnahan. Could he live in one of those houses? Could he be watching us?

I looked over at Mike and could tell that he was thinking the same thing, but neither one of us wanted to say it. We turned our eyes to the ground, looking for evidence.

The empty grave and immediate area did not provide any obvious clues. But as Mike and I searched the rest of the lot, we found several items of interest. Walking around the clusters of pines and low-level ground cover we found a deer carcass and a leg bone thirty feet away from the carcass. We also found a pair of large, dark-green garbage bags, about one hundred feet to the west of the grave site area. They had obviously been there for some time.

My first impression was that these bags must have been examined by the police during their processing of the crime scene. As I walked up to the first bag I noticed that it was full of leaves and pine needles, obviously a fall cleanup from one of the nearby homes, only the owner had been too lazy to take the bag to the dump. The other bag was sitting several feet away, tie-wrapped. Picking up the second bag, I noticed that the ground underneath was pale, dead grass. This garbage bag must have been here when the task force searched just a couple of days prior. Why hadn't they at least picked it up to look inside?

Opening the bag, I was surprised to find clothes. I dumped its contents onto the ground and saw good clothes belonging to a woman and small children. This was not an earth-shattering discovery. Still, you never know whether items like this have any connection to the crime. And you might not find out until much later. It should be routine procedure to collect everything from the crime scene that does not belong there. This bag should have been inspected and documented by the detectives, and then held as evidence. I called Mike over from his own scavenger hunt.

We looked at the clothes until I found a scrap of paper inside one of the pieces of women's clothing. It was a laundry ticket.

"What can you do with that?" Mike asked, looking over my shoulder.

"I don't know." I looked more closely at the laundry ticket. The number on it was legible. This would be pretty easy to trace. "We could find the cleaners, if they are in Spokane. We might be able to get a date and maybe even a customer's name."

"And what will that tell you?"

"I don't know," I said, holding the ticket up so Mike could see it. "One thing I do know is that at a crime scene you've got to account for everything that doesn't fit. And this doesn't fit."

Mike took the laundry ticket and placed it in an envelope, telling me that he had a friend who was a Spokane detective and he would personally give him the clue.

Fourteenth and Carnahan was an evidence-rich crime scene. It was the nucleus of the entire case. That scene would tell investigators everything they needed to know in order to solve the case, if only they knew what to look for and how to interpret it. I truly believe that the killer was dropping clues, hoping that the chase would get hotter.

On the air that afternoon, a caller asked me to do a profile of the suspect. While I don't claim to be a profiler, working detectives do a rudimentary type of profiling in almost every crime they investigate, even if they don't call it that. So I took my best shot, working with the evidence I had.

FUHRMAN: This guy is definitely an organized murderer. He's a predator. He's going out looking for a victim. He's a male white, maybe early to late thirties, no older than the mid-forties. Even in prisons and professional criminals, middle age seems to be a time when their aggression starts to diminish.

The violence has escalated over a period of time. They don't just go from shoplifting to serial killing. This is something that built up and we don't know what's in his head. We don't know if this is something that is conscious, or he is driven by some kind of pathology that's an illness. He could have a criminal record or at least have committed a lot of criminal acts. This is a streetwise guy. You've got to show this guy a little respect for the way he comes in, commits the crime, slips out, and nobody knows the wiser. He doesn't leave a lot of leads. I see this guy as being very organized, fairly intelligent, doesn't have to be book intelligent, whether he got it in prison or on the streets. Clever, cunning. That's how a predator gets his prey. I see a person who can be very personable, that can talk his way in or out of something. Who can actually be stopped by a policeman and end up laughing with the policeman, and he drives away without a ticket with a body in the back of his truck. I see him having a truck with a camper or a van, the type of vehicle where he can conceal a body in the back. He has to transport his victims. As predisposed as he is to go out and find somebody, he doesn't just pick up this woman, have some kind of a sex act with her, or torture and then murder her in the same few hours and then dump the body. I think the contact is more prolonged here, whether it's hours or days. I see this person as being a resident in this county, maybe the city. He's very comfortable with the area. He's comfortable with coming and going. He seems to stick to upper-middle-class areas when he dumps the bodies.

Following the discovery of the Wason and McClenahan bodies, the task force announced that it was intensifying its search for Linda Maybin, a thirty-four-year-old woman who fit the victim profile and had been reported missing November 29.

Was Maybin the next victim? Was she already dead? The killer was only letting us find bodies that he wanted us to find, so I guessed it was up to him.

CHAPTER 10

Melinda Mercer

Melinda Mercer, age 24. Body found December 7, 1997, by a transient in a weed-covered field near railroad tracks in south Tacoma. Cause of death: gunshot wounds to head. White plastic bag over head. Officially linked to Spokane Serial Killer on January 31, 1998.

On January 6, 1998, the task force connected four homicides as being "attributable to the same person or persons."

The victims were Darla Sue Scott, Shawn Johnson, Laurie Wason, and Shawn McClenahan.

The press release stated:

The Task Force will not discuss all the similarities in these four deaths in order to maintain investigative integrity. However, similarities include:

Manner of death: all four had been shot.

Manner of disposition: each was discovered in a semi-rural area near less travelled roadways.

Similar life-style: these victims were highly mobile and not likely to be reported missing immediately.

If only those three similarities were used to link up the murders, then the task force could also include at least seven of the other victims. Clearly, they had something more. We knew that those four victims had plastic bags on their heads. But there was probably some forensic connection, either ballistics or DNA or both.

In addition to the four they were publicly connecting, the task force stated that they were also investigating fourteen other unsolved homicides dating back to 1984. They went on to explain that the task force had already "established with certainty that several of these unsolved homicides are not connected to the last four."

If the task force had made that determination—probably the same cases that Mike and I had eliminated over lunch at the Viking—why were they still controlling these unconnected cases? They should have gone back to their original departments (they were probably all Spokane PD) for non–task force detectives to work. That didn't happen. Instead, the task force maintained responsibility for cases that they were publicly admitting were not connected, although they wouldn't reveal which ones these were. As a result, all unsolved prostitute homicides were protected from public scrutiny.

The task force also stated that during the period of 1984 to 1997 there had been eleven homicides "involving female victims which generally fit the parameters of this investigation which have been successfully prosecuted."

That statement did not specify that the victims were all prostitutes (and some of them probably weren't) or that any of these cases were self-solvers (and some of them no doubt were). The task force stated that they were looking at these cases to determine "which, if any, similarities may be specific to this investigation and which similarities may be only coincidentally connected."

In other words, the task force was looking at the homicides that someone else had solved, to see if any of them might be connected to the ones they hadn't solved. This was very curious. Did the Spokane cops think they had previously caught the serial killer murdering someone else? I hoped that anybody convicted of homicide was still in prison, even from a 1984 case. Clearly that's not what they meant. Were they concerned that they had convicted an innocent man for a murder that the serial killer had committed? I sure hoped not. So what exactly did they mean by this statement? It looked as if the Spokane cops were just patting themselves on the back for solving eleven street homicides during the course of thirteen years.

If that statement was anything more than public relations, then the task force detectives were wasting their time studying eleven homicides that had already been solved when there were at least that many unsolved they should have been looking into.

The task force's problems seemed to come, like their press releases, straight from the top. The task force was administratively top-heavy. There were as many captains, lieutenants, and sergeants as there were working detectives.

Mike and I knew that the working detectives couldn't talk to us, but we wanted to open up a dialogue with the task force leadership. There were certainly enough of them, so we figured at least one of them could find time to come on our program. At the initial announcement of the task force, Mike offered an open invitation to its members. We were willing to accept any ground rules for questioning, and understood that there would be subjects they would be unable to discuss.

No representative of the task force appeared on our show, or, to our knowledge, ever called in.

Mike and I were very sympathetic to Spokane law enforcement in general and the serial killer task force in particular. I had been a cop for twenty years. Mike is a fixture in the community. He has several close friends on the job. We were just starting the regular radio program we called *All About Crime*. The serial killer case was the biggest crime story to hit Spokane since the South Hill Rapist. Of course we were going to cover this story, and of course we would do so aggressively. We expected to be able to develop a relationship with the task force. That relationship would be advantageous to Mike and me, since it would provide information and stories for the radio show. We sincerely hoped that it would be advantageous to the task force as well.

As critical of the task force as we might have been privately, we didn't voice any criticism of them on the air during those first several months. In early 1998, many of the questions Mike and I had about the task force and the manner in which it was conducting its investigation could probably have been easily answered. If only they would have talked to us.

During our overtures to the task force, which were made privately and on the air, we promised that we would sit on information the task force wanted kept confidential—whether they gave us that information or we learned it on our own. By now, Mike and I were conducting our own investigation, visiting crime scenes, following leads given to us by our listeners, and working off the public record. Every shred of useful information we uncovered we sent along to the task force by fax, with a cover memo explaining any necessary background or source material. We didn't expect any thanks or praise. We were just doing what we thought we should do as journalists and as citizens.

During one of our radio shows immediately following the formation of the task force, I stated that I would give a digit from one of my hands to be part of the official investigation. While I certainly didn't expect to be invited on board as a detective, or even a consultant, I did expect them to show me the courtesy of a fellow cop, and at least answer a couple of questions.

Sheriff's department captain Doug Silver and SPD captain Chuck Bown had been appointed as "spokespersons" for the newly formed task force. The stated media policy was "to ensure that [the Spokane PD and the sheriff's department] meet our professional obligations both to release through the media to the public information to which they are entitled and to preserve the integrity of the investigation so that it might be brought to a successful conclusion."

Sounds fair enough. In practice, the task force's media policy was to release as little information as possible, and when information had leaked out or had been independently discovered, neither to confirm nor deny it.

In the absence of solid information, Mike and I were left to find things out on our own. In our spare time, we pondered the curious statements that Silver and Bown made in their press releases and rare press briefings. The closer we examined what little information the task force did release, the more questions we had. Their refusal to answer, or even consider, our questions only made us begin to think that the task force had something to hide. We didn't know what it was—probably just the fear of an old-fashioned police department being dragged kicking and screaming into the media age.

The task force was accustomed to a pliant media corps. From reading the newspapers, the construction of a parking garage downtown seemed far more important than eighteen homicides.

Despite repeated requests for information, the task force wouldn't release anything. They wouldn't even tell us the most basic information about the makeup of the task force—budget, personnel, scope of investigation. After weeks of badgering the task force, they finally released personnel profiles of the detectives.

Rick Grabenstein of the Sheriff's Department. Grabenstein was hired as a deputy in 1975 and promoted to detective in 1982. He is attached to the crimes-against-persons unit.

Fred Ruetsch of the Sheriff's Department. Ruetsch was hired as a deputy in June 1978. He worked in the investigative support unit, crime analysis and property crimes. Ruetsch was promoted to detective in January 1995 and is assigned to the crimes-against-persons unit.

John Miller of the Spokane Police Department. Miller was hired in 1979, promoted to detective in 1994 and joined the major crimes unit in 1996.

Minde Connelly of the Police Department. Connelly was hired in September 1985, promoted to detective in 1992 and is assigned to the major crimes unit.

The Spokane Sheriff's Department was designated as the lead agency in the investigation because the last four victims had been discovered in the county, even though they were being abducted and possibly even killed in the city. Mike and I could both see the potential for interagency squabbling. The city and county cops often worked together, but above them were political challenges that couldn't help filtering down.

Though the city of Spokane was composed of more longtime residents, the county had more people who were relatively new to the area. As money and power shifted from downtown Spokane to the outlying suburbs, pressure for political reform began to grow. Since the turn of the century, Spokane had been run by a handful of powerful families, who had grown accustomed to having the local government (or, when they had Tom Foley as Speaker of the House, the federal government) working for them. Although families like the Cowles, who owned the *Spokesman-Review*, KHQ television (the NBC affiliate in Spokane), and extensive real estate holdings, still had great power and wealth, the changing demographics and political conditions made reform inevitable. Voters began supporting ballot measures like a new city charter and a strong mayoral system to loosen the grip that the downtown power structure still had on greater Spokane.

What does all this have to do with the serial killer task force? The city-county political struggle soon came to affect the task force itself, both externally and internally. The county had much more money than the city; that was one of the reasons why it took the lead in this investigation. Another reason was that the Spokane PD, a city agency, was reluctant to get involved in the first place. Again, this reluctance was not felt by the working detectives. In fact, the original city detectives on the task force were highly experienced, motivated, and well thought of throughout the local law enforcement community. Did the actions of the Spokane PD administration reflect the reluctance of their temporary chief, Roger Bragdon?

The city-county conflict was evident in the very logistics of the task force itself. Until mid-January, the task force did not even work out of a common office. Instead, they worked at their regular desks in separate offices in the Public Safety Building.

"Part of the delay in getting the office is related to logistics," Doug Silver told the *Spokesman-Review*. "Every inch of space here in the Public Safety Building is spoken for, and it was difficult to find space for the task force office."

I've been to the Public Safety Building a few times, and

had meetings in a conference room that was open. The task force had the space they needed. They just couldn't agree on a common working area. The inability of these two agencies even to get together in the same room seemed to me to be more an issue of interagency pettiness than any lack of resources.

Soon office politics spread beyond the Public Safety Building. From the beginning, I had been suggesting on the radio that Spokane detectives get help from other agencies, particularly the Washington State Patrol and the FBI. With Joseph and Hernandez, Spokane law enforcement knew they had a serial killer, whether he was the 1990 suspect or someone else. The FBI should have been contacted in September 1997 to see if there were any similarities in MO or signature with other serial murders around the nation, or even the world.

The task force didn't like getting help from outside. They dragged their heels requesting it in the first place. And once they finally did get it, they didn't take full advantage.

The task force were talking to Canadian authorities in Calgary, Alberta, where a serial killer murdered five women during a nineteen-month period in the early 1990s. Four of the victims were prostitutes, and all of them were discovered dumped around the outskirts of Calgary. I wondered how much information the task force had actually shared with Canadian authorities.

On January 11, 1998, agents from the FBI's Violent Criminal Apprehension Program (VICAP) visited Spokane. The feds stayed for three days, but there were conflicting reports as to how well the meetings went.

The local police said that an FBI profiler was not present.

"You don't start profiling until you've exhausted all investigative leads," Silver told the media after the FBI confab. "We haven't done that yet."

In fact, a profiler had been sent from Quantico. Apparently, the task force didn't expect or want a criminal profile. Why not? Were they unwilling to share the evidentiary details necessary for a profiler to do his job? Former FBI profiler John Douglas told me that this type of reluctance often surfaces. Local law enforcement agencies want profilers like Douglas to help them identify the suspect, yet they won't give them the information they need in order to draw up a useful profile.

According to the task force, detectives from the 1990 task force did not attend the FBI meeting. But two of the 1990 detectives were there. The task force also stated that only three FBI agents came to the meeting. In fact, seven FBI agents were present. A source in the task force told Mike and me that the Spokane detectives had been upset because so many FBI agents had come, when they had expected only a couple.

Why would the task force turn down the free help and expertise of the FBI? Mike and I couldn't think of any good reason.

And we weren't the only ones critical of the task force. Some of the victims' family members were getting angry.

"I really believe if the recent task force had been formed sooner, Shawn and somebody else would still be alive," Kathy Lloyd, sister of Shawn McClenahan, told the *Spokesman-Review.* "It makes me sick."

The task force responded by revising their own organizational history.

"It certainly isn't our position to stand and be defensive or to even get into that," Captain Chuck Bown, commander of the task force, said. "What I will say is that there are two bodies discovered in August. Two weeks later, we resurrected the task force from 1990. That is a reasonably quick response time for a joint investigation and two agencies."

Wait a second. I thought the task force had been formed on December 22, 1997. Now they were saying that the task force from 1990 had been "resurrected" back in September. What exactly did they mean? Had the 1990 team been in mothballs for six years?

Following the Joseph and Hernandez homicides, and while they were still officially being investigated separately by detectives with other investigative duties, two of the 1990 task force detectives had been brought in for a briefing. Apparently that was what the current task force was calling a "resurrection" of the 1990 force.

By the task force's own words, we can conclude that in September 1997 there were no additional personnel or resources committed to either the Joseph and Hernandez cases or the other unsolved prostitute homicides. Even after Johnson and Scott, and all the publicity associated with the forming of the new task force, all that really changed was that the four detectives already assigned to the Joseph and Hernandez cases were taken off their regular assignments and allowed to work these homicides full-time. And two supervisors and two spokesmen were assigned.

If the task force was at least saying that they "resurrected" the 1990 force in September, wasn't that a tacit admission that Hernandez and Joseph were linked to each other and to at least some of the previous homicides? If they did "resurrect" the 1990 task force, why didn't they tell anybody?

In early 1998, they wanted credit for starting a secret task force in September, but they still refused to link Joseph or Hernandez to any of the other victims, or even to each other. It was much easier just to gather all the dead prostitutes together under the serial killer case, and then not have to explain why they hadn't solved them. If they never caught the killer, they would have an excuse why all the other cases were unsolved. If they did catch him, they would be able to clear those cases on his back.

Whatever kind of bureaucratic numbers game the Spokane PD and the sheriff's department were playing with these dead women, there was still the very real possibility that most of them were in fact connected and that the serial killer had more victims than we thought. There certainly were more than four. Even if Joseph and Hernandez weren't connected, there was also Sherry Palmer, Shannon Zielinski, and JoAnn Flores—and let's not forget Teresa-Lyn Asmussen, even if everyone else already had.

If the task force ever stated that any of these grouped homicides, like the 1990 cases or Joseph and Hernandez, were not connected, then they would have to admit that Spokane had more than one serial killer.

The task force administrators wanted to keep everything vague. That's why they wouldn't answer questions. That's why they refused to confirm or deny. They would connect only the victims they absolutely had to, meanwhile pushing all the other unsolved prostitute murders under the protective custody of the serial killer case.

With the task force's tacit and retroactive admission that Joseph and Hernandez were probably the work of a serial killer, the sequence of killings deserved a closer look.

Following the 1990 killings, there were no unsolved prostitute murders in Spokane for two years. Then in 1992 Sherry Palmer was found dead, with multiple gunshot wounds to the chest, and a plastic bag over her head. Roseann Pleasant disappeared, and although they suspected her husband, Brad Jackson, they didn't make a case against him. There were three more unsolved prostitute murders in 1996 (Flores, Harris, and Zielinski), but police didn't start talking about a task force until early September 1997, immediately following the Hernandez and Joseph murders. That tells me that whether or not Hernandez and Joseph were victims of the serial killer, the police seemed to think they were. Why reopen a task force if you don't think those murders are connected? Why do it then and not after Palmer and Pleasant? And what about Flores and Zielinski? Did the police know, or suspect, they were connected, but because the press on them wasn't very intense, they figured they could let those two go unmentioned and therefore unnoticed?

Whether they "resurrected" the 1990 task force in September or formed a new one in December, in the winter of 1998 the city of Spokane still didn't have a real task force.

Doug Silver was asked why there were only four detectives on the task force.

"We have to go with what our resources allow," Silver replied.

If their resources were so limited, then the task force should have reached out for all the outside help it could get. Soon the killer himself would provide them with a golden opportunity to accept such help.

On January 30, 1998, the task force announced that they were working with Tacoma police detectives in the investigation of the death of Melinda Mercer, twenty-four, whose body was found in Tacoma on December 7, 1997.

Melinda Mercer was born on June 27, 1973, in Baker, Oregon. She had graduated from high school and never married. She had left home four years before her death, and had worked as a waitress in several restaurants. She had no criminal history other than two 1988 juvenile theft convictions in Lewis County, Washington, but she was known to be working as a prostitute and involved in drugs. Her parents, John Mercer and Karyl Greenwood, lived near Centralia, Washington.

Mercer had been discovered at 1:30 P.M. by a man collecting aluminum cans by the side of the road in an undeveloped industrial area near some railroad tracks, not far from Ponder's Corners, an area not unlike East Sprague, known for prostitution and a drug trade. Her nude body was lying a short distance from South Adams Road, partially covered with brush. Her clothes were scattered near her body. Her shoes were missing. There was a plastic bag on her head.

The autopsy, conducted on December 9 by chief medical examiner Dr. John Howard, determined that Mercer had been killed by gunshot wounds to the head.

Mercer was last reported seen in Tacoma on December 6.

The task force stated that they believed Mercer's death may have been connected with the four other victims officially linked to the serial killer. "As with the victims here," the task force's press release stated, "Mercer had a highly mobile lifestyle." Other than saying that she had been shot and dumped, the investigators would not give any more reasons why they thought Mercer might be connected.

Mercer was the first body outside Spokane to be linked to the serial killer. The plastic bag on her head was the apparent connection, although there also might have been forensic and/or signature evidence. The bag had already been reported in the Tacoma press, so the task force was unable to suppress that information.

Mercer was killed on December 6 or 7. She was officially connected to the Spokane case on January 31. Why did it take so long?

Spokane should have been putting out teletypes, telling other agencies to look for white females between the ages of sixteen and forty who had been shot in the head with a small-caliber handgun and dumped in a rural location with or without a plastic bag on their heads. If they did this, why did it take them a month and a half to connect Mercer to the other murders? Did Spokane initiate the contact with Tacoma, or did Tacoma police contact the task force?

Mercer's was the only body found so far in western

Washington, while all the other victims were discovered in Spokane. This indicated to me that the suspect lived in Spokane, but had a reason to be in the Seattle-Tacoma area. He knew the region, otherwise he wouldn't be comfortable enough to kill over there. He had probably at least patronized prostitutes in that area before. I grew up in western Washington, and I couldn't tell you where to find hookers in Seattle or Tacoma, but this guy knew the turf.

Still, he wasn't entirely comfortable there. While the Mercer dump site bore some similarities to the Spokane dump sites, it was more remote and more heavily wooded—a steep embankment off the side of the road in a rural area. South Adams Road was not far from the prostitute district of the Sea-Tac strip (where the Green River Killer snatched and killed more than forty women). From what I observed of the site, it was a place easily accessed from the road, but also more secretive than the Spokane dump sites.

He didn't want Mercer's body to be found. This told me that as familiar as he was with the Seattle-Tacoma area, he was not entirely comfortable there, or at least not as comfortable as he was in Spokane. In Spokane, he could be pulled over by a cop and have a reason to be wherever he was. He could be home from the prostitute district in a matter of minutes. He didn't have that luxury in Tacoma. There, he had to account for his time. The longer the body went undiscovered, the more chance he had at an alibi.

Also, once a suspect was identified, police now had a time of death that was much more closely bracketed than any of the prior homicides. Mercer died on the night of December 6, or early on the morning of the seventh. That's a time frame that any possible suspect had better have an alibi for.

Despite the fact that he resided in Spokane, the killer probably had some reason to be in Tacoma. He was no doubt driving, and would have the same van or truck he had used in his Spokane killings. If I were working the case, I would focus on what other business brought him there. Check out what was happening in Seattle and Tacoma around December 6. What would bring the suspect to the area?

Mike and I hoped that the Mercer homicide, and its link with the largest metropolitan area in the state, would ratchet the investigation up to another level of intensity and make it a statewide investigation.

CHAPTER 11

Sunny Oster

Sunny Oster, age 41. Body found February 8, 1998, on Graham Road south of Salnave Road in Spokane County. Cause of death: gunshot wound to head. Clothed in green undergarment, dark blue sweater, gray pants. White plastic bag over head. Body had been recently dumped.

On February 8, 1998, another body was discovered. Police officials publicly speculated that this victim was tied to the serial killer, but they would not disclose any information.

"At this point," police spokesman Dick Cottam said in a statement, "it's not known who the victim is, the cause of death, or even the gender as a certainty."

Doug Silver told the *Spokesman-Review* that the release of too much information had hindered the apprehension and prosecution of serial killers in other communities.

"Suffice it to say that when you look at other cases and other task forces, it hurts," Silver said.

Silver did not specify which cases or task forces were hurt by the release of information. In my study of serial killer cases, I found the reverse to be true, that many cases were not solved because the police were too protective of information. And I could find no example in which a case was seriously jeopardized by the release of information.

As a result of this task force policy, the public knew nothing for days about this apparent homicide victim. The police would not even disclose the location of the body, saying only that it was in a rural area somewhere in southwest Spokane County.

On Thursday, February 12, Concerned Women of Spokane organized a noontime vigil for the killed and missing women. The vigil was held in Riverfront Park, on the steps behind the Spokane Opera House. One hundred fifty people attended the vigil, the first public event associated with the deaths of at least eighteen women.

That same day, the task force issued a press release:

The Spokane-City-County Investigative Task Force says the body found Sunday in the county is that of a woman who died as a result of a gun shot.

Because of the circumstances, the nature of the victim's lifestyle, the manner of death and the disposal of the body in a rural area, the Task Force has assumed responsibility for the investigation.

The identity of the woman has been determined, and detectives have talked with her family members. The Task Force has decided, and the family members have agreed, not to release the identity at this time.

The task force wouldn't even say if the victim had previously been reported missing. It didn't matter, because on the same day the task force issued that press release, the victim's family was already talking to the media.

Her name was Sunny Oster, a forty-one-year-old native of Auburn, Washington, located near Seattle. Oster was last reported seen working as a prostitute in the East Sprague neighborhood around November 1, 1997. The task force had reported Oster missing and had been actively looking for her after the two bodies were found at Fourteenth and Carnahan.

Sunny Oster was born on August 8, 1956, in Centralia, Washington. She graduated from high school and had worked as a nurse's aide. Her parents, Edwin and Anita Kay Oster, lived in Auburn.

Oster had been arrested several times for drug possession and prostitution in the Tacoma area. Her last arrest was in September 1997. She had no criminal record in Spokane, where she was known to be living as late as October 1997. She had recently completed a drug treatment program at American Behavioral Health System, a Salvation Army facility in Spokane. The day after she left the treatment program, Oster disappeared.

Oster had never been married and was the mother of two sons, both of whom she had to give up. Her last known address was the Colonial Motel on Pacific Highway South in Tacoma. Motel owner Ray Holmes told the *Spokesman-Review*, "She was just too friendly for her own good."

Oster was one of several prostitutes living in the motel when Holmes repossessed it in April 1995 from his sister.

"I remember one time she came in here with a black eye and a busted lip," Holmes told the newspaper. "I said, Sunny, just go take a room and sleep for a couple days."

Oster's autopsy, conducted on February 12 by Dr. George Lindholm, revealed that she had been killed by a gunshot to the head.

Even after this information was made public, the task force refused to state where Oster's body was found.

So Mike and I decided to find out for ourselves.

From the beginning, the task force had been very tight-lipped about even the most harmless investigative details. What possible reason did they have to withhold the name of the victim and the location at which her body had been

found? I understood that there were some details that detectives wanted to keep out of the media. I had been there
myself. But this was clearly an attempt to muzzle the press,
and keep them away from the crime scene.

Maybe they had a good reason to keep us away. There
was only one I could think of—the possibility that they
were still surveilling the site, hoping that the killer might
return.

Of course, the announcement that a body had been
found was made, so I didn't see why they would expect the
killer to revisit the grave. Perhaps they thought he had
dropped another double, similar to the Fourteenth and
Carnahan and Hangman Valley sites.

Mike and I believed that the public had a right to know
where dead bodies were being dumped. Besides, we were
curious. If the task force wasn't going to tell us the location
of the latest crime scene, we'd have to find out on our own.

We drove out to southern Spokane County and started
poking around. We visited the post office in Marshall and
asked if the local carriers had heard about anything on
their routes. They told us that the sheriff's department
had been looking for a body out farther, beyond the town
of Cheney.

We made plans to return and canvass the neighborhood.
Before we could, a group of high-ranking law enforcement
officers met with Spokane's top editors and television news
directors. In that meeting, the police asked the media to
suppress any information about the location of the body
found on February 8. Paul Brandt, KXLY television's executive news director, would not agree to these conditions.

Neither would Mike and I.

During the meeting, the police referred to the site as being on Graham Road. Armed with that information, Mike
was confident we could find the precise location. We put
our heads together and tried to figure out how.

While we were busy strategizing, one of the KXLY television reporters uncovered a witness who had seen several sheriff patrol cars driving onto Graham Road from Salnave Road. The witness characterized this as unusual activity. It was rare to see even one sheriff's department car out there. More than one meant something was definitely up.

"If we ask the task force whether they are conducting surveillance, they will not confirm or deny anything," I said.

"We have to give them a chance to stop us from looking," Mike said, "so they can never claim we ruined a chance to catch the killer."

Mike called Doug Silver, and asked if the task force was surveilling Graham Road. Silver would not confirm or deny that the task force had any "ongoing" investigation off Graham Road.

"Doug, if you've got something going on there, just tell us to stay away and we will," Mike said. "We sure don't want to screw things up. It will not end up on the radio, you have my word."

Silver wouldn't tell Mike anything. He wouldn't even tell Mike to stay away from Graham Road.

After Mike spoke with Silver, we sat in the conference room at KXLY. We needed to make a decision. Were we going to continue playing by the task force's rules? They had given us nothing. No information, no respect. We gave them every opportunity to tell us to stay away from Graham Road, but they didn't.

My line of reasoning was that the task force was stonewalling, and meanwhile women were dying. I'd had it with their nonanswers and refusals to confirm or deny, their unwillingness to release information. Not only did the public have a right to know, but it just might help solve the case.

"Screw 'em," I said finally. "Let's go find it."

Mike sat back in his chair with his arms folded. I expected a long and reasoned argument from him, mostly because my own reaction had been somewhat, well, Neanderthal. To my surprise Mike calmly said, "You're right, let's go."

Heading west on Interstate 90 out of Spokane, it doesn't take long before the terrain starts to change. The Spokane Valley lies between the end of the conifer forests and the beginning of the desert. On this February day, it was cool and blustery, but in a few short months the temperature would reach one hundred degrees. This was not my kind of country. Too few trees, and too many rattlesnakes.

As we exited the interstate toward the small university town of Cheney, the landscape was decidedly rural. Cultivated land, cattle, and horses filled in the spaces between homes. In this part of the country, properties are most likely described as either ranches or farms, depending on whether they raise livestock or grow crops. Everybody drives a pickup. They wear jeans and hats every day but Sunday. I wondered whether we'd be able to find out anything. I had grown up in a small northwestern town not unlike this one, and I knew this was a place where people minded their own business.

Driving through Cheney, I told Mike, "I've got a good feeling about this area . . . I don't know why, but I think there's bodies here."

Mike looked around, then got the joke.

"Fuhrman, we're driving past a cemetery."

Graham Road is a dirt and gravel road. The right-of-way was lined with barbed wire fencing, beer cans, and weeds. I looked out at the fields and saw a hawk hover and dive toward his unsuspecting meal. Farther along, a coyote cautiously ventured into a clearing. For a moment my mind drifted back to my childhood. I would spend entire days wandering through pastures and fields hunting with my .22. Back then, time meant nothing and evil was something we watched on the yearly airing of *The Wizard of Oz.* A lot had changed since then, but not the landscape.

Mike's booming voice woke me out of my daydream.

"Why don't we just stop at some of these houses and ask if they've seen any sheriff cars lately?"

"Yeah," I said, shifting back into detective mode. "Let's canvass all these houses. Even if we don't find the dump site we'll know if the cops ever talked to anyone."

We went house to house. Since it was a weekday afternoon, not everybody was home. Still, we were able to speak with several local residents. They were friendly, helpful, and seemingly unaffected by the discovery of a dead body in their community. There was no indication that anyone from the Spokane Sheriff's Department or the task force had ever talked with any of them, or made any attempt to interview them. No business cards had been left on their doors. No follow-up calls. Nothing.

"They must know who the killer is," one woman said. "Why else would they not talk to everyone around here? There's not that many of us."

Mike and I worked the north side of Graham Road, driving the station's KXLY Channel 4 News car onto every property. It was a far cry from driving around Los Angeles in a snappy new Crown Victoria, wearing a business suit, and carrying gun and badge. Here we were, bouncing around in a Japanese import decorated like a birthday cake, wearing Levi's and armed with only a pencil.

At one home a middle-aged woman listened intently to our questions and said, "Why don't you ask Mike Cummings?"

"Mike Cummings?"

"Yeah, he found the body." She pointed toward a bend in the road. "His place is over there, first farm on the left."

We thanked her for the help.

"Good luck," she said as we walked back to the car.

We drove up to the farm and knocked on the door. Nobody answered, and I wasn't surprised. We couldn't expect a farmer to be inside the house before lunch. Walking behind the house I could see a man and a woman moving some cows down by a barn.

I greeted them with a country "Mornin.'"

The man gave a suspicious nod and continued pushing the cows along. The woman smiled at us.

"Good mornin,'" she said. "What can we do for you?"

Mike and I took turns explaining. The man quietly walked over to join the conversation.

"I found her on Sunday while my wife and I were walking our dog."

He pointed in an easterly direction down Graham Road.

"You found the body?" I asked.

"Yup."

He stretched his hand out to me and stated in a matter-of-fact tone, "I know who you are and I'm not talking to anyone, but I'll talk to you."

Mike Cummings introduced himself and his wife Jeri. He looked me right in the eye and gave me a firm handshake. He seemed to be normally a quiet man, but with each question we asked, the words came faster. Finally, he got a little frustrated and asked, "Do you want me to show you where she was?"

We all jumped into the car and drove back down the road.

"I found her over there," Cummings said, pointing toward a cluster of trees by the fence line just ten feet off the road.

As Mike pulled the car over, I was struck by the similarities with the water treatment plant where Shawn Johnson had been dumped—a clump of dogwood trees at the bottom of an embankment off the side of the road.

The terrain was wide open, leaving the dump site visible from a long distance. You could see down the road for a quarter mile each way.

Cummings was an excellent witness. He described how he and his wife and neighbor had been walking down the road around 3:00 that Sunday afternoon when they saw a body facedown in a shallow ditch, approximately ten feet off the roadway, near the dogwood trees.

Oster's body was facing south-southwest, with her left arm outstretched. The right arm was positioned beneath and across the front of the body. The skin on one of her hands appeared to have been abnormally stretched, indicating that the body had been dragged rather than dumped into the ditch. This is known as skin slippage and is quite common. Someone tries to take a wedding ring off a dead body, and all the skin comes with it. Since Sunny Oster had been dead for some time but was not severely decomposed, the skin on her hand merely stretched when she was dragged to the dump site.

Oster was clothed in a green undergarment (possibly a T-shirt), a dark blue sweater, and gray jeans or cords. Her shoes and socks were missing. The lower right back of her torso was exposed and there was blood pooling under the skin, possibly indicating postmortem lividity, which suggested that she died on her back, and at a different location. Lividity occurs when the blood settles to the point of gravity and remains fixed there, no matter if the body is subsequently moved, or how long it lies in its new position.

A white plastic bag covered the victim's head.

Cummings referred to the body as "her." Remembering the comments made by a police spokesperson, I asked Cummings if he could tell if the body was a woman. He said that it was obvious.

One of the detectives who viewed the Oster body stated that they immediately knew it was connected. This was apparent from the plastic bag. That's why they wanted to keep everything about this body secret, because they knew it was connected.

Cummings had seen a number of predatory animals and birds present in the area, but the exposed areas of Oster's skin showed no evidence of animal depredation, indicating that the body had not been at this location for very long (possibly twelve to fourteen hours). There was some water in the ditch and the ambient air temperature at the time of discovery was around forty-five degrees.

I remembered the hawk and coyote I had seen earlier. The exposed skin on Oster's body would have been the first target of ravens, coyotes, or dogs. The body had been here no more than twenty-four hours. She had been killed somewhere else, then dumped here.

Oster was probably dragged with one arm, facedown into the water-filled ditch below the trees. The outstretched arm was the towline; the right arm was pulled underneath her naturally, and that is how it remained. I looked around; the dump site was easily observed. Oster's body was meant to be found—just like Johnson, Wason, McClenahan, and probably most of the others. How many more bodies were out there that would never be found? Were there any nearby?

He drives up and parks on the opposite side of the street. It's early on the morning of the eighth. The suspect struggles with the dead weight of the body. He does not pick her up. Instead, he drags her across the street. Once he gets to the dogwoods, he simply dumps her on the ground. With a sickening soft thud she lands on the frozen road. He is right-handed. To use his left hand to drag her would have caused his heels to come in contact with her head or shoulder. He does not stage her, but she is dragged to this spot to be found.

"You can drive in one direction and drive out the other direction," Mike said, "same as Hangman Valley."

"And the trees are the same as where they found Shawn Johnson," I said. "Dogwood trees are a clue."

"What's he trying to tell us?"

"I don't know. But it's a clue until you know why. I think that kind of coincidence is not a coincidence."

"Stop talking in riddles, Fuhrman."

"What are the odds that he would stop and dump the bodies right at a place where birch trees are?" I asked. "No, he's staging the body again. Both Johnson and Oster were dumped on the west side. He's coming from the north. When they came to rest, the bodies were in the same position. Both facedown."

"Are the dogwoods markers, indicating more bodies somewhere?"

"Either that, or some kind of a statement. It might not even be something that's conscious. He's not going back to these bodies, he's leaving them to be found."

"So what do the trees mean?"

We both thought for a moment.

"Dogwood is part of the birch family," Mike suggested.

"Maybe Birch is his last name."

"Maybe Birch is the street he lives on."

"Maybe Birch is his mother's maiden name."

"Maybe he's a member of the John Birch Society," Mike said.

It was time to go. We gave Cummings a ride back to his home and thanked him for the help. As we shook hands good-bye, Cummings had one request.

"I'd appreciate it if you didn't talk about me on the radio. I don't want to talk to any other people about this."

Mike and I promised to keep his name off the radio. And we did not disclose any of the information we had discovered that day. Despite the fact that the task force was stonewalling us, we wanted to allow them the opportunity either to respond or to give us a good reason to sit on this information.

Graham Road was an evidence-filled crime scene. Whether or not Sunny Oster had been killed shortly before her dumping, the body had been there a short period of time. There was no reported animal predation and little chance that the crime scene had been compromised by weather or witnesses. There was a very good chance that the task force could retrieve trace evidence from her body and clothes.

With Oster we had our first witness who had clearly seen the body at its dump site. Cummings said that the plastic bag appeared clean inside, which indicated that Oster had been dead long enough not to have bled in the vehicle. Maybe the plastic bag had started out as MO and had become a signature.

Or, as Mike put it, "What was once necessity now becomes desire."

Mike and I had a lot to talk about. We stayed away from the Oster case for two weeks, giving the task force a chance to respond. We called and faxed them, asking if they had any comment, even if that comment was for us to shut the hell up. They had no comment, and wouldn't confirm or deny anything.

After two weeks of doing radio shows on auto theft and fraud, it was time to talk about the serial killer. We still hadn't gotten any response from the task force.

During our show on March 12, a listener called in, saying her husband had significant information about a suspect vehicle he saw on Graham Road the morning of February 8. Mike took their phone number, and we called the man after the show was concluded.

His name was Mike Mallinson. He told us that he drove on Graham Road every morning on his way to work. At approximately 4:25 A.M. on February 4 and again at the same time on February 8, Mallinson had seen a maroon 1988–92 GM full-sized car parked along the side of Graham Road. The car was facing north. Its tires were completely off the road and the vehicle was up against the fence. Its lights were off and the engine was not running. The windows were not frosted, indicating that the driver had parked it at that location for less than a half hour. Mallinson's calculations placed the vehicle about 8/10 of a mile south of Salnave Road, right across Graham Road from where Oster's body was found some twelve hours later.

Mallinson did not know this was the exact location of the Oster crime scene. He knew only that a body had been found somewhere nearby, but he didn't know where, and he hadn't linked it to his observation of the car. His description placed the maroon car directly across the street from the clump of dogwoods, the closest place a car could have parked off the road. Mallinson also did not know that a similar vehicle had been connected with the 1990 homicides. A source from the 1990 task force told us that detectives had been looking for a maroon sedan.

This was an explosive clue, and possibly a major breakthrough in the case. We didn't put the information out on the air. Instead, we faxed a memo to the task force, providing all the information that Mallinson had told us, as well as his home and work phone numbers so they could contact him immediately.

The next week we called Mallinson back. He said that nobody from the task force or the sheriff's department had called him.

When I told a retired Spokane cop, with extensive

homicide experience, about the Mallinson clue, he was dumbstruck.

"What would you do if that clue came in?"

"I would drop everything," he said. "This is a hot clue."

The Mallinson clue should have been priority one. We already knew that the Graham Road neighborhood hadn't been canvassed. Over the months, we had passed along other listener tips to the task force. When we followed up on them, very few had been checked out.

Mike and I wanted to help the task force. The question, in our minds, was whether playing along with the task force would actually achieve that. We had already seen how the task force didn't follow even the most basic police procedures for homicide investigations, like canvassing a neighborhood or processing a crime scene correctly. We had seen them ignore priority-one clues.

Mike and I believed that the more the public knew about these killings, the more concerned and involved they would be. Information would stimulate clues and witness reports. The task force was always saying that they could not release information because it might harm the integrity of the investigation. By now, we were beginning to realize they just didn't want to be held accountable.

We felt we had a moral responsibility to put information out that a possible witness might need to come forward, or a possible victim might need to protect herself. To sit on the Mallinson clue would be the same as if we were in Seattle in 1974 and didn't reveal that the "Ted" suspect was driving a light-colored Volkswagen.

Mike and I decided that if the police weren't going to act on this information, we would.

At 11:00 A.M. on March 19 Mike called the task force and left a message for Doug Silver, telling him that we were going on the air at 2:05 that afternoon. They had three hours to call us back and tell us not to disclose this information on the air. Silver wouldn't tell us not to put the clue out, and neither did anyone else from the task force. So we put the Mallinson clue on the radio.

FUHRMAN: We called the task force fifteen minutes before this show and you know what Captain Silver's comment was? We will not confirm or deny anything. Is this a UFO case? Are we talking to the Air Force?

FITZSIMMONS: I'm not angry about this. I'm bewildered and confused. A clue that important, when one week has gone by and no one has interviewed the claimant, that is unforgivable. That is not good police work, under anybody's definition of good police work. You could tell me they don't have the money, they don't have the manpower. We made it simple for them. We gave them the witness's name, address, phone number, best time to call. . . . To say that you don't have the manpower to follow up on a clue like this is saying that you don't have the ability to solve this thing. I don't understand this. I think an explanation is owed. The very witness himself is sitting, waiting at home at this very hour wondering why it is that something as important as a suspect vehicle, which matches the description on a suspect vehicle from three other prostitute homicides, is being ignored. Why hasn't this witness been called?

FUHRMAN: If we can find this out as two nonpolice, unarmed guys just shuffling our feet and asking questions, what can you find out when you have the power of a search warrant? What can you find out when you have the power of a badge behind you? This is not a budget problem, this is a problem of dedication.

The response was thunderous. Some callers were outraged at the task force for not following up on such a good clue. Others were outraged at us for criticizing the task force. Several Spokane cops, both retired and active, called in and tried to defend their colleagues, but even they had to admit that the Mallinson clue deserved immediate follow-up, or at least an explanation why this wasn't done.

Mike called Mallinson several times during the following months, and he still hadn't been contacted by anybody from law enforcement. Seventeen months after we had first informed the task force about the clue, Mallinson told us that he had been interviewed by detectives in July 1999. This was shortly after a meeting with Sheriff Mark Sterk in which I reminded him of the clue.

The task force should have gone door to door along Salnave and Graham Roads, asking everybody if they had ever seen this vehicle. The task force didn't even have to conduct the interviews themselves; they could have relied on sheriff's officers on their regular duty.

They could have used the clue out on East Sprague, showing a photo of the car model and asking prostitutes: Have you dated anyone driving a car like this? Ever seen Sunny Oster or any of the other victims in a car fitting this description? Please notify us if you see it in the future.

They could have circulated a flyer on East Sprague and throughout the county, asking for witnesses to report any sightings of this car, or any people known to drive it that might have been acting in a suspicious manner. They could have put a stakeout unit or video camera at a busy intersection on East Sprague, looking for that car.

Instead, the task force ignored the Mallinson clue. Maybe they knew something that we didn't. Maybe they already had a suspect in their sights, and they knew he did or didn't drive a maroon car. Maybe they were just one step away from catching the serial killer.

Maybe. But we doubted it.

The Spokane PD and the sheriff's department reacted

to our series of radio shows on Oster as if we had given away the president's nuclear launch codes.

Chuck Bown of the task force came over to KXLY and told the station owner, Steve Herling, that Mike and I were coming awful close to interfering with a police investigation. To his credit, Steve said, "If they're breaking the law, arrest them. If not, get out of my office."

Sheriff John Goldman wrote a letter, complaining that Mike and I were coming very, very close to interfering with an investigation.

In an article subsequently published in the *Portland Oregonian,* Sergeant Cal Walker of the Spokane Sheriff's Department was asked if the task force had come over to KXLY to lean on us. "As far as we're concerned," Walker told the reporter, "it never happened."

Bown's and Goldman's reactions were meant to intimidate us and KXLY management. Instead, their pressure tactics had the opposite effect. Now we really started turning up the heat.

CHAPTER 12

Dead of Winter

After our release of the Mallinson clue and the firestorm that followed, the task force issued a press release that deserves to be reprinted in its entirety.

The joint Homicide Task Force is providing the following information to keep the public informed about the status of the investigation:

The investigation team has received 920 tips related to the series of homicides. They have come from a wide range of sources including law enforcement officers, other law agencies, social service providers, and the public.

Captain Doug Silver, co-commander of the Task Force, says: "The fastest and most efficient way for citizens to ensure that their information reaches the Task Force is to call that information directly to Crime Check at 456-2233."

Secret Witness is offering $2,000 cash rewards for information that solves any of these homicides, and multiples of that amount for more than one solution. The Secret Witness 24-hour line is 327-5111.

Callers are urged to use a code name or number to protect their identity.

Capt. Silver notes some tips are coming in second hand after being filtered through entertainment programs in the community. To assure all tips are received by the Task Force, and that the information given is accurately recorded, it's important that Crime Check or Secret Witness be the receiving sources.

A tip may take a matter of hours to investigate, but some have taken several weeks to fully follow up.

Information received so far ranges from people reporting "uncomfortable feelings" about an acquaintance to specific information about unusual behavior or statements that seem suspicious.

All tips are read by a Task Force sergeant, and assigned a specific priority. They are then assigned to detectives based on that priority. Some tips may not be investigated for several months while higher priority information is handled first.

To date, investigators have been assigned 241 tips.

Throughout the investigation, detectives have developed numerous persons of interest. Many have been investigated and tentatively ruled out as suspects. Others have been investigated but have not been conclusively eliminated as suspects at this time.

Capt. Silver asks anyone who has called in information to be patient. "One of our biggest challenges is to handle the vast amount of tips and the information they are generating."

Authorities again urge anyone who has information on any of these homicides to call Crime Check 456-2233 or Secret Witness 327-5111.

"In many similar investigations elsewhere in the county," said Silver, "the key information that led to

an arrest came from a member of the public. Law enforcement needs the eyes and ears of the community."

This press release was clearly written in, response to
Mike and me. By discussing how many clues had come in
and describing how those clues were handled, the task
force was trying to show that they were hard at work, even
if they hadn't followed up on the Mallinson clue.

In the time they wrote the press release, they could have
followed up on the Mallinson clue and a dozen others. For
some reason, they were too stubborn to pick up the phone
and call him. It appeared that they just didn't want to work
a tip Mike and I had generated. When I was a detective, I
worked tips given to me by drug addicts, gang members,
rapists, thieves, murderers, even lawyers. If it came from
the devil himself, I would work a clue like Mallinson's as
soon as it came in.

At the same time that they were soliciting tips, the task
force was describing itself as being inundated with them.
But their numbers didn't add up. The task force had been
in operation full-time since December and part-time since
September. By March 27, 1998, they had received 920 tips,
no doubt ranging from solid clues, like Mallinson's, to calls
from crackpots. That gave them seven months to follow up
920 clues. Let's do the math. Four detectives working forty
hours a week for three months (remember, they weren't
full-time until December 22) is 1,920 man-hours. Four detectives working twenty hours a week for four months is
1,280 man-hours. With more than 3,000 man-hours already committed to the case, they had enough time to follow up on 920 clues.

Of course, they had other duties. During this period,
there were four crime scenes to process, five autopsies to
attend, and meetings with the FBI, the Tacoma police, and

other outside law enforcement agencies. Still, a detective's job is to solve the case. To do that, you've got to work clues, not just count them.

We knew that Sergeant Cal Walker of the sheriff's department was prioritizing the clues. Cal Walker's prior homicide experience, as far as we knew, consisted of only one case, the recently adjudicated DiBartolo murder, in which a sheriff's deputy had been convicted of killing his wife. Now he had the most important job in the task force. By prioritizing clues, Walker was determining what each detective did day to day. Within the organization, Walker probably had more real power than either of the captains.

Whatever was going on internally, it was obvious that the job simply wasn't getting done. As of March 27, 1998, only 241 tips had been worked. What about the other 679? Why did Silver say, "One of our biggest challenges is to handle the vast amount of tips and the information they are generating"?

I didn't understand why the task force was first asking for tips without giving the public any information to work with, and then not processing the tips when they got them. All you need is one clue to solve a crime, but you never know which one it is until you work it. The clue they needed to solve this case could have been sitting in a pile on Cal Walker's desk.

The rest of the press release was an obvious attempt to cover up their embarrassment over the Mallinson clue and other revelations Mike and I had aired on the radio.

Why else would Doug Silver say that the "fastest and most efficient way for citizens to ensure that their information reaches the Task Force" was to call Crime Check? And why was he so worried about tips that were "coming in second hand after being filtered through entertainment programs"?

I have been called a lot of things in my life. But never an

entertainer. Clearly, Silver and the task force were telling people not to give anything to Fuhrman and Fitzsimmons.

FITZSIMMONS: One thing I would hate to think was that if a clue came from this program, from Fuhrman and Fitzsimmons, that it is being discounted. If that is the case, ladies and gentlemen, that is a serious oversight on the part of law enforcement in this community and that cannot be stood for.

FUHRMAN: This is righteous information that we're trying to pass on to help solve this crime.

At the end of the release, Silver stated that key information in other investigations came from the public: "Law enforcement needs the eyes and ears of the community."

I couldn't agree more. The only problem is, the public needs to know that the information they have is important or possibly helpful to the investigation. If no information about a crime is released to the public, then how could anybody know to call in a clue?

The Moxley case provides a perfect example of this. For twenty-three years, Thomas Skakel was the main suspect in the murder of Martha Moxley. In 1998, my book came out naming his younger brother Michael as the killer. There had been earlier reports, which I document in the book, of Michael making confessions to the murder while in a drug and alcohol rehab program in Maine. There were numerous witnesses to these confessions, yet very few of them came forward when it was publicly known that Thomas was the suspect. As long as everybody thought that Thomas was the killer, Michael's confessions didn't mean much. The confession witnesses must have thought they were mistaken or confused, or they didn't want to get involved. The publicity surrounding my book and the subsequent grand jury made it easier for them to come forward.

Mike Mallinson didn't know that the vehicle he saw on the morning of February 8 might have been connected to a crime, until he heard information about the Oster homicide on our radio show. If the task force had succeeded in keeping this information secret, Mallinson and other witnesses might never have come forward.

Meanwhile, the controversy continued.

FITZSIMMONS: My producer tells me we just got a call from a man who described himself as a police officer, but would not go on the air. He said, we supported you Fuhrman, when you were on the O. J. Simpson case, but now we wish you would just stop second-guessing the police here and allow them to do their job.

FUHRMAN: In the Simpson case, I did my job, and I would have welcomed any help in that case if somebody had come forward. And I'm not second-guessing anything. You and I, Mike, we're going out there and we're finding things and we're turning them over to the police. That's not second-guessing, that's helping. What I'm second-guessing is, we come up with good clues, good solid leads that have to be followed up on, and they're not. How is that second-guessing? That's somebody who's not doing anything. You can't second-guess them if they haven't done it.

FITZSIMMONS: By the way, Officer whoever you are, and you're welcome to call us, you know the telephone numbers by heart now. I don't care if you disagree with what we're doing or not, that's certainly your prerogative to do so. But these are citizens who called us, the people who pay the taxes that pay your salary, and they called us with what they saw. We passed on that information, that's all we did. We checked it out to make sure these people were legitimate. And here's what you're really upset about. We're holding you accountable for the information we passed on to you. We're calling them back and asking them whether they were followed up upon.

FUHRMAN: Let me just say something about the officer who wouldn't come on the air. I cherish that support that officers gave me. But is my payment to the officers in this city for their support that I turn my head on obvious clues in a serial killer case? We have made every single effort to give everything to the task force before it is ever spoken on the air, and we get no comment. If the task force said to me, don't bring this out, we're onto something, we can't tell you what, but you'll understand in a few weeks, we'd sit on it.

FITZSIMMONS: Hello, Alan, you're on the air.

ALAN: I don't think they have any intention of solving this case. I think they look at it as they are all prostitutes and good riddance.

FITZSIMMONS: I don't buy that.

FUHRMAN: Me neither, not for a minute. . . . We don't know if those clues have been passed along to a working detective or not. I think that's the first question. Does the working detective, the guy who knocks on the door and picks up the phone, is he the guy who's got that clue, or is it still sitting in a folder on some administrator's desk?

ALAN: Mark, let me ask you. You've been involved in enough of these investigations. Wouldn't that be the first thing you would do is inquire of the closest neighbors to see if they saw or heard anything?

FUHRMAN: I would send somebody while I was at the body site to all houses within a mile in all directions, knock on every door, and leave cards if they're not home. If I got a clue on a Friday night at midnight about a suspect vehicle that was there and unexplained that early the morning a body was found, I would expect to get a call at

12:05 in the morning and I would be at the station, working that clue.

FITZSIMMONS: I think that it's unfair and unreasonable to assume that they do not desire to resolve this case. I think that the guys who are working with clues in the field very definitely want to get this guy in the worst way. Hello, George.

GEORGE: I understand what you're doing, but I just wish you'd stop blasting the cops.

FUHRMAN: I'm not blasting anybody. I just want somebody to follow up on the clue.

FITZSIMMONS: Seven days have gone by and as of 2:45 this afternoon, that same witness is still waiting for a call from the authorities.

GEORGE: I would be willing to bet you that after this program is over that somebody would be calling whoever the heck it is.

FUHRMAN: In seven days, there might be somebody else who's dead. This is not a game. This is a homicide investigation. This is not forged checks. People are dying.

GEORGE: Do me a favor, stop blasting the cops.

FUHRMAN: I'm not blasting the cops. We're giving the information to a captain. If there's a detective on this task force that wants to do it on the QT we'll funnel information to a working cop. I'm not even sure that working cops are getting these clues.

FITZSIMMONS: I have been doing talk radio here since 1974, you find one program where I have blasted cops. I defend cops. I'm not blasting them now. I'm disappointed. I'm not angry. I'm not a know-it-all, but I'm smart enough to know when a piece of information is worthy of somebody's attention and when it doesn't get that attention, as a journalist it's my job, my responsibility, to be curious enough to know why that isn't happening.

FUHRMAN: You don't need to be a cop to figure out that these little pieces of evidence mean something. It could be the greatest coincidence on earth. It also could be the lead that breaks the case.

GEORGE: Well, I just don't know that you're helping any.

Walking out of the station after the show, I found myself scanning the lot for occupied vehicles. The investigation had instilled some fear in me. The instinct that keeps your guard up on the job had long since taken a back seat to retirement. Now, without a thought, that instinct had returned. Only this time I didn't know who I was looking out for—the suspect or the cops.

It was late afternoon in dead of winter. Another snowstorm, which meant I had a two-and-a-half-hour drive ahead of me. Time enough to think and rethink and eventually overthink the case.

For months now, the serial killer investigation had been a nonstop discovery of bodies or search for missing women. It was overwhelming just following the story. I could imagine how the task force was swamped. I had only to remember the fatigue that always came with crime scenes, and in doing so, I felt a certain kinship with those detectives. I knew their job was almost impossible, and no one expected them to succeed. No matter how much I wanted them to catch this killer, the odds were stacked against them.

And here I was criticizing everything they did, or didn't do. Second-guessing them, playing Monday-morning quarterback. The big-city detective comes to the cowtown and shows them how to do it. That's not how I meant it, but I'm sure that's how it came across. I knew I was pissing them off—if not the task force detectives themselves, then at least the police administrators. Well, that was my job, I guess. I was a journalist. And after several months, it still felt more uncomfortable than my first day as a rookie cop.

As I drove into Idaho, the white winter scenery was a stark contrast to my own dark thoughts. I thought about the case, about the crime scenes and the evidence. I found myself distracted by details like plastic bags, foreign DNA, recoverable ballistics, ambient temperature at the time the body was found. None of those facts meant anything right now. Instead, I started thinking about the women. I tried to imagine how they lived, what kind of a home they returned to. I thought about their families and their childhood, how they ended up on the street. I thought how sad they were, what a waste, how their lives had come to nothing. Then he steps in and ends it all, and that's even worse. To be raped and tortured and shot in the head and then raped again and mutilated and thrown away on the side of the road to lie there until some transient finds your body, or what's left of it. No one should die like that. No one.

But that's what he wants. And he wants it so bad he's willing to put aside everything, any shred of conscience or decency or compassion he once had. The only thing he worries about is getting caught. And he doesn't want to get caught, because then he can't kill anymore.

For the past six months, I had tried to think about him as a suspect. I wanted to know what he did so that I might help to catch him. But now I had a glimmer of what he was like as a man. Pathetic. Weak. Cowardly. As selfish and cruel as any human could ever be. The women meant nothing to him. They were just a cheap release, disposable human tissue.

I wondered if what I was doing was actually helping solve these murders, or only driving the suspect to kill more. He wanted the story to go national. He was toying with the task force. I was their harshest critic.

When I was a cop, I could go to sleep at night knowing I was doing good. No matter what happened during the day,

I was trying to help people. Being a journalist wasn't so simple. I had no clear lines of right and wrong, no loyal support group, no camaraderie except for Fitz, and we weren't making a whole lot of friends. I wanted the cops to succeed, but I was also their adversary. Aside from Fitz and some others at KXLY, I couldn't align myself with any of the other media, or they wouldn't align themselves with me. So which side was I on?

As I drove through the falling snow, I thought long and hard, and the only answer I could come up with was that I was on the side of the story. That wasn't good enough. So I thought longer and harder, and finally convinced myself that I was on the side of the truth. But that didn't make it any easier.

CHAPTER 13

Linda Maybin

Linda Maybin, age 34. Body found April 1, 1998, loosely buried in a ditch along Fourteenth and Carnahan. Cause of death: gunshot wound to head. Body clothed and partially decomposed. Evidence of animal predators. White plastic bag on head.

Mike and I expected that more bodies would start turning up. So did the task force.

On February 19–20, 1998, the task force had a National Guard helicopter fly over the crime scenes at Fourteenth and Carnahan and Graham Road. The helicopters were equipped with forward-looking-infrared devices (FLIRs), which the task force hoped would be able to detect the warmth of decomposing bodies in those two areas.

The task force had already conducted an extensive physical search of both areas. What made them think that there might be more bodies in those particular locations? Even if there were additional bodies, they were probably buried, and the FLIRs would not be able to detect them. Also, it was winter, and the bodies would be decomposing only during a narrow window of time each day, if at all.

There was only one more woman fitting the victim profile whom police had officially reported missing. That was Linda Maybin, who had last been reported seen in late November 1997.

I wondered if the aerial and ground searches were intended to find Linda Maybin. I also wondered if they knew that Maybin was dead and buried somewhere. Had the killer been communicating with the task force in some way—telling them she was out there, daring them to find her?

There were other possible explanations for these expensive and high-profile searches. The flyovers could have been an attempt to catch the killer as he revisited a grave site. This is how serial killer Arthur Shawcross had been apprehended. In the late 1980s, Shawcross murdered several prostitutes and street people in Rochester, New York. The victims were mutilated after death and dumped in the woods near the Genesee River. The FBI was brought in, and profiler Gregg McCrary concluded that if the suspect was inflicting postmortem wounds to his victims, then he was probably revisiting them in their grave sites. Using helicopters to perform overhead surveillance, New York State Police first located a fresh body, and then spotted Shawcross nearby. He soon confessed to the murders.

There were many similarities between Shawcross and the Spokane Serial Killer. Perhaps the FBI had suggested aerial surveillance during their January meeting with the task force. Or maybe one of the task force detectives, who were reportedly reading every serial killer book they could get their hands on, had come across the Shawcross story in *Mindhunter* by John Douglas and Mark Olshaker.

"It's a shot in the dark," Doug Silver said about the search, "but we thought we had to try it."

After the helicopter flyover and additional ground searches by teams of volunteers, spokesmen for the task force would not say whether they had found any new bodies. In other words, they hadn't.

For months now the suspect had been running the show. He dropped bodies and the task force responded. After six weeks with no fresh bodies, the task force decided to go out and try to find one. This only demonstrated how well the killer had trained the task force. It reminded me of a dog chasing a stick, and running after the stick even when it wasn't thrown.

It isn't easy to find dead bodies if the killer doesn't want them found. Particularly in a city like Spokane, surrounded by rural areas and vast stretches of wilderness. Only about a quarter of Ted Bundy's estimated one hundred victims have been found. The Green River killings produced forty-nine dead bodies, but there were no doubt many more victims. In both cases, investigators had specific areas to search. The Spokane killer was dumping bodies all over the county. Even if the task force knew for certain that there were more bodies in, say, Hangman Valley, how could they possibly hope to find them?

Or take Fourteenth and Carnahan. The evidence indicated that the bodies of Wason and McClenahan had been dumped only a day or two prior to discovery. Three days after the crime scene had been processed, Mike and I were out there searching for possible clues. Still, we couldn't be certain that more bodies weren't buried right beneath our feet. The lot had been the site of excavations, well drillings, and water table tests. It was covered with fill dirt and gravel, garbage and debris. You couldn't recognize a freshly dug grave among all this disrupted earth, much less one that had been dug several months before.

The task force was at a severe disadvantage. The killer knew where the bodies were buried. They didn't. And as I watched them search for additional bodies, I wondered whether this was the most effective use of their limited resources. The task force was already undermanned, under-funded, and overwhelmed. By their own admission, task force detectives could not keep up with the tips that were coming in. Why were they seeking more evidence, when they couldn't even work the clues they already had in front of them?

Even when they did something resembling proactive police work, like the searches and the flyovers, the task force was still playing the killer's game. By searching for bodies instead of pursuing the suspect, the task force was demonstrating just who was in control of this investigation—the killer himself. And if the task force didn't realize who was in control, the killer was about to show them.

On March 31, the task force stated that there were no more bodies at Fourteenth and Carnahan.

The next day the killer made them eat those words.

On April 1, at approximately 4:50 P.M., a couple was walking their dog in the vacant lot near Fourteenth and Carnahan when they saw a human leg sticking out from beneath a pile of debris.

Police and criminalists quickly responded to the scene. Task force personnel showed up as well. The pile of debris covering the body was slowly removed, revealing a white female, clothed, barefoot, and partially decomposed. There was a white plastic bag on her head.

The body had been discovered right next to the road on Fourteenth Avenue, just a few feet from where the criminalist van had been parked while processing the Wason-McClenahan crime scene. Right where they had just finished searching and made definitive statements that there were no additional bodies in the area. The next day—April Fools'—a body is found.

This was a huge embarrassment. Members of the task force were visibly demoralized. The looks on their faces, their statements and actions, not just on April 1 but for many days afterward, showed an investigative team stunned and confused, unsure what to do next.

At the crime scene, task force spokesmen refused to confirm or deny whether the body had been there during their well-publicized searches. Neither possibility made them look good. If the body had been there, they missed it. If it hadn't been there, then the killer demonstrated that he could dump bodies under their noses at will.

"We believe we searched thoroughly, but we searched with humans," Undersheriff Mike Aubrey said. "I'm not saying this victim was there before, but I'm not saying it wasn't, either."

"I can't tell you how long the body's been here or whether it was missed on the previous searches," task force co-commander Steve Braun said.

Some local residents stated what everybody else already knew.

"He's taunting the police," Theresa Mallory told the *Spokesman-Review*. "He's coming back, and he's laughing in their faces."

Mallory said that if the body had been there long, neighbors, or at least their dogs, would have noticed it.

Sheriff John Goldman himself admitted that the killer might be taunting the task force. Steve Braun was visibly bewildered.

"Anybody who participates in this kind of crime is operating on his own agenda," Braun said, responding to the possibility that the killer was taunting them. "I can't even guess where he's coming from."

"This is something that really bothers us," Doug Silver said.

When asked what it would take to catch the serial killer, Silver said, "It will take time."

Apparently the task force felt that time was on their side, if little else was. As it grew dark the evening of April 1, detectives "secured" the crime scene and left it until the next morning. I was no longer surprised by this. It seemed like standard procedure. In fact, I didn't know of a crime scene that they hadn't left overnight.

The next day, detectives and criminalists returned to finish processing the scene. Fourteenth Avenue was closed and the vacant lot was searched by volunteers and bloodhounds.

At a press conference that day, Silver would not state whether the body was connected to the other prostitute homicides. Though Silver said that a preliminary examination did not indicate the gender, age, or race of the body, or what might have caused the death, the entire city knew that the serial killer had struck again.

Following an autopsy on April 3, the body was identified through dental records as Linda Maybin, a thirty-four-year-old Spokane prostitute and drug addict who had been last seen alive November 22, 1997. She had been officially reported missing on November 29 by Lynn Everson, a social worker with the Spokane County Health District, and her continued disappearance had stimulated much interest from the task force.

Linda Maybin was about five feet ten inches tall, 140 pounds, with blond hair and blue eyes. She was born on April 25, 1963, in Ellensburg, Washington. She graduated from high school, had been married and divorced. Her parents, David Fischer and Jeanne Connot, lived in Blaine, Washington.

Maybin was a crack addict whose friends called her "Barefoot Linda" because she hardly ever wore shoes. She had never gone into treatment for her addiction. A friend said, "Her detox was when she went to jail for thirty days.

"All she wanted was crack," the friend said. "She talked crack. She lived crack."

Maybin was arrested more than a half dozen times for

prostitution. She pleaded guilty to two counts of forgery in Spokane Superior Court on June 23, 1997. She was released from jail on October 6. In the four years prior to her death, Maybin lived in Ellensburg, Cheney, Seattle, and at a low-income motel in Spokane.

In the press release announcing Maybin's identity, Doug Silver made another veiled reference to the criticism the task force had been getting on our radio show.

"I would hope no one would wait until an officer contacts them before letting us know any information that might be relevant," Doug Silver said. "Our detectives are busy following up tips we've already received, and they cannot canvass residents to request information."

Mike and I soon learned that soil samples from Maybin's body did not match soil samples from the grave site at Fourteenth and Carnahan. This absolutely confirmed our suspicions that the body was exhumed from another location. Her body was severely decomposed, and she had been missing since November 22, 1997, which indicated that she had been killed and buried somewhere else, then dug up and dumped around April 1.

The Green River Killer had done something similar on April 1, 1984. He placed a skull by the edge of the road, forming an arrow with other bone fragments pointing directly to where the remains of two more bodies had been dumped.

If the Spokane Serial Killer was paying tribute to the Green River slayings, then the task force was dealing with an intelligent and educated suspect whose motives went beyond violence. He enjoyed playing with the cops, the press, and the public. It must have made him angry when Spokane did not pay attention to him. Linda Maybin was the killer's way of demanding respect.

We also discovered that Maybin had a plastic bag on her head. By the time Silver said that the task force was not certain whether this latest body was connected to the other homicides, detectives had already seen the telltale plastic bag covering her head.

Silver had also said that they could not, by the afternoon of April 2, determine the race or gender of the body. A leg was sticking out from the debris. Surely the witness who first came upon the body could tell what color and sex the victim was, simply from the exposed body part.

I've seen a lot of rotten bodies, some of them very advanced in decomposition, but I could always tell whether I was looking at a man or a woman. Their body shapes and sizes are different.

The race, gender, and identity of the victim were going to be made public eventually. So would the fact that she was connected to the other homicides. How was Silver protecting the integrity of the investigation by keeping any of this a mystery for another day or two? The task force was already embarrassed and demoralized.

That's exactly what the killer intended by the body dump. Linda Maybin's body was staged to be found. It was a statement of control and manipulation by the suspect. He was probably watching them process the crime scene. I could imagine what he was thinking . . .

I am in control. You think you can outsmart me. You think you can find my girls. You think that if you find them, you will find me. You've got it all wrong. You only find the ones I want you to find.

I know who you are. You don't know who I am. I know where you are. You don't know where I am. I know what you are doing. You don't know what I'm doing. You're not watching me. I'm watching you.

I took her out of the grave and I dumped her here. I've had her this long, and now I'm going to put her in your face. I'm in control. I'm in control of the investigation. You don't know me. You won't find me. I can walk through your world with impunity.

Okay, so you'll figure out why she turned up today. But have you guessed anything else? Do you know why I dropped this one? Or why I dropped her here? You think you know? You're probably wrong. There's a message, but you're too stupid to see it.

There's no fool like an April fool.

For months now, I had said that the task force needed to respect their suspect. Now he was directly challenging them to recognize what he was doing and to pay him the proper respect. He was also demonstrating that he was in control of the investigation. When he dropped a body, they jumped. When he didn't drop a body, they would go out looking for one.

The killer was issuing a challenge, and the task force should have risen to meet it. This was an opportunity for the task force to take their investigation to another level. The killer had just given them not just another body and another crime scene, but a glimpse into his own mind.

The crime scenes at Fourteenth and Carnahan deserved to be looked at closely, almost in isolation from all the other homicides. Here the killer was playing a very sick game of human chess. He was exhuming decomposed bodies and dumping them in a vacant lot at the edge of a suburban development. He was partially burying them with leaves and debris from the previous dump sites, to indicate where they had been before. He was exposing body parts so that he could be certain they would be found. He had already stacked two bodies in reverse order of their time of death, to demonstrate that he was at least holding his victims dead in some other location, and possibly holding them alive.

So what did Maybin's body mean?

First of all, the killer was making a powerful statement that he was in control. Even before the Maybin body dump, the task force was dancing to the killer's tune. Now he was manipulating them emotionally—hurting their feelings, making them doubt their own abilities, and causing them to question everything they thought they knew. He was clearly creating depression and dissension within the ranks of the task force itself.

Soon after Maybin's body was found, two Spokane PD detectives asked to be let off the task force. Dan Lundgren and Minde Connelly were, by all reports, the most experienced and capable detectives on the task force. I was later told by a former Spokane PD officer that Lundgren and Connelly quit the task force because of "micromanaging" by Cal Walker. That may well have been true, but from the timing of their departure, it was also clearly a reaction to the events following the Maybin dump.

The chaos within the task force continued long after Lundgren and Connelly were replaced.

The task force spokespersons wouldn't admit that Maybin's body had not been at the vacant lot during their well-publicized searches. Neither would they speculate that the body had been there, but they had missed it.

That's what they were saying publicly, but it's also what they were saying among themselves. A source in the task force told me that the detectives could not even agree whether Maybin had been moved from another grave. Half of them believed that she had been dumped sometime around March 31. The other half felt that she had been there since her death, near the end of November. This second scenario was more than unlikely—once again, the soil and vegetative samples taken from Maybin's body didn't match the surrounding grave site.

I didn't understand why detectives within the task force refused to admit, even to their own colleagues, that Maybin had been dumped just prior to April 1. The only explanation I could come up with was something I had seen too many times before in my law enforcement career. Egos were superseding evidence.

Maybin had been dumped just prior to discovery. Why couldn't the task force simply admit that? And why didn't they make use of this information by releasing it to the public? Here is significant information about the movements and actions of the suspect. There was no reason, other than fear of embarrassment, for the task force to refuse to confirm or deny this obvious fact.

Doug Silver, or one of the other spokespersons, could have described to the press how the killer had exhumed a body and reburied it at a site that obviously had some meaning to him. This would engage the public, get them more interested and more involved in the case. Perhaps there had been witnesses to the dumping. If citizens weren't even told the approximate time that the dumping occurred, how were they supposed to know whether what they saw might have had any connection to the crime?

As far as Mike and I knew, the Maybin body dump at Fourteenth and Carnahan was the best lead this task force ever had. Yet they wouldn't use it to their advantage, because they were so scared of embarrassing themselves.

Instead of going on the offensive with this information, the task force tried to suppress it. Failing that, they used their policy of refusing to confirm or deny to keep what few facts the public did know hidden in a cloud of doubt and rumor. All they appeared to be worried about was whether someone would second-guess them, or catch them making a mistake.

The task force knew the killer was taunting them and they reacted by losing their professional detachment and taking it personally. They saw Linda Maybin's body as an embarrassment, not an opportunity. From the beginning, the task force had been personally very sensitive, and obsessively aware of how they were being perceived in the media and by the public at large. That's one reason why they were so angry with Mike and me. It was as if the task force were actors and not detectives. They were more concerned with how they looked, rather than with what they actually did. And their policy of withholding information from the public had more to do with their own fear of being second-guessed than it did with protecting investigative integrity. Mike and I were tired of this game. And so was the killer.

There is no doubt in my mind that on April 1, the killer watched the Fourteenth and Carnahan crime scene being processed. He wanted to see how the task force would react. And he wanted to see how the public would react as well. He was sick of being ignored and underplayed by the police and the media. By dumping Linda Maybin, he was writing a story that Spokane could not ignore. He wanted the public to fear him, as the police feared him.

If I had been on the task force, I would have welcomed the challenge. Finding the Maybin body would have been exhilarating. It would have energized me, raising the game to another level. The killer was willing to take chances. He had an enormous ego and probably thought he was invincible at this point. This meant he could possibly be baited into a trap.

The killer was feeling confident, and confident suspects can make stupid mistakes. What the task force should have done following the Maybin body dump was to stimulate the killer to further acts of brazenness.

This was the perfect time for a public event associated with the task force investigation that might draw out the killer. They could be fairly certain that he had been there at Fourteenth and Carnahan on both dates that the bodies were discovered. If they held a public assembly to disseminate information and stimulate tips, the killer would probably attend, as long as it was held in a forum that was large enough for him to feel as if he could blend in with the crowd.

Even if he didn't attend this forum, he might react to it. The task force believed that there were more dead bodies somewhere. Why wouldn't they want him to dump another one? With each body dump, there was not only more evidence, but also a greater chance that he might be seen.

I had no doubt that this option was suggested to the task force, at least by the FBI, whose VICAP and serial killer units often tell local agencies to stage such events to draw out the killer and to provoke him into action.

Fourteenth and Carnahan was the site the killer had chosen as a battlefield between himself and the task force. With Wason and McClenahan, and later with Linda Maybin, he threw down a challenge to which the task force did not respond. Instead of engaging him on his own ground, the task force retreated to their windowless office in the Public Safety Building. If they couldn't solve the case from there, then at least they could avoid further embarrassment. Or so they thought.

The killer had just changed the rules of the game. He was supposed to be on the defensive. Instead, he took the offensive, and knocked the task force back on their heels. He was in control of the investigation. He was being aggressive. They were being fearful and reactive. He was chasing the task force, and they were running away from him.

CHAPTER 14

He's Listening

On April 2, 1998, we started the radio show with Doug Silver's press conference, and then talked briefly about the latest body dump at Fourteenth and Carnahan.

FUHRMAN: The suspect feels comfortable at Fourteenth and Carnahan. He dumped two bodies there. The first time he dumped a body and then he returned with another one. He feels confident. You look at this scene, and it's fairly ideal to dump a body. People are not paying attention. People don't have crime in this area. They're not used to it. They're not of a suspicious nature. We were there for a long time and nobody bothered us. We could have shot a gun and nobody would have come to investigate. We could have dumped a body there today.
FITZSIMMONS: Nobody probably would have bothered us.
FUHRMAN: Mike, I could have dumped your body there.
FITZSIMMONS: But then you'd have to do the show by yourself.

The rest of the day's program was devoted to a discussion of school shootings. There had been a couple of recent cases of teenagers shooting up their high schools. It was a troubling subject, and our guest had some interesting perspective on it. As she spoke, I caught myself drifting back to Fourteenth and Carnahan. I had to fight to stay focused on the subject at hand.

During an extended newsbreak, while Mike was busy running the board, I found myself thinking about the killer. He was certainly very smart, and he was doing things on purpose. From the discovery of Jennifer Joseph and Heather Hernandez on the same day to the dumping of a body on April Fools' Day, I felt there had been very few coincidences in this case.

The serial killer was doing all this for a reason. He wanted attention. And he wasn't getting it.

After as many as nineteen victims, the serial killer wasn't a national story. He didn't have a nickname. The city of Spokane had basically ignored him. The only time he got any press was when he dumped a body. Then he dug up Linda Maybin and dumped her body on April Fools' Day. Now they had to pay attention.

Well, the killer definitely won that round. And he was probably feeling pretty good, following the story in the newspaper and on television.

Then it struck me. He was listening to our radio show, right now. Of course he was listening. Why wouldn't he? The newspaper had run an article about Mike and me in March. The TV station had filmed us at the Carnahan scene back in January. And we were doing almost every radio show about the serial killer case. If the killer wasn't a listener from the beginning, he was now.

That realization stopped me in my tracks. Throughout the investigation, I had been standing aside, an interested but uninvolved observer. Sure, Mike and I had been conducting our own investigation, but we weren't part of the task force. We weren't part of the story. Or were we?

He wasn't listening just because it was me. He would

have paid attention to anybody talking about him. Now I was part of his world. We had a connection. A relationship, of sorts.

I shuddered at the prospect. I was on the radio, expressing my thoughts and feelings, bringing my experience to bear upon a very important case. Was I just watching the game, or had I become a player? If I was a player, then what were the rules?

I tried to imagine him sitting at home, listening to the radio. He could have been alone, surrounded by trinkets and trophies of his kills. Looking at Linda Maybin's driver's license, holding a piece of her jewelry or some of her hair. Or maybe he wasn't alone. He could have been at work, listening to the radio, engaging his coworkers in speculation about the murders, none of them ever suspecting that he might be involved. Meanwhile, he was getting off on the secret knowledge that he was the person that everybody was talking about. That everybody was scared of. The killer. The suspect. The fiend. Whatever you called him, he was the one. And only he knew it.

I've faced down thousands of suspects, and none of them scared me as much as this man I couldn't see. It was precisely the fact that I couldn't see him, that I wouldn't know him if I looked right at him, that scared me so much. He could be anywhere. I had no idea who he was or what he would do next. At least the task force knew something about him, even if it was only a fingerprint, or a strip of DNA or a blood type or hair color. I knew nothing, and that's what scared me.

No, I knew one thing. He was listening.

For a month now, Mike and I had been vocal critics of the task force. While we were certain that the killer was taunting the task force by dumping Linda Maybin's body on April Fools' Day, we also wondered whether he wasn't throwing us a bone. Maybe he wanted to draw us into the game. Maybe he felt we would make things more interesting. Maybe we already had.

The killer was definitely reacting to statements and events disclosed in the press. Shawn Johnson's body was dumped the day after an article appeared in the *Spokesman-Review* stating that Johnson was missing. This article was also the first public notice that Maybin had disappeared. Wason's and McClenahan's bodies turned up a couple days after the announcement of the task force. Maybin's body was dumped the day after the task force said there were no more bodies at Fourteenth and Carnahan. April Fools'.

If the killer was dumping bodies in reaction to press reports, what, if anything, was he doing in reaction to our radio show?

Mike and I had no way of knowing whether we were part of the killer's games, but we did know he was listening. From April 2 on, we always sensed his presence. Every word we said had to pass through the calculation that the killer would be hearing it. We tried not to let this fact suppress any thoughts or feelings we might have, but it was difficult not to think about it.

Once I knew he was out there, I started becoming comfortable on the air. The radio shows were easier, my delivery and content smoother. I guess that it was now more like the dangerous, violent, and unpredictable world I had previously inhabited.

From the beginning of our radio dialogue on the prostitute homicides, Mike and I had given the killer one thing he never received from the task force—respect. While Roger Bragdon was publicly hoping the murders were not connected, we were looking for clues that would link them up.

Mike and I both understood that respecting the killer didn't mean we liked him or approved of what he was doing or were taking his side against the police. It simply meant that we acknowledged his intelligence and the control he obviously had over the situation. By treating him with respect, we hoped to draw him out, and perhaps provoke him into doing something brash and making a fatal mistake.

Off the air, we speculated about how the killer was contacting his victims.

"If the killer is a john, the task force must have something," I said. "A witness report, a bad trick. How could the killer pick up girls off the street and not be seen? If anybody wants him caught, it's the prostitutes on Sprague. Not only is he killing them, but he's also cutting into business."

"I think you're right," Mike said. "He's got to be making contact away from the normal street transactions with these girls. He meets them at a place of comfort, where their defenses are down. How else could he snatch them without any witnesses?"

"Prostitutes know what's going on in the street. They're competing with each other for business. They see who the other girls go off with."

Mike and I had spoken to several prostitutes who worked on East Sprague. It appeared that neither the task force nor the Spokane PD was doing any intelligence work on the street. And they were not giving these potential victims much information concerning the homicides. No flyers, no suspect sketches, no "be on the lookout for." Nothing. So we decided to put one of these women on the air.

We sat in the tiny studio, bent over our microphones. Outside, the newsroom hummed with its usual activity. Mike was perched behind the control panels. He pushed a couple buttons and the music came up. Then he slipped easily into his radio voice.

FITZSIMMONS: Stay tuned for *All About Crime* with Mark
Fuhrman. It promises to be an interesting show. April
Scott, our producer, has been able to get a prostitute
from Spokane to come into the studio and talk to us. Be
right back, this is KXLY News Radio 920.

During the break for news, Mike and I had a brief off-
air conversation about our next guest. Even though I was
very comfortable talking to prostitutes as a detective, I
wasn't quite sure how to do it as a radio talk show host.
Mike said he would take the lead, make sure she was comfortable, and bring her along slowly.

April had found the woman through Lynn Everson, the
Spokane social worker, who had appeared on the show before. Lynn worked closely with the prostitutes on East
Sprague, running a women's shelter and the needle exchange program.

The door opened and April led the woman inside. She
didn't need to tell us how hard her life had been—it was
written on her face and body. Her skin was blemished and
scarred. She was overweight but malnourished. Drugs had
taken their toll. Dressing up in her best clothes only made
her look sad and shabby.

I had seen thousands of women like her. They lived on
the street, day to day, with none of the comfort or security
that the rest of us took for granted every day. What led her
into this life? She didn't start out this way, but at some
point she found herself trapped in a hard and dangerous
existence on the streets.

Knowing I had a family and a ranch to go home to
didn't make me feel superior to this woman. Instead, I just
felt more sorry for her wasted body and shattered life. I
knew where she and all the other women had been, where
they were going, and it was all just one vicious circle. From
the street to jail to rehab to halfway house back to the street

again. When they made money they stayed in cheap motels, or maybe a one-room apartment with a hot plate. They worked every day; survival was a full-time job. Drugs, booze, cigarettes, and the cautious friendship of other street people were their only pleasures. They got nothing from physical intimacy—that had stopped being fun a long time ago. They were accustomed to being used and thrown away—by their pimps, by their johns, by society itself. Now a sexual psychopath was killing them—almost a natural progression of the abuse they had suffered throughout their lives.

Inside the studio, the woman was nervous, uncertain, obviously uncomfortable. She was used to being treated with contempt. It wasn't often that people were actually polite to her, offering her coffee, asking if she needed to use the bathroom. Of course, we wanted something from her. That's why she was there and she knew it. We wanted her to talk candidly about her life and her fears. We wanted her to give us a glimpse into a lifestyle which so many of us thought of as sordid, even immoral. We wanted her to bare her soul on the radio.

FITZSIMMONS: Before we take a break, we're going to introduce another guest here. We will call you Rhonda, for the purposes of our conversation. Rhonda is a prostitute. Rhonda is not her real name, but we're going to use it. Her voice has also been distorted electronically so that she can speak to us without the possibility of her voice being detected. Good afternoon.
RHONDA: Good afternoon.

This woman was frightened. Although she lived in constant fear, this was a danger that she could not get used to. Dealing with johns and pimps and dealers and regular assholes was bad enough. Now there was a serial killer preying on her and her friends. Each car she got into, each man she went to a motel with, could be the wrong one.

But she was trapped and she knew it. She couldn't get off the streets, even though those street made her bait for a serial killer.

FITZSIMMONS: Let me ask you right off the top. You are involved in the prostitution industry here in Spokane. Has there been any breakthrough that you can identify among your peers regarding whom we might be looking for in this case?

RHONDA: None. We have no idea.

FITZSIMMONS: There's been no person who has gone away with somebody and then the person not heard from for a long time?

RHONDA: None of us have noticed anything. We try to keep an eye on each other as well as we can, but we're all doing the same thing, jumping into cars, jumping out. Sometimes we don't notice who comes out and who doesn't.

FITZSIMMONS: I think, Rhonda, you would agree also that the john on the street doesn't seem to be, at least in a conventional way, taking you women off the street.

RHONDA: No, when you get in with one, there's just ways that you feel them out and that's the way that most of us girls go. If we feel comfortable, we go. If we don't, we don't. These girls that have been picked up are not in their right frame of mind. Most of these girls are drug addicts, so they're not thinking about the circumstances.

FUHRMAN: They're chasing their habit.

FITZSIMMONS: And they're not paying attention to their own safety.

RHONDA: No.

FITZSIMMONS: What are ways in which the vulnerability can be exploited?

RHONDA: I think it's someone who knows they're addicted to drugs and he gains their trust, dates them a few times, that's when he takes them somewhere and shoots them.

FUHRMAN: It's really interesting to think that this man has targeted the victim first, because we have no indication that this has happened where he hasn't killed the person.

FITZSIMMONS: Where would this person undetected be able to snatch a prostitute that he might have dated once or twice? Because you have not seen somebody who has gone off with somebody and then has turned up missing.

RHONDA: That's just it. If the girl has dated him a couple times, and the rest of us know that he has, and we feel that he's safe, then we just don't pay attention.

FUHRMAN: How long have you been on the street?

RHONDA: Fifteen years.

FUHRMAN: In let's say the last five years, if you can think back, have you ever known somebody to make any statements about, "I met somebody, he's going to take me off the street." Or "I met somebody, he's giving me really good dope." And then all of a sudden you never see that person again?

RHONDA: No. But just recently I had met somebody who had made a comment to one of the girls out there and said that he knows who the killer is.

FUHRMAN: And does this girl think she could recognize him again?

RHONDA: I was with him, too. So I would know who he is if I saw him.

FITZSIMMONS: He's not returned?

RHONDA: I haven't seen him. From my understanding, he just only goes out there from time to time.

FUHRMAN: Rhonda, have you contacted the task force with this information?

RHONDA: No, not yet.

FUHRMAN: Do you think if you looked at a series of photographs of mug books, do you think you got a good enough look?

RHONDA: I would recognize him off the bat. I would know who he was.

FUHRMAN: Could you do a composite? In other words, could you sit with an artist and describe certain features about his face and let that artist draw and guide him into drawing the picture of this person?

RHONDA: Yes, absolutely.

FITZSIMMONS: Let's take a time-out here. This is Newstalk 920, we will be right back.

Rhonda had relaxed a little. On and off the air, she was speaking comfortably with us. Talking to street people, to pimps and prostitutes and drug addicts, you have to approach them in a certain way. If you don't like them, if you don't respect them, they'll know it and they won't cooperate with you. They might not be book smart, but they're often very savvy about other people. If you approach them with a relaxed manner, treat them with respect, even empathize with them, you'll get what you want. And that's information and understanding. You want to understand them, their life, the people with whom they are involved.

I'd seen too many law enforcement officers who couldn't deal with street people in a respectful and empathetic manner. So had Rhonda.

Earlier in the show, Mark Olshaker, John Douglas's coauthor, had been doing a phone-in from his car on the way back from the airport. He switched over to a landline and joined in our discussion with Rhonda.

FITZSIMMONS: And we welcome you back, we've got Mark Olshaker, coauthor with John Douglas of *Mindhunter*,

Journey into Darkness, and *Obsession.* And Rhonda, who is a prostitute here in Spokane. Rhonda, let us talk a little bit about how the police are dealing with the women in the prostitution industry here. Do you see very many police? Do they interview you? Do they talk to you?

RHONDA: I've seen them, and the only way they talk to us is to check and see if we have any warrants, or any contact with them recently. None of them have ever asked us if we have any information about the murders.

FUHRMAN: How about detectives?

RHONDA: No.

FITZSIMMONS: Now there has been a sheet circulated over the last week or so, which is an information sheet designed essentially to get vital statistics on you women so that if you turn up missing they are going to be able to identify who you are and, of course, if they find a body, they might be able to identify the body, but this is a sort of a do-it-yourself kind of thing, isn't it?

RHONDA: Yes.

MARK OLSHAKER: I'd like to ask Mark Fuhrman a question if I could? Mark, in your experience with the LAPD, how much value do detectives put on prostitutes' accounts and testimony? They're out on the street a lot. Are they well thought of as witnesses, or do they tend to be discounted?

FUHRMAN: I think it's on an individual basis, not only for the detective, but for the person you're talking to. The mutual respect is what gets you somewhere. If you respect them and treat them like a human being, when you go out there and ask them a question, say "I need some help, I need you to ask some questions around," you buy them a meal, treat them with some respect, it goes a long way. That's the way I operated and so did anybody I ever worked with. Same thing with heroin addicts. Yeah, I don't agree with their lifestyles; yeah, I don't agree with them using drugs. But prostitution and drugs are probably your two best sources of information on the street. So if you want to know what's going down after the sun goes down, you better get in there and talk to people. You've got to mean what you say and you've got to back up your word. Rhonda, what I just said, would that go a long way with you, if a detective in plain clothes came out and talked to you the way he talked to his neighbor and just basically asked you, we need help, and we need help from all your friends?

RHONDA: Yes, it would. It would be enlightening actually, if they just talked to us like we were normal people.

FITZSIMMONS: Do you feel neglected by them?

RHONDA: Yes, I do. Sometimes I do. The only times they want to say anything to us is when they think we're doing something wrong. I know prostitution is illegal. But they don't want to get to know us on a personal basis.

FUHRMAN: I think I'd rather know a lot more prostitutes than I would politicians.

FITZSIMMONS: Do you think that there's a lot of information on the street that would be useful to a swift conclusion to this investigation? Do the women know something that the police could use?

RHONDA: Not just the women, some of the dealers out there, some of the users, if they would just go talk to them without making them feel threatened maybe they would get more information.

FITZSIMMONS: Let me ask you, Rhonda, are you very frightened?

RHONDA: Yes. It's been kind of a rough week with the recent body just found. A lot of people are more nervous now. It relaxes after they find them and they find out who it is, but then it's still in the back of everybody's mind that he's still out there.

FITZSIMMONS: Now, with the finding of Linda Maybin, the last of the missing women from the Spokane area have been accounted for. And of course most of those, tragically, who have been on the list have turned up dead. Does that mean, Mark Olshaker, he's going to start taking additional women?

MARK OLSHAKER: That's quite possible, unfortunately. It's also possible that he may be coming in and out of the area. It's also possible that he's got something going in some other jurisdiction as well. That's one of the things we're very poor at in this country, correlating major crimes between one area and another. We've got seventeen thousand police and law enforcement agencies in this country and unfortunately they're not very good at talking to each other.

FITZSIMMONS: Rhonda, did you know Melinda Mercer? She was a prostitute in Tacoma. Do you ever remember her being in Spokane?

RHONDA: No.

FUHRMAN: That leaves a lot of space between Spokane and Tacoma. I don't think we've accounted for every missing woman between here and Tacoma. To think that the police or the community have found all the victims of this serial killer is crazy.

FITZSIMMONS: What are people saying about Maybin on the street, Rhonda? Did you know her?

RHONDA: Just by passing by and seeing her, not personally.

FITZSIMMONS: She was referred to as Barefoot Linda. Why was that?

RHONDA: Because she never wore shoes.

FITZSIMMONS: No matter the time of year?

RHONDA: Well, when it was snowing, she'd probably have them on. But in the summer, the concrete could be ninety degrees and she's out there walking on it, no shoes.

FUHRMAN: It's chilling. It's almost like he saw that and she became an immediate target just because she was like he preferred to see his victims at the end.

FITZSIMMONS: Rhonda, let me ask you, do you feel that the risk is higher now that the list of missing women has been exhausted?

RHONDA: Yes, I think what he'll be doing is going out there and gaining other girls' trust. And right now, as far as I know, there aren't very many girls out there who are addicted. So he's going to sift them out before he tries something else again.

FITZSIMMONS: Might this not present an opportunity for the task force?

FUHRMAN: The victimology is what's going to solve this case. You've got to find the common denominator of how he's targeting these victims and acquiring their trust, without any one of them escaping alive.

FITZSIMMONS: Rhonda, have you seen an increase in police presence in the prostitute district as of late?

RHONDA: Somewhat, but they don't ever pull over and just talk to us and ask us if we've noticed anything or if we've seen anything unusual.

FUHRMAN: I don't want to second-guess, but detectives are the ones that need to be out talking with these girls, not patrolmen. Patrolmen have the radio chipping at them all the time. They can't really get into in-depth conversations or investigations out on the street. They're just chasing the radio.

MARK OLSHAKER: And it's not really good policy for a prostitute to be seen publicly with a uniformed officer.

FUHRMAN: Exactly, you can stand there in a suit and talk to just about anybody, and no one will notice. You stand there in a uniform, and it's kind of obvious.

FITZSIMMONS: So what you're saying, Rhonda, is that you want detective contact, not patrolman contact.

RHONDA: Yeah, that would be great. The outreach van that's out there every Wednesday night. If just one of the detectives on the task force would sit in there and maybe see the girls as they come in and just look at them, at least know who they are, then maybe they'll gain a little more trust of these girls.

MARK OLSHAKER: My partner, John Douglas, has always said that the way you solve crimes is through the help of the public. The public is your best partner. The public that you need to focus on most clearly is the prostitute community, because they are the ones who are being targeted.

FUHRMAN: With such a small number of people you're talking about, you could probably bring them all in on one meeting and it could be a step toward catching this guy.

RHONDA: I really think the detectives need to come out there and do one-on-one with the girls and gain their trust.

FITZSIMMONS: Let me ask you, Rhonda, do you know of anyone presently missing?

RHONDA: There is one girl out there who hasn't been out there for a long time, but she is addicted, and she's just recently been going out there to support her habit and I haven't seen her in about a week. I haven't heard from her, and she was calling me every day, just about. I don't know if she's left town or put herself into rehab.

FITZSIMMONS: Rhonda, thank you very much for coming on the air with us. We know that it took a good bit of courage, and we appreciate it.

Rhonda said a quiet good-bye and April escorted her out of the studio.

As I watched her walk out of the studio and back to the street, I wondered if Rhonda would be alive next week, next month, next year. I wondered if the killer would go out looking for her now. I wondered if she died, who would miss her, and if she wasn't murdered by the serial killer, whether anyone would even notice, much less care. And I wondered would I have had her on the radio show if there wasn't a chance that she might be the next victim?

We finished up our business and the show ended, and I looked at Mike for his usual comment. He said "good show" if it was and "see ya next week" if it wasn't.

This one was a good show.

CHAPTER 15

Melody Murfin

Melody Murfin, age 43. Reported missing May 20, 1998.

In what was becoming Spokane's favorite pastime, a woman walking her dog discovered human remains in a vacant lot on Sunday, April 19, 1998, at approximately 7:00 P.M. The woman first found a skull, which appeared to be human. Nearby were several other bones, also thought to be human. These remains were lying among debris at the base of an embankment at the northwest corner of Seventh and Sherman.

Police spokesman Dick Cottam stated that the cops didn't know whether the remains belonged to a male or female, and this time, at least, that statement had some validity. Until there was some indication as to the gender and possibly the cause of death, this most recent body find would be handled by the city's Major Crimes Division and not the task force.

The area where the remains were found had been covered with heavy brush until the autumn of 1997, when a group of volunteers cleared it. This indicated to me that the body was probably dumped in the fall, after the cleanup.

There was no follow-up information released to the press. When I requested specific information concerning identification or classification of these remains, I was denied.

On April 23, Doug Silver issued a press release announcing that the task force had met with representatives of eight other law enforcement agencies to discuss the serial killer case. The meeting had been held March 26 at the Regional Justice Center in Kent. Along with the Spokane PD and sheriff's office representatives were others from the Everett Police Department, the King County Sheriff's, the Pierce County Sheriff's, the Seattle PD, the Snohomish County Sheriff's, the Tacoma PD, the Thurston County Sheriff's, and the state's Attorney General's Office.

This meeting was not the first contact with other agencies, but it certainly indicated that other Washington State law enforcement agencies were interested in knowing whether the serial killer might be responsible for homicides in their jurisdictions. Melinda Mercer had already been confirmed as a serial killer victim in Tacoma, and these other agencies had dead and/or missing women whom they hoped might be accounted for.

I had no idea why the task force waited nearly a month to tell the public about this meeting. No information came out of it—no suspect or vehicle descriptions, no warnings to potential victims, no announcements of new bodies, or even the names of additional missing women.

I knew that it was often difficult to get law enforcement agencies to work together and share information, even on a crime as serious as this one. We had seen how reluctant the task force had been to release even the most basic information to its own public. And we were afraid that they might be treating other law enforcement agencies the same way.

In a serial killer case with a highly mobile suspect who had already murdered women on both ends of the state, the Spokane Task Force would be seriously jeopardizing their investigation if they didn't share information with state and local agencies that might be able to help them solve the case. I was not at all confident that they had taken full advantage of the opportunities that the March 26 meeting provided.

The local media consisted of two different groups. There were career Spokane journalists, many of whom didn't want to rock the boat or piss off their sources, even if those sources gave them very little information. And there were young and hungry journalists on their way up the ladder and out of town. Spokane is market seventy-seven media, an entry-level post, and not a place where an ambitious young reporter wants to spend more than a year. These reporters had a tendency to burn their sources, since they had no ties to the community and knew they weren't going to be around much longer. Many Spokane cops had been burned by the media before and were determined not to let it happen again.

I could understand, if not agree with, the task force's policy concerning the release of information. What I didn't understand, and had seen before in my own department, was their reluctance to share information with other agencies.

Information is powerful only if you use it. It doesn't gain interest just sitting somewhere untouched. In fact, it loses value. That's not to say every detail about a case should be released. With a judicious disclosure of information, a detective can unearth new information or understand the information he or she already has in a new context.

When you're interacting with other law enforcement agencies, particularly on a serial homicide case, it's vital that a detective give these agencies enough information to enable them to help. Teletypes describing MO, ballistics, victimology, and other possible connectors should be issued, not just within the region, but nationwide. The word has to get out. Other agencies need to know what the task force is looking for before they can help.

Following the embarrassment of April Fools' Day, the task force appeared to be providing more information to the public. Even these disclosures were odd. Near the end of April, the task force made a pair of announcements regarding two separate discoveries of what they called evidence from the vacant lot on Fourteenth and Carnahan where three bodies had been found.

First, on April 28, 1998, they reported that eight days prior, deputies had discovered two shirts at Fourteenth and Carnahan, near the Linda Maybin crime scene. The shirts were put on display during a press conference, at which Doug Silver stated they were relevant to the case. The only reason he gave for their relevance was the location in which they were found. Evidence of sexual activity—what kind of evidence or activity, Silver would not specify—was also discovered nearby.

"We're trying to determine the reason for these items being discarded at that particular location," Silver said, asking anyone who had information about these T-shirts to contact the police.

One of the shirts had what authorities called "probable bloodstains." Since the shirts had been found on April 19, the task force had time to take them down to the crime lab for at least preliminary analysis. It would take only a matter of minutes to determine whether those stains were human blood.

If those stains were blood, then it wouldn't take much more forensic testing to determine whether they belonged to somebody connected to the homicides. The task force obviously had the victims' DNA. I thought they also had the suspect's DNA (because there was no apparent signature, it appeared to me that DNA was the evidence that allowed them to connect the six cases). Typing the bloodstains from the shirt, they could have first matched the sample for blood type. If the blood type matched any of the victims, or the suspect, then they could perform more extensive testing to determine if the DNA matched.

The shirt with probable bloodstains was an extra-large blue T-shirt with Sun Valley and a skier on the chest. The other shirt was lavender, missing its label, and had no visible markings or stains. These would appear to be the shirts of a male and female, respectively. Did they belong to the killer and one of his victims? Police weren't saying.

When asked whether the serial killer was taunting investigators or revisiting dump sites, Silver responded philosophically: "The possibilities are endless, they really are."

The next day Gary Darigol, a local television reporter, found empty pornographic video boxes at the same location the shirts had been discovered. The reporter turned these boxes over to the task force, who would not release any specific information concerning them.

Since the pornographic video boxes were discovered by a journalist, it was impossible for the task force to control the release of that information. Maybe they were connected, maybe they weren't. The shirts were more interesting, because they reportedly had been discovered by detectives more than a week before the press conference. If they had wanted to, the task force could have suppressed any information concerning this possible evidence. I wondered why they went public with the shirts.

There were three possibilities I could think of:

1. The Task Force thought that the shirts were connected to the killer (probably because the blood sample matched either the suspect or one of the victims).

2. They were so confused and demoralized, they didn't know what they were doing.
3. They wanted to appear as if they were at least doing something, so they announced the discovery of evidence that they knew was not connected.

In late April, the task force conducted another set of flyovers with FLIR-equipped helicopters. In announcing these renewed searches for decomposing bodies, the task force stated that the February flyovers had been unsuccessful because of the cold winter weather and snow cover. They also stated that this second round of aerial searches had been suggested by the helicopter flight crew.

On May 13, the task force announced that it had established a toll-free tip line and a post office box for citizens to call or mail in tips. It took them five months to get these very basic logistical operations in place. Prior to May 13, the task force was taking tips on the countywide Crime Check line, and serial killer calls were first heard by a civilian employee who then directed them to the task force. Even after the task force established their 800 number, the phone was still answered by a secretary and not a detective. And the secretary worked only from 8:00 A.M. to 4:00 P.M. The 800 number was discontinued after a little more than a year.

By this time, Mike and I had no idea what the task force was doing, much less why. We had already gotten into trouble overestimating their abilities. Nature hates a vacuum. In the absence of solid information concerning these homicides, it was easy to start suspecting that the task force was simply not up to the job. Our suspicions were partly confirmed when Mike and I were called out to Hangman Valley by some local residents who complained that they smelled something decomposing in their backyard.

Mike and I met with the residents, then performed a

foot search along the creek behind their house, which was almost within eyesight of the sewage treatment plant where Shawn Johnson had been found. We didn't see anything, but that didn't mean there wasn't something there to find.

After searching the creek, we asked the residents whether anyone had spoken to them. They hadn't been contacted by the police, not after Darla Sue Scott or Shawn Johnson. So Mike and I drove around the rest of the neighborhood, knocking on doors and speaking to every resident who was home. None of them had been contacted by the police in any manner.

I couldn't believe it. Two bodies had been found in the area, and the police had never canvassed the neighborhood. That is one of the first things you do in a homicide investigation. It's basic police work, the kind of stuff they drill into you at the academy. Patrol officers arrive at the crime scene. They secure the scene, establish the perimeter, detain any suspects or possible suspects for detectives, and collect witnesses. They document all vehicles in the neighborhood, noting down license plate numbers and descriptions. Then they go out and canvass the area, knocking on every door and asking every inhabitant if they saw or heard anything. They find out if anyone else might have been home when the homicide occurred and make arrangements to interview them. Once the detectives arrive, patrol gives them all the field interview cards from the interviews and a list of documented vehicles. They tell the detectives anything that these people said or if they were or were not home. Then the detectives go back and talk to the most interesting witnesses first and then the ones who weren't home or didn't want to talk to the patrol officers.

All this should have happened the first day, while the detectives and criminologists were still processing the crime scene. I didn't understand why they hadn't.

Mike and I went back to the station, our feet sopping wet from tramping along the creek bed, and announced that once again the task force had failed to follow one of the most basic procedures of homicide investigation.

We figured there were more bodies, if not in Hangman Valley, then somewhere. With the discovery of Maybin's body, there were no more missing women—at least none the police would officially report or publicly discuss.

With the discovery of Darla Sue Scott's body on November 5, 1997, the Spokane PD and the sheriff's department began reporting missing women who fit the victim profile. Shawn Johnson, Laurie Wason, and Lonna Marie Hughes were the first reported missing. Linda Maybin and Lois Jean Spicer were also reported missing. Both Hughes and Spicer eventually turned up alive.

In late January 1998, the task force reported that in addition to Oster and Maybin, Margaret Marion Streeter and Jessica Fitzgerald were also missing. Detective John Grandinetti of the Spokane PD was assigned to missing persons, and people with information about these missing women were urged to call Grandinetti directly.

In order to make certain that the women calling in were who they said they were, Grandinetti had information that only the missing women would know. When they called in, Grandinetti would ask them questions to corroborate their identity.

"We're really concerned about their safety," Doug Silver said, stating that some of the missing women might be reluctant to come forward because of outstanding warrants. "That's not what we're after. We just want to verify that they're not missing."

Of course, these women were missing. That's why the police were looking for them. What I think Silver meant to say was that they wanted to verify that these women weren't dead, but he did have a point. Why would a drug-addicted prostitute want to report to the police even if she didn't have outstanding warrants? There was no incentive. These women spent much of their time avoiding police. This was particularly true in Spokane, where the police had no rapport and very little contact with the prostitute community.

A standard vice unit arresting prostitutes and johns could have developed useful intelligence, and possibly saved lives. A retired Seattle vice cop, who now lived in Spokane, called up and told Mike and me that he would drive down East Sprague during the past two years and see the same prostitutes on the same street corners every day. This indicated to him that the Spokane PD wasn't working prostitutes.

"I guarantee you that had proper enforcement been done, most of those prostitutes would be alive today," he said. "It would have taken me maybe one night, two different cars, three changes of clothes, and I would have those girls in jail. Or they'd move out of town."

Much later in the investigation, the task force developed better rapport with these women. By then, of course, it was too late. As soon as the bodies of Jennifer Joseph and Heather Hernandez showed up, the cops should have planted themselves on Sprague. This was one of the few connections they had to work on. Each of the victims, except Melinda Mercer, was associated with the prostitution and drug trade in that neighborhood. That's where the killer was finding his victims. The task force should have been out on the street, interviewing the women, arresting johns, telling people to write down license plates and vehicle descriptions.

The women on Sprague had seen the serial killer. They knew him, even if they didn't know who he was. Here was a resource for information that the task force was basically ignoring.

Not only did the task force ignore the women as possible witnesses, they soon began ignoring them as potential victims. In the same manner that they clamped down on any information concerning the homicides themselves, the task force released very little information concerning missing women. Tina Marie Gray and Aubrey Lynn Shults were both reported missing and both found alive. The task force then said that all the missing women were accounted for except one—Melody Murfin.

Melody Ann Murfin was a forty-three-year-old prostitute and drug addict. She was four feet ten inches tall, 120 pounds, with reddish brown hair and hazel or green eyes. She had dentures. Murfin had been on the task force's missing list before, but detectives located and interviewed her in March 1998. She had no recorded prostitution or drug arrests, but was known to be a prostitute and drug addict.

Murfin had been charged with theft in the spring of 1997 and was scheduled to appear in Spokane County Court on June 15, 1998, but she did not show up.

Murfin might have been staying at a motel on Aurora Avenue North in Seattle. An informant I will call James Smith told Mike and me that he picked up a woman named Melody at the motel sometime in the first week of May 1998. Smith said that he had dated Melody for sex, because his wife was dying of cancer and he needed some company. On May 13, he returned to the motel and was told by the proprietor that Melody had been picked up on May 11 by King County police detectives.

On June 10, 1998, the *Seattle Post-Intelligencer* published an article about Murfin's disappearance. After reading the article and recognizing the photo of Melody, Smith went back to the motel and tried to get some information from the proprietor, who told him, "Go away, you're upsetting my wife."

Murfin was last reported seen alive on May 20, 1998. On June 6, Lynn Everson reported her missing. Three days later, the body of a woman was found on Mount Spokane, near where Sherry Palmer and Shannon Zielinski's bodies had been discovered. The task force responded to the scene, as it was now stated policy to call them out to any crime scene where a body had been dumped. On June 12, Doug Silver confirmed that the body was female. She was described as having light hair and being short in height.

"Part of the problem," Silver said, "is the body is so badly decomposed that they're unable to do what they would normally do to a body as far as getting measurements and being able to look at the vital organs, this type of thing."

A witness was reported to have seen a suspicious vehicle driving in the area near where the body was discovered. The task force did not release a description of the vehicle so that other witnesses might be able to come forward with additional information. Though Silver urged the public to call in any clues regarding this vehicle, or any other suspicious persons or activity in the area, he would not give them any information, despite the fact that they had at least a vehicle description.

A month later, the Spokane PD reported that this homicide had been turned over to the sheriff's department, indicating that the body was somehow proven not to be connected to the serial killer. Neither the Spokane PD nor the sheriff's department actually stated why they did not connect this body, nor did they tell the public whether the investigation was successfully concluded or remained open. One thing they did say was that this was not the body of Melody Murfin.

At approximately 9:00 A.M. on June 15, a maintenance worker in Riverside Park was looking for a lost picnic table when he discovered a decomposed body submerged in the

Spokane River near the Carousel. The body was found trapped beneath a floating catwalk just west of the Howard Street Bridge. This was not far from the Post Street Dam, where Teresa-Lyn Asmussen had been found.

Once again, investigators would not say whether the body was male or female.

"We don't know who it is or how long it's been there," Lieutenant Jim Culp of the Spokane PD said. "There's not much left to it, just a little flesh here and there."

Despite the previously stated policy that the task force would respond to any crime scene where a body had been dumped, no representatives came to this crime scene, and Culp said that the task force would probably not get involved in this case until more was known about the victim.

Once again, police announced that this body was not Melody Murfin. No further information was made public about the identification or classification of these remains.

I figured that just because the task force was not announcing missing women didn't mean there weren't more of them. Even if they weren't victims of the serial killer, there would still be women disappearing, dropping out of sight, leaving town without notice, any number of possibilities. Especially women who fit the victim profile.

So I asked the task force for all missing person reports for women between the ages of eighteen and forty. Dave Reagan, task force public information officer, told me that I could not have those reports because the release of such information would hurt the investigation.

Missing person reports are public documents, along the lines of civilian complaints. What reason do the police have to keep that information secret? If they don't make missing person reports public, how are these people supposed to be found?

In the beginning of this case, the task force went public with the names of eight missing women because they thought it would help them find these women. Then the women started turning up dead. Maybe the task force made the same time line connections that I had—just about every body dump occurred after one of their statements about missing women in the press. Now maybe if the task force just stopped mentioning missing women, the serial killer would stop dumping them.

I learned that there were some eighteen to twenty missing women who fit the victim profile. These women were being considered by the task force as possible victims, according to someone who actually processed the missing person reports.

In a meeting with Mark Sterk, who replaced John Goldman as Spokane County sheriff, I was able to confirm that there were more missing women. In Sterk's own words, "There are a *lot* more missing women." The emphasis is Sterk's.

Though he would not specify whether those missing women were from the Spokane area or elsewhere in the state, that comment indicated to me that the serial killer had probably killed several additional victims, and that missing women were simply no longer being reported.

How could Spokane not have any more missing prostitutes? Even if they were not reported missing, how could they be certain that there weren't women disappearing from East Sprague? Spokane is a city to which prostitutes often travel in the warmer months, coming from western Washington, Oregon, Nevada, and California. Heather Hernandez came all the way from Phoenix. If her body hadn't been discovered, how would anybody even know she had been in Spokane?

During the fall and winter, the women out on East Sprague are mostly locals. And the victims from late 1997 and early 1998 reflect that. Scott, Johnson, Wason, McClenahan, Oster, and Maybin had all been in Spokane for years. We can assume that the transient prostitutes might have kept away from Spokane after it was known that a serial killer was killing women there. As Mike said, "It's become a little too risky to play this particular stadium."

We can't assume that no prostitutes arrived from out of town. Before the Joseph and Hernandez bodies were found, there was no need to keep track of who went missing from East Sprague. It was entirely possible that the suspect killed several more transient prostitutes during the summer of 1997, but for some reason their bodies never turned up. We can't be sure whether he wasn't targeting girls from out of town, picking them up on East Sprague, talking with them to determine where they were from, how long they had been around, and whether they would even be missed.

Lynn Everson handed out cards to the women on East Sprague. The cards read, "Do you want to let us know . . . That you are OK . . . About a bad trick . . . That someone is missing," and gave a local phone number for the women to call. Lynn was working hard to keep track of these women. Unless someone called that number, or made some other form of contact with Lynn, either through her needle exchange program or women's shelter, how would she know who was on the street and who wasn't?

Since the police were downplaying the possibility of a serial killer in the fall of 1997, those women didn't know they were at risk. It wasn't until after the discovery of Darla Sue Scott that the police started publicly asking about missing women. Once they stopped releasing those names, the local prostitutes could have been lulled into a false sense of security. Transient prostitutes working the circuit might have heard that Spokane was safe again.

I still couldn't understand why the task force kept mentioning Melody Murfin. After Scott, the only victim who had not been reported missing was Melinda Mercer in Tacoma. And she had been found shortly after she was killed. We already knew that all the other victims were meant to be found. The killer could have been dumping bodies that the task force was specifically mentioning. Was that why they kept mentioning Melody Murfin?

In a November 7, 1999, article in the *Portland Oregonian,* Cal Walker refused to confirm or deny the existence of additional victims, which to Mike and me meant there were more missing women. If they didn't have other missing women, Cal Walker would have simply said so.

Doug Silver as much as admitted that there were more missing women.

"With the nature of prostitution and such," Silver said after one body find, "we don't hear about all the missing women. Unfortunately, we don't know how many others are missing. . . . How many don't we know about?"

At the April 28, 1998, press conference announcing the discovery of the two T-shirts at Fourteenth and Carnahan, Silver stated, "We have located over forty people at this time that have been missing or reported as missing persons."

If they located forty, why did we only hear about a fraction of them? And how many were reported missing whom they did not find? That question the task force wasn't answering. As long as these women were not identified in the press, then the task force didn't have to acknowledge them as possible victims.

Why would a task force, unwilling to connect murders on bodies that they did find, want to link one in which the body had yet to turn up? This made the Murfin case seem even more bizarre.

On July 17 the task force "redoubled their efforts" to find Melody Murfin. After that, they simply began referring to her as a victim of the serial killer, missing and presumed dead.

In order to presume somebody dead, you need evidence. If the task force received any indication that Melody Murfin had been abducted or killed by the suspect, they didn't share it with the public. If they found her body and were surveilling the grave site, waiting for the suspect to return, then this was one of the longest stakeouts in the history of law enforcement—and there would be very little of her left to revisit.

Think of the unnecessary pain and trauma inflicted upon Murfin's family. It would be more than just embarrassing if the task force stated that Murfin was a serial killer victim, and then she turned up alive. They were also putting themselves at severe liability risk.

Any number of things could have happened to Melody Murfin. The killer could have dumped her body in order for it to be found and somehow the discovery was prevented. Weather and/or predators could have destroyed, removed, or concealed the body. Maybe the suspect dumped her in an area where he expected she would be found, but people for some reason stopped walking their dogs there. Maybe the people of Spokane had grown so accustomed to finding dead bodies that they no longer even noticed them.

We don't even know that Murfin was taken in Spokane. She could have gone back to Tacoma and was either abducted or met with some kind of foul play there. She could have been killed and dumped anywhere between Spokane and Seattle. Or maybe the serial killer didn't want her body to be found.

CHAPTER 16

Michelyn Derning

Michelyn Derning, age 47. Body found July 7, 1998, concealed under a hot tub cover and other debris in an overgrown field in the 200 block of North Crestline in east Spokane. Cause of death: gunshot wound to head. Plastic bag on head. Derning was killed and her body was dumped only days before it was found.

As spring turned to summer, Melody Murfin was still missing, and no more bodies were found. Everybody figured that the killer had gone away.

Every Thursday our routine was the same. First do any fieldwork, mostly visiting or revisiting crime scenes, and interviewing possible witnesses. Then lunch at the Viking, where we alternated picking up the tab, and then back to the radio station, where we would sit in the conference room and try to unravel the mysteries of a serial killer and the police chasing him.

On July 7 a transient walking through a vacant lot in the 200 block of North Crestline about 6:30 P.M. discovered a body. The body, naked except for a plastic bag over her head, was partially hidden under a pile of debris, including a hot tub cover, and dumped near a tree to the north of a building housing a firm called Systems Technology. The transient had apparently been camping near the body for three days before he noticed the smell.

Police arrived and secured the crime scene, closing off traffic on Main and Crestline for several blocks. When detectives arrived, they decided to wait until the next morning to process the crime scene.

That made six crime scenes we knew of at which the detectives had left the body overnight. As irresponsible as it had been in the other crime scenes, this was even worse. The victim had not been there for a long time. Days, perhaps even hours. There was a very good chance that evidence of rigor mortis was still in her body. The medical examiner might have been able to establish a more accurate time of death. There was a very good chance of fresh evidence, and possibly pursuing some early leads, but the detectives wanted a good night's sleep, so they went home.

There's no excuse and no good reason to leave a homicide victim at the crime scene, whether guarded or not, while the detectives go home and wait until morning. I don't know how those detectives slept at night, knowing there was a fresh body, and other evidence, just sitting there.

A press release issued the night the body was found had the familiar refrain: "The age, gender and condition of the body were not known."

The next day, Spokane police still hadn't figured out whether they had another serial killing on their hands. Detectives from both the Spokane PD and the task force returned to Crestline to process the crime scene. The city police and task force detectives conducted what they called "parallel investigations" until it was determined that this body was a victim of the serial killer.

The body was identified as Michelyn Derning, a forty-seven-year-old prostitute and drug addict. The autopsy, conducted on July 10, 1998, by Dr. George Lindholm, determined that Derning died from a gunshot wound to the head. Her body was cremated later that day at a local funeral home.

Derning had been in Spokane for about a year, moving there from San Diego. She was born on February 18, 1951, in Jacksonville, North Carolina. Her parents, Edmund and Joann Derning, lived in Oceanside, California. Edmund Derning was a Marine Corps colonel. Michelyn was born in Virginia, graduated from high school in Virginia Beach, and briefly attended Palomar College in San Marcos, California. She worked as an executive secretary in a San Diego engineering firm.

She started taking drugs as a teenager. Amphetamines were her drug of choice. She was married in 1985 to a man who worked for the Federal Aviation Administration. They divorced in July 1992. Two years later, Derning filed a domestic violence complaint against another man. From her first marriage, Derning had a son, who lives with his grandparents.

Michelyn Derning had no arrest record, but was known to be involved in drugs and prostitution. In March 1998, her boyfriend obtained a restraining order against her after he claimed she severely damaged his car.

Derning moved to Spokane in April 1997, with no personal belongings and no identification. Gregory Landis, her longtime friend, helped her get an apartment and a telephone. She applied for welfare and food stamps. She worked as a ranch hand, an in-home nursing assistant, and other odd jobs in Spokane. She rode her bike everywhere.

Derning was last seen alive on July 3, 1998. She was supposed to go to Priest Lake with Gregory Landis. When she didn't show up for the trip, Landis said that he wasn't surprised, since Derning was a "free spirit." When her body was found, Derning had not been officially reported missing.

The discovery of Derning's body was met with surprise and disappointment. The serial killer had not gone away.

When her body was found, Doug Silver told the *Spokesman-Review* that perhaps the serial killer had not stopped killing between Maybin and Derning, that maybe other bodies just hadn't turned up yet. Why else would Silver speculate that there were other bodies, unless he knew of other missing women, either in Spokane or elsewhere in Washington? Silver often said things that weren't especially well thought out, but his ideas had to come from somewhere. If there were more missing women, why wasn't Silver, as spokesperson for the task force, telling us about them?

Once it was officially determined that Derning was a serial killer victim (probably through ballistics and preliminary DNA), the police went into action, showing an energy and willingness to share information that had been regrettably absent through the prior investigations.

During the forty-eight hours following Derning's autopsy, Spokane PD detectives assisted the task force in canvassing the neighborhood. A flyer was printed up with Derning's mug shot and a series of questions directed at possible witnesses: "Have you seen this person? When and where did you see her last? Who did you see her with last? Was there a person or vehicle that you can describe? What was she wearing when seen last?"

Roger Bragdon, now acting Spokane PD police chief, held a press conference at which he made public more information about the Derning homicide than had ever been previously disclosed.

Since Derning's body was found so close to the apparent time of her death, police had fresher evidence and a good chance that a witness might come forward.

"This time, we have a better chance of someone being able to come forward and possibly provide us some information that might send us in the right direction," Bragdon said. "It might just be the break, it might just be the luck we've been looking for."

Perhaps after the April Fools' fiasco, the task force had been humbled. Maybe they were learning on the job. Maybe they finally listened to the FBI, or other agencies that were pressuring them to loosen their grip on information. It didn't matter why. What mattered was that for the first time in nearly a year's investigation, the task force was being aggressive and relatively open. For the first time, the task force had a victim who had been missing only a couple days. But they had already waited, first overnight to process the body, and then until after the autopsy to make sure that she was linked to the other killings. At least they were doing something now. After nearly a year of stealth investigating, the police were finally out on the streets, trying to find clues.

Since Derning had been dead only a couple days, her body was relatively fresh and intact. An autopsy would be able to answer many questions about her death and anything that happened to her body either before or after. They would be able to get a good toxicology report to determine whether she was under the influence of drugs. Any potential witnesses would have fresh memories, since she had been last seen on July 3, probably the day she was killed, only four days earlier.

"Number one, we rely on the general public in cases like this," Bragdon said at the press conference. "Somebody saw something."

That was probably true in the Derning case as well as the previous homicides. If the police had mobilized in this manner following any of the other body finds, who knows what the task force could have discovered. Unfortunately, it was too little, too late.

The frenzy of investigation, police mobilization, and publicly disclosed information that took place on July 9 and 10 should have been going on since August 26, 1997.

Jim McLaren, a news reporter for KXLY who was at the press conference, briefed us on everything that Bragdon had said and gave us updates on the police investigation.

We interrupted our show to do an extended newsbreak on the Derning homicide and related police activity.

FUHRMAN: Well, the first thing this homicide tells us is that the killer is back, or else he never left. The hopes that he had left—well, that's over. He is definitely with us, and he isn't going anywhere.

FITZSIMMONS: I found the suggestion that he might have left the area to be quite premature, frankly. Just because a couple months had gone by with no new bodies being found. That was wishful thinking, not a statement of fact. The city and apparently the police had been hoping that the killer had left town and they would not have to continue this serial murder investigation that appears to be going nowhere.

FUHRMAN: Now let's hope that the task force gets the resources and the support they need to see this investigation to its completion. This is victim number eight— even though Mike and I think he's killed twelve or more women. In the Green River case, at victim eight they had thirty-five people working on the task force. This is the time to put egos aside and ask for some help. We need a statewide task force. We've already connected homicides in the Seattle-Tacoma area. They have some outstanding homicide investigators over there who could really help out this task force. I don't see why we're not getting people loaned to the Spokane Task Force from other agencies. We already know he's killing women on the other side of the mountain. The Washington State Patrol is another great tool. This guy is getting from point A to point B someway, and he's probably taking state highways and freeways.

FITZSIMMONS: Let's also recall that in the Green River case, by the time they found the first few bodies, he had already killed forty-nine women. That doesn't necessarily mean that that's the case here. But we could have a lot more victims that we simply haven't found yet.

FUHRMAN: We could be at the tip of the iceberg only acknowledging eight cases here. And I'm sure investigators in the Seattle-Tacoma area and throughout the state are reinvestigating all their unsolved homicides, to see if any of them connect up with this suspect.

FITZSIMMONS: Well, one thing, this story is going to go national. What kind of pressure does a national story put on local authorities?

FUHRMAN: They don't have to pay attention to it, so long as they're doing what's necessary. This could be another Ted Bundy. This is a major serial killer who's working in Spokane. And the people who are saying, "I hope he goes away," they should think about what will happen when the national press comes here. Spokane law enforcement is going to be subjected to scrutiny like they've never felt it before. It's time to start forgetting about traffic and burglaries and put twenty-five people on this case.

FITZSIMMONS: The task force says it hopes it gets lucky.

FUHRMAN: Luck has nothing to do with it. Homicides are solved because you work hard enough to ask the right person the right question. People don't run into the police station and confess to something like this. And if the task force is waiting for somebody to get pulled over with a body in the trunk, I don't think this is going to happen. This guy has probably killed two dozen women, and we don't have an eyewitness to anything.

This is going to come down to a lot of tedious, hard work, and finding common denominators with the victims and getting out on the street.

FITZSIMMONS: There is no excuse not to step this up into a full-scale investigation. I don't know why they're sitting on this. It's time for the county commissioners, it's time for the city council and the mayor, it's time for the people who control the purse strings to provide the dollars to fund a sizable enough task force to pull in the net around this guy. They can no longer ignore this situation as just prostitutes getting killed and there's no reason for us to get upset about it.

The task force mobilization ended after forty-eight hours, without apparently finding a clue or witness that brought them any closer to the killer. The story didn't go national. No more bodies showed up. Spokane went back to business as usual.

There was still a good deal to investigate. Derning was an interesting case. In some ways, she fit the victimology and MO, but in some ways she didn't.

Derning was a drug addict and prostitute. Although the Spokane PD issued a press release telling news organizations not to refer to Derning as a prostitute, several neighbors reported that she did, in fact, trade sexual favors for cash. She also had one of the more stable lives of any of the victims. She lived in an apartment that had been secured for her by her longtime friend Gregory Landis. She had gone through a drug treatment program and was working on a ranch. She attended church, at least on occasions. Does that mean that Derning had put the street behind her? Maybe, maybe not. But here we had a victim who had a life outside of East Sprague.

Studying victimology, you look for similarities, or for striking differences, among the victims. Where did Derning's life intersect with the other victims'? In this case, the connections with East Sprague were fewer and easier to investigate.

Her friend Gregory Landis was investigated and eliminated as a suspect. I spoke to him months after Derning's death at his new home in Tucson, Arizona. Landis told me that the task force detectives had given him a polygraph examination, during which they asked him if he had killed Derning, if he had ever hit her, and if he owned a small-caliber firearm.

He also said that Derning didn't know any of the other victims. I asked him how he knew that, and he said that he had asked her. Whether Derning had told him the truth or not, she had certainly traveled in those circles, but she had been on the periphery of the East Sprague life. It was entirely possible that she was telling Landis the truth. She certainly was aware that a serial killer was murdering prostitutes, but for some reason she went away with the suspect.

On June 15, 1999, Landis got a call from one of the detectives in the task force. They wanted a blood sample from him. Landis allowed the Tucson PD to take a blood sample, and they sent it up to Spokane.

In a newspaper article published on July 10, 1998, Landis spoke openly and in depth about his relationship with Derning. Later I interviewed him, and he was very candid. He was the first known suspect I had spoken to, and his description of how the task force handled him told me a lot about the kind of investigation they were conducting.

The blood test confirmed what I had already suspected—they had DNA from the suspect. Since they took a blood sample from Landis, I would assume they had foreign DNA on Derning, but I also thought they had foreign DNA on at least the other seven that they were officially connecting up (Scott, Johnson, Wason, McClenahan, Oster, Mercer, and Maybin). For the task force to connect these victims, but not the others, despite the similarities in victimology and MO, made me think that the connective evidence had to be the suspect's DNA.

That the task force asked Landis if he had hit Derning indicated to me that there was some kind of hematoma, probably on her face or somewhere on her body, which was inflicted shortly before her death. If this was the case, then Derning was beginning to look a lot like the Brisbois case—a struggle followed by homicide, the body discovered in a relatively short period of time after being dumped.

In addition to the DNA and ballistic evidence, there were some very general similarities between Derning and the other cases. She was a prostitute and drug addict. She was shot in the head, and a plastic bag was wrapped around her head. She was killed in one location and her body dumped elsewhere.

What was more interesting to me were the differences between that lot on the 200 block of North Crestline and the other dump sites of victims we absolutely knew were connected.

Derning was an uncharacteristic kill. She was dumped almost immediately after she was killed. She was hidden by debris, leaves, and a hot tub cover, but she wasn't buried. More important, the dumping of her body seemed to indicate that the suspect wanted to delay her being found. In all the other connected cases, except for the possible exception of Darla Sue Scott, it was clear that the killer wanted the bodies to be found. There was also the possibility that he was making a public statement with this body dump. After the task force and the city of Spokane seemed to think that he had left town, Derning's body emphatically stated that he hadn't gone anywhere. That he was still in business.

The more I thought about it, the more the Derning case

didn't fit. It was the same suspect, of course, but something was different. He didn't show the same control or premeditation that he had exhibited in his previous murders. For some reason he didn't cherish Derning, and even though all her clothes and personal effects were taken from her, I would be surprised if he had kept them as souvenirs.

Then why did he kill her? I wondered if she could be a witness or have had some personal connection to either the killer or his victims. Perhaps he killed her not because he wanted to, but because he had to. She could have seen him with one of his other victims. She could have been his way of procuring these women, or getting the drugs that he might have used to bring them along and keep them happy once he had them.

Or maybe the Derning homicide was an accident, or at least unplanned.

He hasn't killed in a long, long time. The feeling is building up inside him. He has to do something. It's the Fourth of July weekend, everybody's headed out of town. Sprague is nearly empty. When he sees her, he knows that she's desperate. Maybe she's back on the needle, or whatever she does. She's not really his type. But beggars can't be choosers.

Once he's killed her, he doesn't take her out into the woods. There will be no cherishing this one. She was just a victim of convenience. An easy, and necessary, kill. He dumps her body in the alley, covers her with garbage, and drives away.

I began to wonder whether this killer was as intelligent and in control as we had initially thought. Whatever the motive, Derning's homicide did not appear planned or controlled. Maybe the beast just took over.

Derning made me reexamine the other killings, particularly the ones that were not officially connected: Sapp, Lowe, Brisbois, Palmer, Zielinski, Flores, Joseph, and Hernandez. If those early homicides were the work of the same suspect, and I believed that they were, then he could have been developing his MO. By Scott and Johnson, we began to see a more consistent MO, with the plastic bags on the head, and the bodies dumped in a rural location where they could still be easily found. Derning was a throwback to the earlier homicides. Was the suspect regressing in his MO? Was he losing control of his homicidal urges? Or was he just not quite as clever as I thought?

In my mind, I had built this suspect up as one of the craftiest, most cunning, most calculated serial killers since Ted Bundy. He obviously demonstrated great control, most of the time. There were also events, like Brisbois and now Derning, which indicated that sometimes he nearly lost it.

As evil and as smart as the killer no doubt was, one thing we tended to forget was that he was human. A serial killer might be the hardest class of criminal to catch, but he's still a criminal. And even the best have their bad days. Of course this suspect was going to make mistakes. In our desire to make him superhuman, we overestimated his abnormality and underestimated how ordinary he might in fact be.

I figured we had to start thinking about him as we would any other suspect, still giving him the respect that his intelligence and pathology deserved, but also realizing that he was not Hannibal Lecter. This wasn't Hollywood, after all. This was Spokane.

CHAPTER 17

Patricia Barnes and Connie LaFontaine Ellis

Patricia Barnes, age 61. Body found August 25, 1995, in 15900 block of Peacock Hill Road in rural area of Kitsap County, Washington. Cause of death: gunshot wounds to head and chest. Linked to Spokane Serial Killer on September 24, 1998.

Connie LaFontaine Ellis, age 35. Body found October 13, 1998, in ditch along 108th Street in Parkland, near Tacoma. Cause of death: gunshot wound to head. Body in advanced state of decomposition. Plastic bag on head. Officially linked to Spokane Serial Killer on January 8, 1999.

After a brief flurry of activity following the discovery of Michelyn Derning's body, it appeared that the task force was back to business as usual. If one more dead body wasn't going to stir things up, then perhaps changes in the highest ranks of police administration would. And that was just about to happen.

Both local law enforcement agencies would get new chiefs before the end of 1998. The Spokane County Sheriff's Department was gearing up for an election. And Spokane police chief Terry Mangan had stepped down after eleven years on the job. Roger Bragdon was appointed acting chief, but city leaders said they wanted the new Spokane PD chief to be someone from outside the department.

In August 1998, following an eight-month, nationwide search that examined twenty-six candidates, Alan Chertok was selected to be the new chief of the Spokane Police Department. Chertok, an East Coast cop with a great deal of experience and a military background, appeared to be well qualified for the job. He was young, energetic, an experienced administrator, and seemed to have the necessary political skills. A lieutenant commander in the Navy Reserve, Chertok came from the Newport News, Virginia, police department, after serving for many years in Prince Georges County, Maryland.

During one of our early conversations, Chertok told me, "Police work is pretty simple. Initially, you treat everybody with the respect you would give your mother. And then you take the bad guy to jail and do whatever he dictates you do. That's police work—go out there and get bad guys."

Chertok was very aware of the need for changes in the Spokane PD. He knew that the force had to be modernized and reorganized. A lot had changed in law enforcement, and it was time for Spokane to catch up. He was also aware of the delicate political situation that he had just stepped into. The city of Spokane, and particularly its police department, was resistant to change. Chertok spent the first few months in office meeting with his officers and community leaders.

At first, Chertok was welcomed enthusiastically by City Manager Bill Pupo, the city council, and leaders in the minority communities. Coming from departments back East with sizable minority populations, Chertok was seen as a chief who could take the theories of community policing and make them effective in practical application.

Despite Chertok's reception in the civilian community, there was discontent among the city cops almost from the beginning. Apparently, many felt that their new chief should have been picked from their own ranks. The favorite within the department had been Deputy Chief Roger Bragdon, who now served under Chertok as assistant chief.

In just a matter of days, Chertok ran into trouble. A state Department of Licensing clerk complained to City Hall that Chertok had treated her rudely while applying for a driver's license. Then, in January 1999, Chertok got into an argument with a patrol officer when the officer refused to jump-start a police vehicle. After a six-week investigation into the matter, City Manager Bill Pupo issued Chertok what he called a verbal reprimand.

I talked to Chertok about the jumper cable incident. A police vehicle had a dead battery, so Chertok told a patrol officer to jump-start it. The officer responded that he didn't have any jumper cables. Chertok demanded to know why a patrol officer wouldn't have jumper cables in his car. Instead of following orders, the patrol officer beefed his own chief. The fact that the Spokane Police Guild (the employees' union of the Spokane PD) backed the patrol officer only demonstrated how, despite whatever support Chertok might have had in the community or among the politicians who had selected him, there was still a great deal of resentment against him in the department he was now, at least officially, in charge of.

Chertok was taking the reins of a very insular, Old Boy police department. An example of just how insular the Spokane PD could be was the story of how my friend Tony Bamonte solved the oldest open murder case in America.

During the day, Tony served as county sheriff in Pend Oreille, a rural county northeast of Spokane. At night,

Tony went to Gonzaga University in Spokane, studying toward a master's degree in organizational leadership. For his thesis, Tony wrote a history of law enforcement in Pend Oreille County. During his research, he came across the 1935 murder of Newport, Washington, sheriff George Conniff, who was shot during the robbery of a local creamery. The case was in Tony's jurisdiction, so he reopened it. His investigation led to a retired Spokane PD detective as the suspect.

In the 1930s, Spokane PD headquarters was known as the Stone Fortress. Many of the cops were involved in rackets, bootlegging, robbery, and the thriving black market in rationed food, particularly dairy products. Using good old-fashioned detective work, Tony proved that Clyde Ralstin, a notoriously violent and corrupt Spokane detective, shot Conniff during a robbery he committed along with his criminal associate Acie Logan.

Ralstin's fellow cops helped cover up the murder. Patrol Officers Dan Mangan (no relation to former Spokane PD chief Terry Mangan) and Bill Parsons (who became Spokane PD chief) helped dispose of the murder weapon in the Spokane River. Fifty-four years later, Tony went down into the river and recovered the murder weapon. Clyde Ralstin died shortly afterward, and Tony closed the case.

Even two generations later, Spokane cops were still defending Clyde Ralstin. During his investigation, Tony kept getting stonewalled by cops who knew what Ralstin had done, but didn't want Tony getting to the bottom of it. George Conniff was a cop. Another cop murdered him. And the rest of the department helped the killer get away with it—in 1935 and in 1989.

The Spokane PD is still insular and doesn't take to outsiders. That's one reason why they didn't like Alan Chertok.

Chertok was trying to reorganize a department that needed to change. The rank and file, or at least the guild leadership, was against him. His political foundation outside the department was shaky. And there was a serial killer working in the city.

Soon after Chertok came aboard, two additional bodies found in western Washington were linked to the Spokane Serial Killer.

The first of these cases occurred three years prior, when the body of Patricia Barnes was discovered in a rural area in Kitsap County, Washington, on August 25, 1995. Barnes was sixty-one years old. She had no arrests and no convictions, was known to be an alcoholic, but not a drug addict. Her autopsy revealed that she had been drinking earlier in the day, perhaps at a Seattle bar. The cause of death was gunshot wounds to the head and chest.

Barnes's naked body was found wrapped in a sleeping bag. She had been dumped in a ditch near some woods in a rural area just north of the Pierce County line. Barnes had suffered massive head trauma.

Barnes was a homeless woman who was frequently seen in the Pioneer Square area of downtown Seattle. She was known as the "towel lady" because she often wore a towel or bandanna around her head, reportedly to hide scars from a fire.

She was last reported seen in the company of a white male, thirty-five years of age, with reddish blond, wavy hair, blue eyes, and a muscular medium build, between the hours of 3:00 P.M. and 4:00 P.M. on August 22, 1995, in downtown Seattle. A composite of the man was drawn on August 27, and distributed to the media in the Seattle-Tacoma area, but apparently produced no solid leads.

On September 24, 1998, Doug Silver held a press conference announcing that task force detectives had been investigating the Barnes homicide because she had a "similar lifestyle" to the other victims. Silver also stated that Barnes was killed "in a similar way."

Silver said that the task force detectives believed that the man she was last seen with might have been connected to the murders of the women officially linked to the Spokane Serial Killer. "We cannot say if this case is definitely related to the serial killings," Silver said. "But it's close enough."

The task force released the 1995 composite of the Barnes suspect. More than a year after the Joseph and Hernandez homicides, the citizens of Spokane saw their first real clue (prior to that time there had been no suspect descriptions, no vehicle descriptions, nothing). It had been generated by an outside law enforcement agency.

The task force had apparently been working on the Barnes case for some time before making this announcement. The task force had been informed about the homicide and briefed on its particulars. Then a Spokane detective traveled to Bremerton, Washington, to discuss it with local officials. Soon after that, Silver held the press conference.

At his press conference, Silver released the 1995 composite in hopes that the sketch would generate new information regarding the Spokane homicides.

The Spokane press treated the suspect composite as the first step toward solving the case, and Silver did not dispute that. "This is the closest we have to an individual that we can focus on," Silver said. "I consider this a very good lead."

Looking at the composite, I figured that the task force was going on more than just the witness description from back in 1995. They must have had other corroborative evidence. The suspect was reported as having reddish blond hair. So they must have retrieved foreign hair matching that description from at least one of the Spokane victims. But they didn't.

The second western Washington case took less time to be linked to the Spokane suspect. The task force had been initially called in on a homicide of a twenty-one-year-old woman who was found on August 21, 1998. She had been shot in the head and dumped near an area of Tacoma known for its prostitution and drug activities. This homicide apparently was not the work of the Spokane killer, or else they did not find any evidence to link it with the other cases.

Then in October, the task force was called to the Tacoma area again. Task force detectives went out to Parkland, Washington, to review the homicide of a then-unidentified female, whose body had been found in a wooded area southeast of Tacoma on October 13. She had been shot in the head with a .25-caliber weapon, and there was a plastic bag wrapped around her head. A .380 bullet was recovered at the scene. The body was so badly decomposed that it took medical examiners two weeks to identify her as Connie LaFontaine Ellis, a thirty-five-year-old native of North Dakota.

Connie LaFontaine Ellis was born on August 21, 1963, in Belcourt, North Dakota. Ellis left her family and daughter on North Dakota's Turtle Mountain Indian Reservation in 1983. Her father, Emil LaFontaine, was a Chippewa Indian. Her brother and sister lived on the Spokane Indian Reservation. In 1993, Connie moved from Spokane to Tacoma, and married Rick Ellis. After they got divorced, she traveled between Spokane and Tacoma. She returned only once to North Dakota, when her mother died.

Ellis was a heroin addict who supported her habit through prostitution. A mother of three, her two sons had both died, one from a heart condition, the other from sudden infant death syndrome. Her daughter was grown, and a mother herself.

Ellis had been convicted of second-degree burglary in

Pierce County in 1992. She served an eight-month jail sentence. She was also convicted of trafficking in stolen property in Kitsap County in 1994. She was sentenced to thirteen months in prison.

She worked as a prostitute in Spokane and Tacoma to support her heroin habit. She was last reported seen in Spokane in May 1997, a month after she had been convicted of a misdemeanor theft charge. She was known to carry a .380 automatic in her purse.

In the early days of the Ellis investigation, there were signs of inter-departmental squabbling. Doug Silver complained that the Pierce County investigators were tough to reach.

"Their investigators are very busy," Silver said. "The lead investigator on the case has a lot of other things going on. It has been hard for us to get in touch with them."

"We're not going to join the task force," Deputy Ed Troyer, spokesman for the Pierce County Sheriff's Department, shot back. "We'll work with Spokane. We're sharing everything we have with Spokane. But they have all the information at this point."

Ellis's homicide was officially linked to the other Spokane cases on January 8, 1999. The Spokane Sheriff's Department said that the delay was the result of their being "thorough."

"It's nice that they did that officially, but it's not news to us," Ed Troyer said. "That's what we believed all along."

Since the death and discovery of Melinda Mercer on December 7, 1997, Tacoma law enforcement was familiar with the MO of the Spokane Serial Killer. Even though Ellis's body was decomposed and went unidentified for two weeks, they must have contacted Spokane as soon as they recognized the plastic bag, small-caliber gunshot wound, and rural dump site. No doubt the task force knew about Ellis within days of her discovery. Still, it took nearly three months for them to link her to the other serial murders.

On November 3, Sergeant Cal Walker, Undersheriff Mike Aubrey, Lieutenant John Simmons, and Captain Steve Braun went to Seattle to "brief detectives about the latest developments" in the serial killer case.

I don't know why they sent four administrators and no working detectives to Tacoma. That might have had something to do with the lack of communication. It also reinforced the rumors I had been hearing about "micromanagement" and "administrative problems" inside the task force.

"We're going to talk about the need to cooperate and so on," Aubrey told the *Spokesman-Review.* "This isn't a sit-down between detectives to compare notes. This is about improving communication."

Troyer said that the task force hadn't spoken to Tacoma detectives until November 2.

"This is a long-term investigation," Spokane sheriff John Goldman responded. "Sometimes it takes some time to get together on the telephone."

After their conversation on the second, task force investigators were unwilling to say that Ellis was connected to their suspect.

Emil LaFontaine, the father of the victim, said that investigators from both Pierce and Spokane Counties had told him that his daughter was the victim of the serial killer more than a month prior to the official confirmation.

When asked if Pierce County would get involved with the Spokane Task Force investigation, Troyer said, "There's no reason for us to have anybody over there at this time."

Whoever was to blame, there had obviously been a breakdown in communications and cooperation between the two agencies. Women were dying; this was no time for turf politics.

Now there were at least two confirmed victims in western Washington, and probably three. Once Melinda Mercer's body had been found on the West Side, the Spokane Task Force needed to be expanded and made statewide. Three murders on the West Side made this only more necessary and, I thought, inevitable.

The Washington State Patrol, King County Sheriff's Department, and other agencies with missing women or unsolved homicides needed to take part in the Spokane investigation. The task force had controlled all the information on their cases for more than a year now, and they were apparently getting nowhere. It was time to expand the task force, bring in these other jurisdictions, and get more experienced detectives to look not only at the cases within their agencies' purview, but in Spokane as well. How would we know if the Spokane Task Force hadn't overlooked an important clue? A fresh set of eyes might be exactly what this case needed.

I hoped that the new leadership at the Spokane PD and the sheriff's department would effect these and other necessary changes. There were some positive signs. For example, task force detectives were finally seen working East Sprague, and developing a rapport with the prostitutes there. Although Chertok was already embattled, he showed signs of leadership and resolve, as well as an openness that his predecessors had lacked.

When a new leader was poised to take over the sheriff's department, I was also initially impressed.

Incumbent sheriff John Goldman had announced that he would not run for reelection. In the fall election, former state legislator and city police sergeant Mark Sterk ran as a Republican against Democrat Jim Finke, a sheriff's department lieutenant. Since World War II, the county sheriff's office had been a Democratic stronghold. In the 1998 election, the officers' union broke with tradition and endorsed Sterk, the first time anyone could remember the union backing a Republican candidate

during a primary. Cal Walker was an active Sterk supporter, going against Goldman, his own superior officer,
in the election. According to my sources, Walker helped
deliver the union for Sterk.

Sterk was elected handily. One of his first priorities, the
sheriff-elect promised, would be to give the task force more
latitude.

"I plan to step back and let the trained homicide detectives on the task force do their jobs," Sterk told the
Spokesman-Review as he celebrated his victory at a GOP
party in the Bayou Brewing Company. He also told reporters of his plans to replace many of the senior administrators in the sheriff's department, including the head of
detectives, with his own people.

Mike and I were hopeful that Sterk would make much
needed changes and bring a new attitude of proactive police
work and openness to the media. Though the city of
Spokane is predominantly Democrat, the county has a Republican majority. Two out of three county commissioners
are Republican. There was now a Republican in the prosecutor's office and a Republican sheriff, so there was some
philosophical continuity between the political establishment and the new sheriff. Being a former cop and an accomplished politician, Sterk seemed to have the tools
necessary to balance political pressures and the interests of
his own rank and file.

Sterk apparently had a completely different view of
press relations than his predecessor. As a state legislator,
Sterk had dealt with the press in a very up-front manner.
Mike felt that Sterk couldn't change his press relations
without completely losing his credibility. He certainly
didn't seem like the kind of sheriff who would come to
KXLY and complain to our news director that we were getting awful close to interfering with a criminal investigation, as John Goldman had earlier that year.

Sterk had a great reputation in law enforcement and had the support of the rank-and-file officers. The press portrayed him as a man of progressive law enforcement ideals, one who cared a great deal about his community. Fitzsimmons knew Sterk and described him as educated and competent and, most important, a man of his word.

Our hopes seemed well placed. On Friday, November 13, 1998, Sheriff Sterk was briefed by John Simmons and Cal Walker of the task force. A few days after that briefing, Sterk discussed the case with the *Spokesman-Review*. His remarks were very cautious, complimentary, and politic. He spoke well of the personnel on the task force, saying that they were doing their homework, cooperating well with other agencies, and sharing information, but also keeping some information secret "in order to maintain the integrity of the investigation." The need to protect information seemed to be an issue with which Sterk was very concerned, as he returned to it several times. He said that the release of information had been very detrimental to morale among the task force detectives, and that two detectives had left the task force because of it.

I figured that Sterk was referring to Dan Lundgren and Minde Connelly, by all accounts the two most experienced and competent detectives on the task force. But was that the true reason these two city detectives had left? Remember, one of Sterk's briefing officers was Cal Walker. Could Walker have been trying to blame the departure of Lundgren and Connelly on someone other than himself?

After the briefing, Sterk also said that he hoped to add four new detectives to the task force, two of them coming from his department and two from the Washington State Patrol. This would bring the task force up to twelve detectives, two sergeants, and two clerks. Two captains and two lieutenants were also working on the serial killer case part-time.

Sterk wanted to get the WSP on board and broaden the scope of the task force. "This thing is evolving into a statewide task force, rather than just a local task force," he said.

I was glad to hear Sterk say that.

Sterk believed that the task force did not have sufficient personnel to track down all the leads it was receiving. He stated that during the previous year, some three thousand tips had come in from the public. Sterk gave the impression that the lack of personnel was allowing these tips to go cold.

"You can't just leave them sit because you may end up with egg on your face down the line if you miss this guy and you had the information sitting in the office," Sterk said.

Sterk also outlined his plans for personnel changes within the task force, saying that he would replace Captain Doug Silver with Lieutenant John Simmons as co-commander of the group and the senior sheriff's department officer on the task force. At the time of his promotion, Simmons was a twenty-eight-year veteran of the department, having supervised the Major Crimes Unit for five years.

Sterk was emphatic in stating that the task force would remain in place indefinitely.

"What I've heard so far from the community is, 'This is what we want you to do. This needs to be resolved,' " Sterk told the newspaper. "I agree with that."

When asked how the task force might catch the Spokane Serial Killer, Sterk responded, "I think that basically this guy is going to make a mistake."

The following week, at a law enforcement conference in Chelan, Washington, Sterk and Chertok met privately to discuss the serial killer case. They promised to work closely together and support each other in their new positions. Both new leaders had said publicly that the serial killer case was the top law enforcement priority in Spokane. But the question remained, what were they going to do about it?

One of the first steps taken by Chertok and Sterk was to put up a billboard in the East Sprague neighborhood, with the faces of sixteen murdered prostitutes under the headline, "Help us find our killer!" They also put the same sign on Spokane city buses.

This was a good start to raise public awareness about the homicides and possibly generate some leads. The selection of the victims indicated to me that although the task force had officially connected only eight of the victims, they were unofficially considering another eight to be connected as well. These eight victims were Sapp, Lowe, Brisbois, Palmer, Zielinski, Joseph, Hernandez, and Murfin, who was still missing and presumed dead. Add the three West Side murders, and the unofficial body count was twenty-one.

That body count could possibly be higher. On October 23, 1998, hunters found a human skeleton in a remote area of Quincy Lakes Wildlife Refuge. The body was so decomposed that anthropologists were called in to determine the skeleton's gender and other identifying characteristics. Four days after the body was found, members of the task force went to Grant County to speak with authorities there. At the time, Doug Silver said the skeleton had not been connected to the Spokane Serial Killer.

The task force stated that the reason the Grant County investigators had summoned them was "their expertise in processing outdoor crime scenes."

In late December, forensic scientists helped create composite sketches of the young woman whose skeleton had been found. She was said to be racially a mix of black and Caucasian, between the ages of sixteen and twenty-one. Her height was estimated at between five feet two and five feet seven. Her hair was a naturally dark brown that had been dyed a lighter color. Time of death was estimated to be anywhere between April and October 23 (the day she was found). The cause of death was a gunshot wound to the head.

After the sketches were released, but not to the Spokane media, Doug Silver said that the task force still had not connected this victim to their suspect, although they also would not rule out that possibility.

There was no follow-up information, and task force representatives repeatedly refused to comment or answer any direct questions concerning this possible victim.

Also in late December, the Washington State Patrol agreed to provide a detective to the task force. Despite the fact that the state patrol would pay the detective's salary, the task force had initially balked at having an outside investigator join their group. Task force members said that they didn't have enough clerical staff to support an additional detective, and wondered whether a state patrol detective would be able to work well with sheriff's department and Spokane PD personnel. Chertok and Sterk stepped in, and made the task force take on the extra help.

I hoped Chertok and Sterk would change the way the task force was operating. I was eager to meet both these new leaders, so I invited them to appear on the radio show. I was hoping to gain their trust, in order to work together on the serial killer case. Mike and I were tired of being stonewalled by the task force detectives and looked forward to Sterk and Chertok as being more open and cooperative with the media and more competent in pursuing the investigation.

We were willing to do anything that would help the case. We would solicit leads, develop them, follow up on them, and then even sit on the information that we discovered if the police wanted us to. We both believed that the task force needed to be held accountable. They had done it their way for a year, and it hadn't worked. The task force needed to change the way they were doing business, in both their investigation and their dealings with the media.

And we hoped that Sterk and Chertok felt the same way.

We invited Chertok and Sterk on the radio show for a "Chiefs' Day." We wanted to give them both an opportunity to talk about their concerns, their plans, their goals. And we wanted to open a dialogue with them.

I must admit I was a bit surprised when both Sterk and Chertok agreed to come on the radio show. As the day approached, I wondered how they would react to me, whether they would act like cops or politicians.

Chertok was the first to arrive. As soon as he introduced himself, I felt at ease. He may have been average in height, weight, and appearance, but he had an air of confidence, almost a swagger to his attitude. I could tell immediately that he was not just book smart, but also very experienced and streetwise.

Sterk arrived a little later, just before we were about to go on air. At first glance, I liked Sterk as well. He had a very open attitude and a warm, engaging smile. At the radio station, Sterk worked the room like a politician, friendly and respectful, but not giving away anything and never letting his guard down.

During the show, we talked about local law enforcement issues, discussed each new leader's plans for their departments, and scrupulously avoided any discussion of the serial killer—which obviously was the biggest law enforcement challenge facing Spokane. I didn't want to open that can of worms. At least not yet.

Chertok and Sterk knew that Mike and I were very interested in the serial killer case, and they were probably ready for some pretty tough questions. So we must have really thrown them when we didn't mention the serial killer at all.

On the air, Chertok and Sterk were a little more guarded and politic in their statements than when we were talking casually.

After this first Chiefs' Day program, whenever Mike and I discussed the serial killer on the radio show our remarks were more diplomatic. We were no longer so critical of the task force, wanting to avoid alienating the new leadership, in whom we both had great faith. Now Mike and I focused our investigation and comments on the suspect himself. No longer were we critiquing the police. Now we were trying to help them catch the killer.

Of course we wanted to help solve the case, but I was also planning to write a book. And what better sources could there be than the two men who were ultimately in charge of the task force? It seemed that the best way to start with Chertok and Sterk would be to verify information I already possessed to make certain that it was accurate.

On April 27, 1999, a badly decomposed body was discovered in Snoqualmie, in the Cascade Mountains east of Seattle. The body was found when a dog had taken a human hand from the dump site and placed it in his own food bowl. The dog's owner saw the hand, and had the dog lead him back to the body, two miles away from his home.

The body was identified as Jennifer Diane Justus, a twenty-six-year-old Seattle prostitute and drug addict. Doug Silver said that there was no apparent connection to the Spokane killings. There was no follow-up, and my specific questions as to the classification of the Justus homicide were never answered.

Aside from unclaimed bodies like Jennifer Justus and the skeleton found in Quincy Lakes, no official victims had been discovered since Connie LaFontaine Ellis. Once again, Spokane seemed to forget about the serial killer. The *Spokesman-Review* ran very few follow-up stories on the homicides. The editorial columns and letters to the editor showed more interest in issues like potholes and garbage collection.

This seemed the perfect time to let Sterk and Chertok know that I was planning to write a book about the Spokane Serial Killer. I wanted to stir things up a little. If I couldn't wake Spokane out of its complacency, perhaps I could light a fire under its top cops.

Mike and I arranged another Chiefs' Day radio show, just a few days after the Spokane Sheriff's Department had a child homicide.

When eleven-year-old Christopher Wood was found dead, strangled, and dumped down a snow-covered embankment some forty miles north of Spokane, the sheriff's department immediately pulled all available detectives off their regular duty to assist in the investigation. The neighborhood where the boy lived was canvassed by detectives. A total of thirteen detectives worked on that case, four more than were assigned to the task force at that time.

Two days before Christopher's body was found, his house had suspiciously burned to the ground, and Christopher was reported missing. His father, Robert Wood, was considered a "person of interest" in his son's murder, and was held in the county jail on unrelated theft charges until detectives could make a case against him. Once he was arrested, he hung himself in jail.

Detectives on the Wood case asked the public for assistance. They released a detailed description of Robert Wood's vehicle. They described the possible route the suspect took to the crime scene, and asked for people who drove that route within a four-and-a-half-hour window of time to call Crime Check.

The case was solved in a matter of days. And it showed that Spokane law enforcement can devote resources and manpower to solving a murder. When they want to.

On the air, I commended both leaders for the great

work they were doing, particularly Sterk for the job he and his office did on the Wood case. We talked about a wide variety of law enforcement issues, but once again, I didn't bring up the serial killer. It might have gone unmentioned if one of my last callers hadn't asked about it, wondering if the police and the community had lost interest in the case. Chertok told the caller it was unavoidable that public attention would lag as long as there weren't any breakthroughs or new activity. He assured her, "Don't worry, we'll catch this guy. It just hasn't happened yet."

After the show was over, I told Sterk and Chertok about my planned book on the Spokane Serial Killer. To my surprise, both of them supported the idea and offered to cooperate with me on it. The most they could promise at this point was the corroboration of specific investigative facts I had already developed on my own, to ensure that the book was accurate. Still, that was a good start.

Compared to the official cooperation I got on my first two books, it all seemed too easy. I had two chief law enforcement officers willing to cooperate on the book.

Whenever things are going well, I get a little nervous. The events of the next few months showed that I had good reason to be skeptical.

First, Alan Chertok got into trouble.

On April 15, 1999, Chertok appeared at a local high school criminal justice class. When a student asked him about the task force, Chertok went on to describe the present state of the investigation. As an example of some of the crazy tips that came in from the public, he cited that even former Spokane police chief Terry Mangan had been named as a possible suspect.

A few days after making this remark, Chertok found himself the target of an official investigation conducted by the sheriff's department. Mark Sterk, whose relationship with Chertok had previously been supportive and cordial, seemed to be bowing to pressure from his men on the task force. Following his department's investigation, Sterk said that the investigators had verified that Chertok had made those remarks, but that Terry Mangan was not being called back to Spokane for an interview.

Then the task force issued a press release that only added fuel to the fire.

The recent controversy regarding statements Spokane Police Chief Alan Chertok made to a Ferris High criminal justice class appears to be winding down to a discussion of whether or not the police chief was joking when he commented on aspects of the Spokane Homicide Task Force and its investigation.

The investigators assigned to this unit see one issue of overriding importance in this matter. Despite the policy of the Spokane County Sheriff and Spokane City Police Department prohibiting discussion of the case by other than official spokespersons, Chief Chertok held an open, public discussion of the investigation.

As is necessary in any difficult criminal investigation, issues regarding solution of the case are discussed among detectives, supervisors and support staff that are not revealed to the public. This is the reason a single spokesperson is appointed, and information debated and approved by detectives working each area of the case.

The killing of Spokane-area women is a serious matter, taken seriously by the investigators charged with its solution. It is not a joke, and is certainly not a matter to be discussed in a cavalier manner in an open forum which might jeopardize solution of the murders.

The investigators assigned to the Spokane Homicide Task Force hope the focus of the Spokane community remains on the solution of this string of murders, and on justice attained for its many victims.

Detectives continue to solicit any tip or information the public can provide regarding these homicides. Each and every tip will be taken seriously and thoroughly pursued.

This press release, put out under Sheriff Sterk's name, signaled the beginning of the end of Alan Chertok's police career in Spokane. Sterk forwarded the results of his investigation to Spokane County prosecutor Steve Tucker for consideration of possible charges of interfering with an investigation or official misconduct.

A police chief makes a joke about how ridiculous some of the tips were that had come into the task force, and suddenly he's up on possible criminal charges. The seriousness with which the task force, Sterk, and Tucker handled this entire matter only made it look as if Mangan was a suspect.

The vultures were circling, and Chertok's days as chief were numbered. The Spokane Police Guild issued press releases questioning Chertok's credibility and leadership. City Manager Bill Pupo gave the chief a nine-month job evaluation that was decidedly negative, stating, among other things, that Chertok hadn't accomplished much, though Pupo had told Chertok to spend the first several months of his tenure establishing relationships in town. In fact, Pupo had scheduled many of Chertok's meetings. Chertok had told Pupo that he had a lot of ideas for administrative changes, but he wanted to implement them slowly, and Pupo had agreed. Then he criticized Chertok for doing exactly what the chief said he would do, and what the city manager had agreed to.

When the nine-month evaluation came due, the political climate had shifted dramatically. Pupo didn't want to continue supporting Chertok if it meant bucking the system. The task force, the Spokane PD rank and file, Sterk and his sheriff's department, and others in local politics were all against Chertok. When Pupo took their side, Chertok didn't stand a chance.

Following his negative evaluation, Chertok went on vacation. The next day, he was formally cleared of any criminal wrongdoing in the Ferris High School incident by Steve Tucker. Then Pupo retroactively suspended Chertok from his position as chief, saying that he had reviewed Chertok's actions and decided they merited a suspension.

Three weeks later, Chertok resigned from the position, agreeing to a $65,000 buyout of his contract.

Chertok wasn't the first good cop that Spokane lost to politics.

"Some of the best police officers we ever had in this town have long since retired before their time," Mike told me, "because they just didn't want any part of it. Many of them are out of law enforcement altogether. It's usually the politics, and not the street stuff, that burns them out. They loved police work, they just hated the politics of being a cop in Spokane."

Alan Chertok was another good cop lost to the Spokane PD. He probably didn't realize it at the time, but Chertok walked into a no-win situation in Spokane. And he didn't help himself by having an outspoken, sometimes brash, personality. Still, he deserved a chance, and Spokane didn't give him one.

Once Chertok was forced out, Roger Bragdon reassumed the position of acting chief, and the city government began the search process all over again. From the beginning of this new search, Mike told me that this process would probably not result in another outside hire.

Mike was convinced that the Spokane PD was going to stick with one of their own. Although Bragdon did not meet the formal qualifications, because he did not have a college degree, Mike predicted that the college requirement would be waived.

Of course, Mike was right. The college requirement was eventually waived and Roger Bragdon was officially sworn in as the chief of the Spokane PD.

Now the Spokane cops had one of their own back in command. Or, as Mike put it, "The inmates are in charge of the asylum again."

CHAPTER 18

"Waiting for Another Body"

FUHRMAN: When a politician makes a promise, when a politician shakes your hand and says, I'm going to do this because it's good for the county and the investigation and I want your book to be accurate, and then they go sideways, isn't there something wrong here? A man's handshake should mean something. Mark Sterk's doesn't.

Once Alan Chertok got fired, he stayed in Spokane. I invited him to Sandpoint to go fishing. We went out on Lake Pend Oreille on a cold and gloomy day, pretty typical for June. The fish weren't biting, and Alan looked a little green out there on the choppy water. We talked about the case, but he couldn't give me much information. I understood. It wasn't his case any longer, and he couldn't give up information for which he was not responsible. At least Alan caught a fish, even if it was too small to eat.

Spokane had lost a good cop, and I lost a good source. There was still a lot that I knew about the evidence, even if I couldn't get it officially confirmed. For example, I knew the task force had DNA evidence. They were taking blood samples from suspects, and they had to have something with which to compare it. I also thought that DNA was at least one way (the other being ballistics) that the task force was connecting the cases that they would officially admit were connected.

If they had DNA, what kind was it? DNA evidence can come only from blood, saliva, semen, hair follicles, or tissue. If there was DNA evidence on more than one victim, it probably wasn't blood or tissue, as those would be left on the victims only as a result of an altercation. And aside from Kathy Brisbois and possibly Michelyn Derning, we had no indications of a struggle being common to all eight officially connected cases.

Saliva is very difficult to detect. While the suspect could have left hairs on one or more of his victims, I was more interested in the possibility of semen being the source of DNA evidence. With prostitutes, of course, it would not be surprising to find foreign semen when oral, vaginal, and anal swabs are taken during the autopsy. If eight of the victims had semen with matching DNA, then the task force was onto something. All they needed to do was to find the right suspect and match his DNA to the samples they found on the victims. Of course, finding the suspect is the challenge.

I wondered if the task force was up to it. After what I had seen so far, there was no reason for me to have any confidence in their investigative abilities. At first glance, the fact that they had DNA seemed like a great advantage, but it also could hinder, rather than help, their investigation.

I hoped that the task force detectives were not expecting the DNA evidence by itself to solve the case. Just because the suspect was leaving DNA didn't mean they didn't have to investigate. If they were just taking polygraphs and blood samples from suspects (as we had seen them do with the two Joseph suspects and Gregory Landis), that was just dartboard detective work. Maybe they'd get lucky and find the right suspect. Maybe they wouldn't.

What if they did find the right suspect and he refused to submit a blood sample? Would the task force be able to develop enough evidence to write a search warrant that a judge would sign?

Even with good DNA evidence, you still have to use old-fashioned detective work to find your suspect. From the few examples I had seen firsthand—such as the Mallinson clue and the lack of neighborhood canvassing, for example—I was not at all confident that they had the ability, training, or experience to catch this killer. Any detective who would walk away from a body and leave the crime scene until the next morning, not just once but on six separate occasions, at least lacked stamina.

On April 14, 1999, Spokane Task Force detectives served a search warrant on a South Hill home, while saying that there was no connection, at that time, with the serial killings. A thirty-five-year-old doctor was a suspect in the kidnap, rape, and assault of a female prostitute in downtown Spokane. The woman told police that on February 16 a man fitting the doctor's description forced her into his Toyota 4-Runner at gunpoint, drove her to his home, and sexually assaulted her.

While continuing to state that the search warrant was not connected to the serial killings, the task force did admit that because they had "developed additional information regarding this incident," they felt it appropriate to investigate the crime.

When directly asked whether the search warrant was connected to the serial killer case, Cal Walker responded, "I'm not going to say whether it is or if it isn't. We are investigating what appears to be a separate incident."

So why were they there? Walker said that the task force

had solved other crimes that weren't related to the serial killings, but he wouldn't specify which ones.

The case of the doctor looked like a dispute over payment, not a kidnapping and rape. The task force eliminated him as a suspect, probably through DNA comparison.

In May, the Spokane Task Force requested police in Dothan, Alabama, to contact a "person of interest" for questioning. The man was held overnight, interrogated by Alabama investigators, and then released.

"There was no reason for arrest, at least on our end," Dave Reagan said. "We called them and said, 'Hey, if you run into this guy, ask him these questions.' "

Apparently, the suspect refused to answer questions. Members of the task force said they had no plans to interview the suspect themselves, although they would keep him in their files. The task force would not disclose this suspect's identity or say why they were interested in him.

Since the October 1998 discovery of Connie LaFontaine in Parkland, Washington, there had been no new bodies. This meant that either the suspect had stopped killing or we simply weren't finding his bodies. The task force was still active, even if the killer wasn't. And the evidence from twenty-four victims was all there. The solution to these crimes lay somewhere in that evidence, if only the detectives working the case had the determination and the imagination to find the killer.

Meanwhile, a serial killer was working in Portland. On May 7, 1999, the body of Lilla Faye Moler was found in Portland's Forest Park. Police stated that Moler had been dead in the park for two months. During a search of the area, another body was found, this one Stephanie Lynn Russell, who was likely to have been killed within a week of being found. On June 2, the body of Alexandra Nicole Ison was found on a steep ravine in Forest Park. Ison was a teenage runaway with a history of drug abuse. Russell also had a drug record, and Moler was a prostitute. All three women had been strangled.

The Portland Police Department formed a task force of twelve detectives to solve the three murders. The difference in MO made me think that this wasn't the Spokane killer. Still, the cases needed to be looked at closely.

Soon after the announcement of the Portland Task Force, three Spokane Task Force members drove to Portland to meet with their counterparts there. They spent two days driving back and forth, and one day meeting with the Portland cops.

A little more than a month after forming their task force, Portland police arrested Todd Alan Reed for the three murders. Reed, a thirty-two-year-old laborer from north Portland, had previous arrests for sexual assault and kidnapping. He was not a suspect in the Spokane killings.

In June 1999, Stephen Weeks, my old partner from the Moxley case, came out to Idaho to help me with the book. It was time to stir things up a little.

June also brought the fifth anniversary of the murders of Nicole Brown Simpson and Ron Goldman. Instead of the anniversary of their deaths being marked by solemn remembrance, it was celebrated by a morbid media circus. I had several requests to appear on television programs. As much as I wanted to leave the Simpson case behind me, I decided to appear on *Good Morning America* and a few other programs.

Since *Good Morning America* is taped at 4:00 A.M. Spokane time, I planned to spend the night before in Spokane, so I wouldn't have to wake up at 1:00 A.M. Since I was going to be in Spokane anyway, I decided to see if Sheriff Sterk was available.

I had previously tried to get Sterk alone and speak casually with him, but for one reason or another, he could never find the time. I understood that since he had just been elected sheriff, he had a lot of responsibilities, some of them necessary and important, others simply unavoidable. Before I left for Spokane on the night of June 9, I called Sterk at home and asked if we could get together the next day. As usual, he was booked solid, starting with an 8:30 breakfast meeting.

"That's fine," I responded. "Why don't we meet for coffee at seven o'clock?"

Sterk hesitated, apparently unprepared for my being available so early.

"Come on, I'll buy you breakfast," I said. "I've never known a cop to turn down a free meal."

We both laughed and he finally gave in, agreeing to meet me at Cavanaugh's Restaurant.

Steve and I got to the restaurant about fifteen minutes early so I could load up on some much needed coffee. Steve and I discussed what information we wanted to get from Sterk and agreed that with the limited time available the best we could hope for would be to establish trust and communication. We wanted to get him committed to some specifics beyond his previous vague promises of cooperation.

Sterk showed up alone and on time. He was dressed in casual business attire—a sport jacket and tie—and seemed comfortable. We exchanged greetings, and I introduced Steve. Sterk sat down next to me in the booth. From my training in police interrogation, I am always very conscious about where people sit and thought that Sterk's sitting next to me was an odd choice considering the fact that he would be addressing me directly during most of the meeting. Was he more comfortable sitting next to someone he knew? Or did he not want to have to make direct eye contact with me?

As our meeting began, I noticed that Sterk had some apprehension regarding Steve's presence. I explained that Steve worked with me on my books, during both the investigation and the writing process. Sterk seemed a little more comfortable, but still directed most of his attention to me.

When the waitress came to take our orders, Sterk took only coffee. I told him to order whatever he wanted, since *Good Morning America* was picking up the tab. Sterk, who doesn't look like a man who ever passes up a meal, said he didn't want anything to eat.

I was struck by Sterk's caution. He wasn't wearing his uniform, because he didn't want to be seen "on the job" talking with me. And he didn't want to let me buy him breakfast, because he didn't want to appear compromised. As if I could buy him with breakfast.

Our conversation started out cordially and superficially enough, mostly focusing on Sterk's new job as sheriff and the many different issues he had to deal with. Eventually, of course, the subject turned to the serial killer.

As the waitress took away our plates and my elbows found the table, I began directing the discussion toward the investigation.

"It seems as if the killer is dormant, at least in a cooling-off period," I said. "What is the task force doing?"

"The investigation is at a dead end right now," Sterk said with a candor that took me by surprise. "The detectives are just sitting around, waiting for another body."

I didn't respond immediately, partly because I couldn't believe what I had just heard. The chief law enforcement officer in the Spokane area—the man in charge of the men in charge of the serial killer investigation—had just stated that the task force was doing basically nothing. Apparently they had no leads, and were not trying to work the thousands of clues that they already had. The admission was so damning, there was no reason for Sterk to say this unless it was true.

And Sterk kept talking, matter-of-factly.

"Unless another body is found soon," he continued, "the task force will probably be disbanded in the fall."

My first reaction, upon hearing these admissions, was to advise Sterk not to say things like this in public, but that was my old cop loyalty. I stopped myself from warning Sterk to be careful, or even to shut up. My curiosity and my need to get the story superseded any sympathies I might have had for Sterk, his career, and the detectives on the task force. It was my job to get the story, and let the chips fall where they would. Sterk was giving me explosive information, a great story. And he was just getting started. I had learned from interrogating hundreds of suspects that once they start talking, it's often best just to shut up and listen. That's what Steve and I both did.

Sterk was silent for a moment, as if he realized that he had just let the cat out of the bag and was trying to decide whether to try and chase it down or let it go.

After a long and awkward silence, I tried to get him talking again.

"My sister-in-law works for Microsoft," I said. "And I have already talked to some people over there in the Law Enforcement Group. They might be able to donate some equipment, software, and maybe personnel if you asked for it."

Again Sterk was silent. Even something as significant as free database support from the largest software company in the world was not as pressing now as the position he found himself in.

So I tried another tack.

"There has to be a common denominator between the recent killings and the 1990 cases," I said. "Because if it's not the same guy, then you have at least two serial killers, and you can't catch either one of them."

"How can there be twenty-three dead prostitutes," Steve jumped in, "all of them unsolved and only a few of them connected?"

Sterk took a deep breath and fidgeted in his seat. He seemed to be very interested in the physical characteristics of his coffee cup. Finally, he started talking again, effortlessly and without his usual caution.

"The task force is handling all twenty-three homicides."

Bingo! He was telling us that most, if not all, of the killings were connected by some form of evidence or signature.

I wanted to keep Sterk talking, so he wouldn't start to backslide on us. After this admission, I felt that more would be forthcoming. I didn't want to give him a chance to think and reconsider what he was giving us. It occurred to me that we were interrogating Sterk. This was the first time I had ever interrogated a cop.

Steve had learned enough about interrogation technique to know what to do next.

"Are there more missing women?" he asked, pushing the conversation in another direction and catching Sterk off guard.

"There are a lot more missing women," Sterk said readily, putting a certain emphasis on the word "lot."

Mike and I had uncovered the fact that a .22 pistol was used in the 1990 killings and also at least some of the more recent deaths. But we had never been able to corroborate this report.

"The task force is giving polygraphs to suspects, asking about a .22-caliber gun," I said. "No doubt that's the gun being used to kill these women."

"Yeah, there's a .22," Sterk said.

"So, you've put out a teletype—"

"Huh?"

"Yeah, a teletype to all the law enforcement agencies in the Pacific Northwest, that if they come across any .22-caliber with certain lands, grooves, and twists, then hold it for ballistics tests."

Sterk didn't answer.

"You've done that, haven't you?"

He still didn't answer. He just looked at me.

Sterk's silence indicated to me that they hadn't sent out any teletypes of that nature. This was basic police work, communicating with other agencies to see if something turns up. If they weren't sending out teletypes on ballistics, and they weren't canvassing the neighborhoods where the bodies had been found, and they weren't following up on tips like the Mallinson clue—then just what were they doing?

I couldn't get distracted by the implications of all I was hearing. I had to get as much information as possible, before Sterk realized what he was doing and clammed up.

I asked him about DNA.

"We know there has to be rape involved at some point," I said, "and I would suppose that at least some of the victims have DNA material left by the suspect."

"Not only rape," Sterk said, "but sexual torture and necrophilia."

No one had ever mentioned sexual torture or necrophilia. Steve and I exchanged glances—we couldn't believe what we were hearing.

"So you do have DNA?" I asked.

"We've got enough DNA to match to a suspect if we ever find him."

"On several of the victims?"

"Yes."

Why was he giving us all this? I could tell that Steve was as surprised as I was. Both of us were trying to do about four things at once—retain and memorize everything as close to verbatim as possible, understand the significance of what he was saying, think of what to ask him next, and figure out why he was spilling the beans like this. He was speaking in a manner designed to impress. He clearly was not making any of this up. He wasn't speaking hypothetically or offering up speculation. This was the unvarnished truth coming straight from the source's mouth. Still, I had to ask myself—why?

Remember, Sheriff Sterk had just spent a term in the Washington State legislature. Before that, he was a traffic cop. So even though he was, at that moment, the ranking law enforcement officer in all of Spokane, he had very little, if any, homicide experience. This morning he was one of the boys, talking evidence over a cup of coffee with an LA homicide detective and his partner from New York.

"Did the dumping of Maybin's body on April Fools' Day kind of demoralize the task force?"

"I have to admit he is taunting us, particularly in that case," Sterk said, appearing somewhat demoralized himself.

He looked at his watch and apologized for having to cut our meeting short, but he had another appointment. Before he left, Sterk made a point to tell us that he was going to meet with the task force later on that day and brief them on how they would cooperate and what kind of information they would be able to share with us, or at least verify for us.

Steve and I thanked Sterk for taking the time to meet with us, and then he left.

Once he was out of earshot, Steve and I looked across the table at each other and the same words came out of our mouths at exactly the same time.

"Can you believe what he just gave up?"

All we had hoped for out of that meeting was to estab-

lish a relationship and figure out how we could work together. Instead, we got several vital pieces of information,
and a picture of a task force clueless, demoralized, virtually
inactive, and waiting to be shut down.

"This is too easy," Steve said. After working with me for
four years, Steve has a tendency to be a little pessimistic, if
not downright paranoid. "Why would he give us all that information? Are we being set up?"

I had thought the same thing while Sterk was talking.
But everything he said had the ring of truth. And it was all
damaging to him and the task force. There's no way, if he
was making it up, he would have told us the specific evidence he did, particularly since it corroborated some of my
previous theories. Even if everything that Sterk told us was
the truth, I was a little concerned about any future cooperation. Information had gushed out of Sterk, some of it of a
highly confidential nature. I wondered whether he might
start backsliding on me.

I knew Mark Sterk was a politician. But Mike told me
that he was a man of his word, and I supposed that meant
something. Still, I had to make sure that he would live up
to his promised cooperation.

As I sat around the house on Sunday morning, June 13,
drinking my first pot of coffee, waiting for everyone else to
wake up, I began reconsidering the breakfast meeting with
Sterk. Sterk had given me his business card and made a
point to put his home phone number on the back. I didn't
want to ruin his Sunday, so I waited until after dinner to
call.

He was at home when I called, and we exchanged some
small talk before I got down to business. First, I apologized
for calling him at home. Sterk said, and he sounded pretty
convincing, that he didn't mind.

"What can I do for you?" he asked.

I told him that I was starting to put together my research needs and was wondering if I could get the autopsy summaries and the missing person reports for any known prostitutes.

The silence was deafening.

Finally, Sterk responded, with an edge to his voice, "Mark, I never said we were going to turn over reports to you. Just help you confirm information you developed so that it is accurate."

The backsliding had already begun. I decided to press him a little.

"Well," I said, "from our conversation Thursday morning, and all the information you gave us, I got the impression that we were going to be on the inside."

"Then I think you got the wrong impression."

"Okay, so what will I be able to get from the task force?"

"We need to go over that with Captain Simmons," Sterk said. The recently promoted Simmons was the task force commander, and Sterk's subordinate. His name hadn't come up in our breakfast meeting, but now Sterk was leaning on him like a crutch. Still, I didn't want to let on, so I just acted as if this was the greatest news I had ever heard. Sterk and I arranged a conference call between the three of us on June 15.

Since I wanted my own witness, I included Steve on this conference call. The atmosphere on the phone line was tense. Sterk kept referring to our "misunderstanding" that the task force would share any reports. At the same time, he promised everything that we were legally entitled to under the Washington State Disclosure Act. Nobody said anything about the information that Sterk had already given us at the breakfast meeting, although I knew that Sterk was waiting for Steve or me to bring it up.

"It's not in anyone's interest to go through a formal legal process to get legally releasable reports, and I certainly don't want to make any lawyer rich," Simmons said. "We can give you anything available under the law."

I knew as well as anybody that in a situation like this, the law was whatever somebody wants it to mean. Still, we kept everything cordial and set a date for another meeting, this time with Sterk, Simmons, and representatives from the task force on Thursday, June 17.

That day, Steve and I drove to the Public Safety Building. We knew that because of his previous disclosures, we still had Sterk in the bag. He had already committed to some level of cooperation, even if he was doing a little two-step trying to dance out of it. We'd get something, at least. Besides, this was only our first real shot at them.

We entered the Public Safety Building and went to the sheriff's desk to announce ourselves. As we waited for the task force members to emerge from their windowless office, I noticed several glass cases in the lobby, filled with items of historical interest in Spokane law enforcement, dating back to the turn of the century.

One of the cases had a Thompson submachine gun in pristine condition, surrounded by photos and a police blotter from the thirties. As I scrutinized the blotter entries, two casually dressed detectives approached us.

We met sheriff's department sergeant Cal Walker and Spokane PD sergeant Al Wilson, and they led us toward a nearby conference room. As we passed the glass case where the Thompson was, I remarked, "That's a nice gun."

"Yeah," Cal Walker said with an angry sarcasm. "Tony Bamonte probably found that one, too."

Al laughed along with him. This was obviously a sore point with both of the men.

Tony is a friend of mine, and they must have known that. It was curious, though, that they were still angry at him for what they must have thought was embarrassing their police department. Well, my opinion was that the only person embarrassing the Spokane police was Clyde Ralstin, and all the other officers who'd helped him cover up the murder of a fellow policeman. Besides, I already knew that Tony Bamonte didn't think much of Cal Walker—and I consider Tony a good judge of character.

We followed the two detectives down a long hall. I felt as if I was walking into any other modern police department: the off-white gloss enamel paint; the cheap linoleum waxed to a high shine; the hum of a faulty air conditioner; the smell of burned coffee. The conference room was done in standard police station design: a Formica-topped conference table with a faux walnut finish and Naugahyde office chairs that were made to be uncomfortable so you wouldn't fall asleep during long meetings.

The two detectives sat together across the table from Steve and me. They didn't offer us coffee.

I began by saying how I had met several times now with Sheriff Sterk, and he had promised his cooperation.

"That's fine," Walker said. "We'll give you everything we give anyone else."

"Yes, but—" I was about to detail my own specific requests for information, when Cal Walker tossed a manila envelope across the table at me.

"These are all the press releases that the task force has issued," Walker said, his face reddening as he spoke. "It's all we've given anyone else. And it's all we're giving you."

I could feel the temperature rising in the room.

"Your boss, Sheriff Sterk, told me he would at the very least make sure that our information was accurate," I said.

"We will not confirm or deny anything that you come up with," Walker said.

I glanced at the other detective, who hadn't said anything since we sat down. I got the distinct impression that he wanted to be anywhere else but here. Too bad, here he was.

"We have been sitting on a lot of information," I said. "Most of it coming from Sterk. If you won't 'confirm or deny' it, then I guess I'll just start putting the information out on the radio."

Neither detective responded, so I gave them a few examples of what we knew.

"You're looking for a small-caliber handgun. You're polygraphing suspects. Taking blood samples for DNA. Haven't put out any teletypes on weapons."

Nothing.

"Or maybe we should talk about necrophilia . . . sexual torture . . . and how about the other missing women that nobody is talking about?"

Walker's face turned a brighter shade of red. He stared at me and said, once again, "We will not confirm or deny anything."

We went back and forth on this for several minutes, and got exactly nowhere.

No punches were thrown. No angry words spoken. Everybody was civil and polite. And as we smiled and shook each other's hands, we were all saying "fuck you" in our minds.

From the Public Safety Building, Steve and I went back to the radio station to brief Mike on the meeting. Our guarded optimism was now confirmed paranoia. Mike did not seem surprised, but he did point out that by not contradicting us, Walker had just confirmed everything that we told him Sterk had said. Then Mike told us to write up a letter containing detailed minutes of our June 10 meeting, to give Sterk a chance either to verify or challenge our recollections of what he had said.

The next day, I called Sterk at his office. I told him about Cal Walker and his childish attitude.

"Cal Walker is in charge," Sterk said carefully. "I have to be guided by his and the task force's opinion about disclosure of information."

"No, you're in charge, Sheriff. He'll do what you tell him."

"I have to take Walker's opinion into consideration. He's my sergeant and I stand by him."

"You're his boss," I said. But Sterk didn't have an answer to that.

As soon as I hung up with Sterk, Steve and I drafted a letter recounting the details of our June 10 breakfast meeting, which we sent to the sheriff. His response was curious.

In a letter dated July 12, Sterk stated that when he was talking about all the MO and evidentiary details, he was just recounting some of the questions the media asked him about. He went on to say that I misunderstood his promise of cooperation.

"The last paragraph of your letter is insulting. Your follow-up phone call on July 7, 1999, was the same. I assume your comments were intended as a veiled threat."

Threat, insult. It really didn't matter now. I was a local journalist, writing a book about the most serious crimes to have been committed in Spokane since the turn of the century. During the research of that book, the sheriff himself made unsolicited statements about a very sensitive investigation. Unless he lived up to his word, he would leave me no choice other than to publish what he said.

What Sheriff Sterk told us at the breakfast meeting was certainly worse than anything Alan Chertok ever said in public. Here was the top law enforcement officer in eastern Washington, an elected official and the commander of the task force, disclosing evidentiary items of incredible sensitivity, on the record, to a journalist and a witness. If, as the task force always argued, disclosure of such information would damage investigative integrity, then Sterk had seriously jeopardized the serial killer case, potentially hobbled the task force, and left his officers totally exposed.

CHAPTER 19

The Town Hall Meeting

More changes came with the November 1999 election, some good, some bad.

Spokane voters approved a new city charter, with a strong mayoral system. For years, the city manager and city council had run Spokane without much real accountability, and city government served the powers who owned and operated Spokane for years.

"The landed gentry used to meet in the Empire Room in the Lincoln Building," Mike told me. "There, they would decide what the city was going to do, and the government would just go along."

The city government was organized and run not to serve the people of Spokane, but to benefit the landed gentry. Mike said that "the local government is beautifully designed to allow a handful of people to control things." The new city charter and a strong mayor would hopefully begin to change things.

Statewide, Washington voters passed Initiative 695, which cut the motor vehicle excise tax and lowered the tag fee to $30. Much of the $550 million annually raised by that excise tax went to local government. Spokane's city government, which was already experiencing a budget crunch, lost approximately $3.9 million in state revenues. One-third of that shortfall was shouldered by the Spokane Police Department, whose budget was reduced by $1.3 million. As a result of the I-695 cuts, or so they said, the Spokane PD pulled its five detectives off the task force on December 24, 1999.

County Commissioner John Roskelley requested that the city contribute two detectives to the investigation. City Manager Henry Miggins, who had replaced Bill Pupo, replied, "The present situation is unfortunate, but I believe Chief Bragdon's decisions are appropriate."

"There are ten women dead," Roger Bragdon said. "And there's still a lot of work to do. But patrol can't absorb that kind of hit."

Two-thirds of the Spokane PD force worked on patrol. There were forty-eight detectives. While no jobs were actually lost by the budget cuts attributed to I-695, several programs were cut or eliminated, and the task force detectives were sent back to their original assignments at Crimes Against Persons. At the same time those detectives were pulled off the task force, the Spokane PD established a new detail for recovering stolen property, which employed the same number of detectives. What was more important to the Spokane PD—murdered women or stolen televisions?

When I was on the LAPD, voters passed a similar initiative. The budget cuts were absorbed by a hiring freeze. For a couple of years, we didn't hire or train any new recruits. Administrators figured out a way to manage with reduced allocations, and we kept doing our jobs. Until they figure out a better way of doing it, and I doubt they ever will, law enforcement will be a branch of civil service. There's always going to be a shortage of resources. You just have to find a way to work with what you're given.

FUHRMAN: I'd say we aren't close to an arrest or even a good suspect, because if they were I am sure they would stick around to bask in glory at catching the guy. You can blame Prop 695 all you want, but the city still has to investigate murders. It's about time that you start asking some accountability for the dollars they spent on this task force.

FITZSIMMONS: The five city detectives that are being removed are simply being reassigned, but if they were close to a solution, they would have to feel that a move like this would compromise a solution. It's quite clear they're not making any headway.

FUHRMAN: Why would you dismantle a task force that is leading the most important investigation in the city?

Soon after the city dropped out of the task force, Mike and I started hearing rumblings that the Spokane PD had never wanted to be involved in the serial killer investigation from the beginning, and that the city's contribution to the task force was negligible.

The whispers we heard about the Spokane PD's lack of enthusiasm for the task force had come, for the most part, from the sheriff's department and people close to it. Mike and I saw a reluctance on the part of both administrations. First, they didn't want to link up the killings, and it took them four bodies to form a task force (even though those four cases were probably connected to at least six previous homicides). Once the task force was established, we saw very little investigation. Of course, we weren't privy to what was going on in the task force's windowless office in the Public Safety Building. We did know that detectives weren't out on Sprague, and they weren't working the leads that we gave them. In addition to the Mallinson clue, we had passed along information on at least a dozen other clues and witnesses. Several of these witnesses were not contacted for months.

The only visible activity on the part of the task force was

their investigation of Brad Jackson, the estranged common-law husband of Roseann Pleasant, a Spokane prostitute who had been missing since 1992. Jackson was arrested for the murder of his and Roseann's nine-year-old daughter Valiree. (In October 2000, he would be convicted of her murder.) Jackson looked like a good suspect in the serial killings. He was connected to Pleasant, Sherry Palmer, and other prostitutes, and he matched the suspect description in the composite flyer from the Barnes homicide. The task force took a blood sample from Jackson, but he was apparently cleared of suspicion in the serial killings.

We were about to see whether the sheriff's department was actually more dedicated to solving the serial killer case than the Spokane PD had been, because they were now in complete control of the investigation.

With the city detectives gone, the task force now consisted of four sheriff's detectives, one detective from the Washington State Police, and a handful of sheriff's administrators (Sergeant Cal Walker, Corporal Dave Reagan, Lieutenant Doug Silver, Captain John Simmons, and Undersheriff Mike Aubrey). To outside observers, it looked as if this case would never be solved, and I wondered whether Sheriff Sterk was going to break up the task force. He had said the task force would be disbanded if they did not have a big break before the fall of 1999. It was now the winter of 2000, and the task force was at half strength. Was the city's departure the first step toward its ultimate dissolution?

On Thursday, February 24, I went into the station to do a show on the shooting of Amadou Diallo in New York City and the growing corruption scandal in the LAPD. There was no news on the serial killer case. No more women were reported missing. No more bodies had been found. The investigation was noticeably quiet. Even the family and friends of the victims were silent. The city's urgency to catch the serial killer now seemed to lag behind the Lincoln Bridge project, the Bloomsday Marathon, or even a Nordstrom white sale.

That Thursday, like every Thursday, I forgot to bring my electronic security card, so I had to go through the front door of KXLY and have the receptionist buzz me in. I grabbed my mail and paycheck, said hello to everybody. That Thursday, like every Thursday, Dominique said, "How are you, Mr. Fuhrman?" Jamie the deejay said, "Fuhrman's here, it must be Thursday." Rick Miller peeked around his cubicle wall to ask me what was on the show today, and I pretended I didn't know yet. Then I went to find Mike, who for some reason was smiling.

"What's up?" I asked.

"Sterk just sent out a press release."

"What, another update on how many clues they haven't had time to get to?"

Mike shook his head, still smiling.

"The task force is holding a town meeting next Monday at the Public Safety Building," Mike said. "They are going to give information and answer questions."

"They've never given any information and never answered any questions before," I said. "What would make you think they're going to start now?"

"Does that mean you don't want to go?"

"Of course I'm going."

We stood in Mike's cubicle with the police scanner chattering in the background. It was all routine stuff, but the radio codes and choppy dialogue brought me back to the years when I was in a police car. Now I was sitting in an office cubicle, listening as it played in the background.

"Why are they holding this meeting?" I asked.

"I have no idea." Mike shrugged. "I guess we'll find out on Monday."

We met at the station following Mike's Monday afternoon show, then drove to the Ram for dinner. The meal quickly turned into another strategy meeting. We had no idea what the task force was up to. We figured they were either desperate for help, or about to disband entirely. Maybe this was the one last push before they simply gave up.

"It doesn't make any sense," Mike said.

"Nothing they ever did made any sense," I replied.

"You think there's another body?"

"We would have heard about it by now," I said. "Do they want to elicit more tips?"

"They're already buried in clues," Mike said.

"Maybe they are trying to draw him out," I said.

"Maybe they want to provoke him to move a body."

"Like Murfin's," I said. "Or they hope he comes to the meeting. They talked to the FBI, who told them to have a big media splash, then photograph the meeting, surveil the parking lot, take down everybody's license plate. But I doubt the FBI said to hold it at the police station."

"Let's take your car," Mike said. "Because you're probably already a suspect."

On the drive over, Mike asked me if planned to ask a lot of questions. I had thought about it and decided that it would be better if I said nothing. The task force probably wanted me to ask questions, especially about the maroon car on Graham Road. They could be setting me up, and I wasn't going to play their game.

Mike understood immediately. After a couple years with me, he had become just a little bit paranoid himself.

"How should we play it?" Mike asked. "Should I ask questions?"

"They know we're partners," I said. "Your asking a question is just the same as if I asked it myself."

There were a lot of questions we did want answered: Why was the task force considering Melody Murfin a homicide? Why wouldn't they release missing person reports? Were Jennifer Joseph and Heather Hernandez con-

nected? What about the 1990 cases? Would the unconnected prostitute homicides ever be cleared?

I've never been afraid to ask questions, but sometimes
you can get answers by just sitting back and listening. If
Mike or I stood up in the town meeting and took on the
task force, then all of a sudden we would be players rather
than observers. We both agreed that we would learn more
by just watching this time. There was a reason the task
force was going against character and holding a public
meeting. If we paid attention, we might be able to figure
out what that reason was.

We arrived at the city-county complex and drove
around for several minutes before we found a legal parking
space (the last thing we needed was a hassle with the
Spokane police). When Mike and I walked up to the city-
county complex, we saw a security officer standing in the
parking lot.

"Why don't you go up to that nice young man," Mike
said, smiling, "and give him your license number."

"No, I'd rather make him work for it."

It was 7:30 P.M. The meeting would start in a half hour,
and the hall was already nearly filled with people. I recognized several of the family members, not just from their
faces in the media, but also by the way they looked and
acted. Though they were dressed more casually than others
in the audience, their faces were serious, even sad. I've dealt
with I don't know how many family members of murder
victims, and whether they're rich or poor, prominent citizens or people living close to the street, there's a grief that's
universal, a wound that will never be healed.

In the front row, I saw a group of middle-aged men
wearing last decade's suits with this year's ties, or else mul-
tifunction sport coats over slacks. These were obviously the
detectives. Seated near them were two well-groomed men
with dark suits, starched white shirts, and conservative ties.

These were obviously FBI. Before we sat down, a police cadet handed Mike and me a flyer with the photos and names of eighteen victims. We looked at each other skeptically. Before this meeting, it had been difficult to get a "good morning" from the police. Now they were handing out flyers.

We sat down near the back, and I tried to make eye contact with Cal Walker. Whether he saw me or not, he wouldn't look at me. The stage area was busy with technicians testing microphones and uniformed deputies milling around, arranging stacks of papers. There were video cameras focused on the stage. I turned around to look at the elevated back row of seats and saw another video camera, this one manned by a deputy who filmed the audience as they entered. Several still photographers walked around, taking shots of the stage and the audience. It was easy to distinguish the media from police photographers and video technicians, as the media had much better equipment, and didn't look so suspicious.

"I just hope that's not the way they do surveillance," I said, pointing out a cop photographer.

"Well, he could always get a job with *Candid Camera*," Mike replied.

The auditorium was about half full when Sheriff Sterk entered from the rear of the stage and walked to a podium, where he shuffled some papers he had brought in with him. He was in uniform, with a gun belt.

The sheriff, Cal Walker, and a couple of detectives had a brief conversation. After conferring with Sterk, Walker started working the first few rows of the crowd, talking to victims' families and members of the media.

Even before the event began, the cops on stage looked very nervous and uncomfortable. The whole town meeting seemed out of character for Spokane law enforcement. It reminded me of Bill Clinton's media events whenever he was dragging in the polls. Only the Spokane cops weren't as skillful as Clinton. I wondered if this was a genuine attempt to help solve the serial killer case, or if it was just media politics.

As he began the meeting, Sterk seemed surprised by the turnout. He said it showed that "this is an important case in this community, and they want us to solve it."

Then there was a series of introductions. Sterk, Cal Walker, Dave Reagan, and John Driscoll, from the county prosecutor's office, all made themselves known to the crowd and then proceeded to warn the audience that while they would be free to ask questions, there would be many questions they simply wouldn't answer.

This was all very strange. If you're not going to answer questions, then why hold the meeting at all? If there are questions you're not going to answer, why not just wait until they're asked?

After introducing all the task force detectives, Sterk turned the meeting over to Dave Reagan, who introduced two FBI agents, a special agent from the Seattle office, and one from the Spokane office. Neither one of the FBI agents had much to offer, and they didn't seem too happy to be there.

Sterk discussed the personnel cuts attributed to I-695. The task force had been basically cut in half. The city detectives had been taken from the task force, and the county was footing the entire bill for the investigation. They had applied for some federal funding, which might be available under recent federal legislation that allowed the FBI to get directly involved in intrastate serial killer cases.

From what Mike and I knew, the relationship between the task force and the feds had been very strained. Between their disastrous January 1998 meeting and now, something had changed. Everybody was at least pretending to get along. We also knew that there had been bad blood between Spokane and Tacoma over the Mercer and Ellis cases, but Cal Walker was now making it sound as if the two jurisdictions were working side by side.

Something else had changed. I remember the victims' families being very upset with the task force. I had spoken to several of them months earlier, and they were not at all happy with the way the task force had conducted its investigation or dealt with them. Now they were very vocal in their support of the task force.

Sterk stated that he and the task force had spoken to the victims' families an hour before the meeting. During the question-and-answer period, several family members stood up, as if on cue, and said that the police were doing a great job. Each one also said that the task force needed more support, specifically more money.

Something had also changed between the task force and the women on Sprague. Cal Walker even admitted it, saying that communication between the police and the prostitute community was leaps and bounds better than it had been before. For nearly two years, there was no rapport whatsoever between the task force detectives and the working girls. We knew that because the girls talked to us about it. They claimed that the police would speak to the women only to hassle them, or to get information about them in order to identify their bodies should they be found dead. The task force detectives had not been seen out on Sprague during the first year of the investigation. Now they had this great relationship with the victim population?

Sterk kept on referring to the task force budget. He asked the audience (the meeting was being televised throughout the Spokane region) to contact the county commissioners and tell them to raise more funds for DNA testing and a crime analyst.

Sterk was lobbying hard for more money. He was a politician, that was his job. After all the talk about money,

Sterk said that even if he didn't get the extra funding, the task force would continue the investigation.

During our June 10 meeting, Sterk stated that the task force was at a dead end, waiting for another body to drop, and ready to be disbanded. Something else had changed.

Sterk admitted that the task force had DNA evidence in nine of the cases. He didn't divulge the source of this DNA evidence—then or now.

Sterk talked about how the task force was confident that this DNA evidence would help them find the killer. I wondered why he was releasing this information. First, he was begging for money. Now he was saying that they just needed to find the right suspect. Maybe it was all just politics. The DNA disclosure was a way for Sterk to get more funding.

Walker stated that they had used DNA to eliminate two thousand suspects. In other words, they had gone into databases for sex offenders, recently released felons, and other available DNA pools. Walker also said that there were $200,000 worth of DNA samples waiting to be tested. If the suspect was a secretor, and they had his blood type, then they didn't need to test every DNA sample. They could eliminate samples through blood type, and then do DNA tests only on samples that matched.

But it sounds better to say you have $200,000 worth of DNA tests waiting to be processed, whether you actually need them processed or not.

This confirmed my suspicions that the task force was leaning on DNA to solve the case for them. Rather than actually investigating these homicides, they were just bringing in suspects, asking for blood samples, and hoping they matched the killer's.

Maybe that's what the meeting was about, I thought.

"They want the suspect to hear this," I whispered to Mike, as he hurriedly jotted down notes. "They want him to react in some manner. Like move another body."

Sterk said that both Brad Jackson and Terry Mangan had been eliminated as suspects. These were not earth-shattering revelations. Mike and I both knew that a blood sample had been taken from Brad Jackson around the time of his arrest. If Jackson had been the killer, the task force would have announced it months ago.

Mangan, on the other hand, was never a serious suspect, at least as far as we knew. Apparently the rumors about his possible involvement were serious enough for them to have taken a blood sample from him. That could have been one reason why the task force was so upset by Chertok's offhand remarks at Ferris High School concerning the tips alleging Mangan's involvement in the homicides. Did the task force really think that the former Spokane police chief could be the serial killer? Or were they just being extra careful?

Once again, old-fashioned detective work could have eliminated Mangan without the embarrassment and expense of a DNA test. He was the chief of police. Just about every minute of his day was accounted for. By comparing Mangan's schedule against the homicide time line, they could have proven he wasn't available for one or more of the murders. Melinda Mercer and Michelyn Derning were both found within days of their deaths. The task force should have been using those approximate dates for alibi questions to eliminate or exclude suspects.

After Chertok's comments, and the unfortunate fallout they provoked, the task force should have formally cleared Mangan. Instead, the rumors persisted for months. Several people had mentioned the possibility of Mangan's involvement in the killings to me, through the radio show and other contacts. The task force did Mangan no favors by waiting until February 2000 to clear him.

The meeting was opened up to the audience. Several people had very good questions. Family members got up and said the task force needed more money.

One person asked about the moving of bodies, specifically the dumping of Linda Maybin's body on April 1, 1998. In response, Cal Walker stated: "We're not aware of a body being moved from point A to point B. That's not saying that it hasn't happened. We're just not aware of it at this point."

That was flat-out ridiculous. I knew that at least Johnson, Wason, and Maybin had been moved. Johnson hadn't lain undetected at the sewage treatment plant for a month. The soil samples from Wason didn't match the site at Fourteenth and Carnahan. If Linda Maybin had been at Fourteenth and Carnahan since late November 1997, the criminalists would have tripped over her body on their way to process the Wason and McClenahan crime scene. The soil samples didn't match, either. Those bodies were moved, and everybody on the task force knew it, including Cal Walker.

One of my radio listeners, whom I hadn't met before, asked Fred Ruetsch about the Mallinson clue.

Ruetsch first stated that the clue was too generic, that if he had followed it up, it would have produced some 25,000 cars. That was ridiculous. Mallinson's description was detailed and precise. I doubted that there were 250 cars matching that description in the area. Then Ruetsch said that he had personally followed up the clue, but he neglected to say that it took him seventeen months to do so. He also didn't say that back in March 1998, when the task force initially said the clue had been followed up, Mallinson had not yet been contacted.

Through the course of the meeting, what surprised me the most was the attitude of apparent humility that Sterk and the task force were constantly assuming. I'd never known them to be humble, and this was the most uncharacteristic aspect of a highly uncharacteristic evening.

"This is a learning experience," Sterk said, referring to

the task force investigation. "We're not like the Los Angeles Police Department."

"We will not do everything perfect," Cal Walker said. "This has been on-the-job training. We had to stop and re-assess what we were doing and how we were doing it, be-cause it appears that we haven't been doing it right."

Walker went on to say that he thought the suspect was in the database, but "we haven't come across the right guy and if we have, we didn't recognize him."

"We're hoping with the information that we release tonight," Sterk said, "that we'll be able to narrow our focus in the investigation."

But they hadn't released any information, aside from the fact that they had DNA evidence. The names, pictures, and time line information that they often referred to was common knowledge to any newspaper reader. I had been saying for more than a year that they had DNA evidence in the cases that they were officially linking to the serial killer. The meeting only confirmed that.

Sterk and Walker both referred the audience repeatedly to the time line, asking them to think about people they knew, and whether they would be available to commit these crimes.

Sterk called for "someone, a friend, a relative, a student, a cabdriver, or a wife," to come forward with information.

"We will solve this case when we run across the right suspect," Sterk said again. "Once you give us the right per-son, we will solve this case."

Then he grimaced and said, "We will catch this killer."

From what I knew of Mark Sterk, he would never make a promise like that unless he already knew it was a lock.

All of a sudden, it came to me. I knew why this meeting had been called in the first place. Why Sterk disclosed that they had DNA evidence. Why he promised that they would catch the killer. Why Cal Walker had suddenly learned to be humble. Why he had said that they knew the killer was in the database. Why relations with the victims' families and the prostitutes on Sprague had all of a sudden gotten so much better.

I leaned over to Mike and whispered, "They've got the suspect."

"Then why don't they arrest the son of a bitch?"

CHAPTER 20

The Arrest

During the late winter and early spring, I had been away on several business trips, mostly associated with the arrest and arraignment of Michael Skakel in the Moxley case. As a result, there was a lot of work to do around the ranch. In addition to the normal spring chores, I also had to get the horses trimmed and shod, and build a fence around the round pen, and finish renovating the bunkhouse.

Meanwhile, business kept distracting me. The phone was ringing constantly, so I started taking it with me around the ranch. Otherwise, I wouldn't get any chores done.

On the morning of April 18, I was out in the front yard, clearing some of the branches that had fallen during the winter storms, when the phone rang. It was Mike, and I could tell from his voice that something really big had happened.

"They've made an arrest at six-thirty this morning," Mike said, his voice charged with excitement. "A guy named Robert Yates."

"Is he the serial killer?"

"I don't know yet. I'll be able to find out more later."

Mike asked me to come on his afternoon radio show

that day, and I agreed. I put the phone down and took a deep breath. If this guy was the serial killer, then all hell was about to break loose. Spokane would be the focus of the kind of media attention it had never experienced before, not even with the Kevin Coe case. This was major, major news. A serial killer with at least a dozen victims—and probably many more—caught by a task force that was severely inexperienced, undermanned, and given hardly any support from the community.

Well, I hoped this guy was the suspect. I wanted to see what he was like. I wanted to learn more about what he did and how he did it, maybe even get a glimpse into why. And now I could finish the book that didn't have an ending before. Most important, the killings would stop.

Later that day, Mike sent me a fax with the latest information on the arrest.

Suspect: Robert Lee Yates, Jr.
White Male Age 47
Address: 2220 East 49th Avenue
Spokane, WA 99222

Yates was arrested around 6:30 A.M. 4/18/00 on North Market Street in Hillyard. He has been charged with 1st Degree Murder . . . "in connection with the death of a prostitute many months ago."

Authorities have seized a vehicle, but have not disclosed what make, color, or model. Police officers have cordoned off an unusually large 10-block area and have been going door to door questioning neighbors. They are saying that they will be investigating this area for several more days.

Authorities have served a search warrant on Yates, and are taking a DNA sample from him at this time. Search warrants have also been served at both the suspect's home and also at his (as yet undisclosed) place of employment.

Later that day, when I got on the radio with Mike, we were truly excited for the task force. I congratulated the detectives on their arrest and stated that it looked like they had done what I had been saying all along: "Solve one, solve them all."

Of course, it was still premature to say that Yates was the serial killer, but the activity surrounding the arrest seemed to indicate that they were looking for evidence connecting him to the other murders. Since they had DNA to match against his sample, once those results came in, the task force would know for certain if Yates was the killer. Right then, Yates had been accused of only one murder of an unnamed prostitute.

Off the air, Mike and I wondered for which murder Yates had been arrested. Apparently, they had really good evidence on one case, and used that to arrest him and to get a blood sample, so they could connect him to the others.

Mike sent me another fax with more detailed information about the suspect.

Robert Lee Yates Born May 27, 1952 in Oak Harbor, Washington

Married (1976)—Wife is Linda D. Yates, formerly of Walla Walla, Washington.

Children: 5 (4 daughters and one son, ages 11–23) . . . Oldest daughter not at home.

Occupation: Presently: Temporary worker—Kaiser Aluminum Mead Work Started: December 1998.

Previously worked for Pantrol, Inc. 2214 East Riverside Avenue

Military: 18-years Active Army—Helicopter Pilot—Warrant Officer for Washington State National Guard Company A, 185th Airborne Battalion—Fort Lewis, Washington—(just completed two-week training camp on Sunday 4-16-00)

Criminal Record: No Previous Convictions . . . In 1998 Yates was arrested in connection with assault (non-sexual) of his 19-year-old daughter during a domestic dispute . . . Charges dropped . . . 4-18-00 . . . Charged with one count of First Degree Murder.

Vehicles: Yates liked to work on old cars . . . Owns a blue Honda Accord . . . Older Plymouth Road Runner . . . Once owned a 1977 Chevrolet Corvette which he sold in 1999. That vehicle was where blood samples were obtained, that led to the break in the case. A Honda Accord is also under police impound.

Key Evidence: Blood residue and a button found in the Corvette is that of one Jennifer Joseph, whose body was found on August 26, 1997. Also—a search warrant was served on the suspect and a blood sample taken. The Washington State Patrol Crime Lab in Spokane says the blood DNA matches DNA obtained from twelve other victims.

Preliminary Court Appearance Wednesday April 19 at 2:00 P.M. $1.5 million cash bond imposed. Arraignment likely to be delayed pending filing of more counts.

Even this basic information provided me with a lot to think about. Yates grew up in Oak Harbor, a small town on Whidbey Island, just up the Puget Sound from Seattle. He was a replacement worker at the Kaiser Mead plant, working in an aluminum smelter and training as a crane operator. After eighteen years in the Army, he left before full retirement and now served as a helicopter pilot for the

Army National Guard. He was in the sixty-sixth Aviation Brigade, which trains once a month in Tacoma and had served on guard duty during the time periods when Melinda Mercer and Connie LaFontaine Ellis were killed.

Not only was he familiar with western Washington, but he was available in Tacoma for at least the Mercer and Ellis homicides. I would bet that he had also been in the Seattle-Tacoma area, whether on Army duty or visiting family, around the time Barnes was killed.

Yates was a helicopter pilot for the National Guard. Hadn't the National Guard provided the helicopters and pilots for the task force's February and April 1998 FLIR fly-overs? And hadn't the second flyover, after the dumping of Murfin's body, been suggested by the flight crew themselves? A couple weeks after the arrest, I asked Mark Sterk himself if Yates had been one of the helicopter pilots. Sterk told me that they didn't know yet. Well, it was an easy enough question to answer; all they had to do was check the flight plans, or just ask whoever went up with the helicopter.

Even if Yates hadn't flown one of the helicopters himself, he would be able to speak to the pilots who did, and certainly could have gotten a great deal of information and insight into the task force investigation.

Yates didn't have a criminal record. That was one detail that didn't exactly match the suspect profile I had done on an early radio show. I wasn't surprised. Often serial killers are able to keep their records clean, because their only criminal activities are associated with the murders.

Yates was married with five children. The assault charges against his daughter were evidence of domestic violence. The fact that he could maintain a family life, however dysfunctional it might have been, while killing more than a dozen women, indicated a highly developed sexual psychopathology.

FUHRMAN: What do you say to your father once you know he's killed twelve women?

FITZSIMMONS: If it were a family member of mine, and I know it would be a hope against hope, but I would want him to tell me he didn't do it. I'd want to believe that. People often believe their loved ones are innocent, even in the face of overwhelming evidence.

FUHRMAN: You go from normal one day to my father, my husband, my brother is one of the most infamous serial killers in the last thirty years. Robert Yates knows what he did or didn't do, whether he's completely without a conscience or what. But his family doesn't have the same tools to deal with this kind of evil.

The Yates family expressed their support of Robert in a letter distributed to the media: "Bobby is a loving, caring and sensitive son; a fun-loving and giving brother; and an understanding, generous and dedicated father, who enjoys playing ball, fishing, and camping with his kids. Bobby is the type of person you would want to have for your best friend."

That's the person they saw, or wanted to see. Bobby's victims saw someone quite different.

The serial killer is evil walking like a man. And sometimes he can walk among us and no one will suspect him. Ted Bundy was very active in Republican politics in the Seattle area—many thought he could run for office himself. John Wayne Gacy served as director of the Polish Constitution Day parade in 1978, where he was photographed with then First Lady Rosalynn Carter. And Gacy dressed up as Pogo the Clown, performing in local charity circuses and visiting sick children in hospitals. Working as a freelance photographer taking class pictures in local schools, Wayne Williams walked in and out of the very classrooms where police had just been warning students about the Atlanta child murderer.

The mask of sanity can hide the face of a killer so effectively that even his family doesn't recognize it. Sexual psychopaths can switch back and forth between their sickness and the world around them, camouflaging themselves like chameleons to blend in with their environment.

Somehow Robert Yates was able to live both lives. He could be married, raise five children, hold down a job, fly helicopters for the National Guard. And at the same time, he was picking up prostitutes and killing them.

Robert Yates Jr. grew up on Whidbey Island, in the Puget Sound. He was the third generation of his mother's family to live on the island, which is connected to the mainland by a bridge over Deception Pass. At the south end, a twenty-minute ferry ride gets you to Mukilteo, just north of Seattle.

At least on the surface, it appears that Yates had a normal Pacific Northwest childhood. He was very active in sports and the outdoors. He rode a Honda motorcycle, hunted black-tailed deer, and fished for coho salmon. During the summer, Yates worked on farms over on the mainland, picking peas. He was a good athlete, pitching for the Little League team that his father coached, then for the Oak Harbor Wildcats and Skagit Valley Junior College in Mount Vernon. He had a 7–1 record in his junior year of high school and also earned a letter in football.

The Yates family lived in a dormered home overlooking the water. His father was a civilian employee at Whidbey Island Naval Air Station. His mother, Anna Mae, was head of housekeeping at Whidbey General Hospital. Yates had three sisters. One of Yates's uncles was a farmer. Another uncle had an airplane and his own landing strip, which piqued Robert's interest in flying.

Yates's father was an elder and his mother a deaconess in the Seventh-Day Adventist Church. It was a small congregation of fewer than one hundred people. Robert Jr. helped his father and other parishioners rebuild the church after a fire.

Neighbors in Oak Harbor called him Bobby to distinguish him from his father.

"This is a kid who was never in trouble," family friend George Cantrell told the *Spokesman-Review*. "He was always practicing his upbringing—and it was a good one."

"He didn't drink. He didn't smoke," childhood friend Al Gatti said. "We didn't give in to peer pressure, that wasn't our thing. Our thing was hunting and fishing and hiking."

Robert Jr. graduated from Oak Harbor High School in 1970. "I really can't remember him ever being mad," classmate Harry Ferrier told the newspaper. "He was easygoing and well-liked by the rest of the students, by the faculty."

According to classmates, Yates always had a girlfriend in high school, but he didn't have a date for the senior prom.

Yates attended Skagit Valley College from 1970 until 1972, earning an associate's degree in general studies.

In the mid-1970s, his mother was stricken with cancer. Robert Sr. would drive his wife into Seattle four times a week for treatments. Anna Mae died in 1976. Before her death, she suggested that her husband marry the widowed wife of a family friend. Robert Sr. followed that advice and moved to Arizona with his new wife.

After two years of premed studies at Walla Walla College, Yates married Linda Brewer in 1977. Brewer was a local girl, the daughter of a prison guard. Yates enlisted in the Army shortly after getting married.

In the Army, Yates trained as a helicopter pilot and eventually taught other pilots. He was reportedly quiet, methodical, and patient. After serving eighteen years, being stationed in Germany, Fort Hood, Alabama, and Fort Drum, New York, Yates left the Army two years short of retirement.

The Yates family moved to Spokane in April 1996. At

first they rented a home in the quiet, upscale neighborhood of South Hill. They later bought a house in the same neighborhood. Their house was in the south end of the neighborhood, where the homes are more modest. Driving from the Yates home, it is a straight shot down Freya Road to get to the prostitute district of East Sprague. The Hangman Valley and Fourteenth and Carnahan dump sites are also nearby.

Once they moved to Spokane, Yates had trouble finding work. In the summer of 1998, he was laid off from his job at Pantrol, whose offices were near the East Sprague district and where the body of Michelyn Derning was found. In December 1998, he took a job as a strikebreaker at the Kaiser Aluminum plant, making $13.75 an hour as a crane operator.

A family friend said that one of Yates's daughters complained that her father was frequently gone from the house. Yates's neighbors in South Hill said that he and his family were quiet and polite. One neighbor, a native German, said that Yates once spoke to her in rudimentary German. Several neighbors reported that they often saw Robert Yates washing his cars, even in winter. One neighbor stated that he washed his cars "excessively." It was also reported that Yates had a cab-over camper in the front yard for some time, although no vehicle matching that description was ever registered to him. The task force issued several press releases looking for this vehicle. They apparently thought that he used the camper as a satellite location where he might have taken his victims or stored their possessions and other evidence, including the weapons used to kill them.

Yates reportedly owned several handguns, including a .25-caliber automatic, but none of the weapons were found when his house was searched. Yates was interested in computers, but reportedly refused to connect to the Internet because he didn't want his children exposed to pornography. When his house was searched, several pornographic videotapes were reportedly found.

Following his arrest, Robert Yates was held on suicide watch at Spokane County Jail. The Yates family was moved to a local hotel while police searched their house. The sheriff's department took the family shopping at Target to buy new clothes. A local high school forwarded math and science homework for one Yates daughter, and an elementary school sent homework for Yates's son. Before their homework arrived, the Yates children spent a morning swimming in the hotel pool.

Linda Yates and her four daughters visited Robert in jail, but his son did not come to visit him. His two sisters, Shirley Hess of Deer Park, Washington, and Linda Welsh of Basin, Montana, also visited Robert. Once they were able to get back their possessions, the Yateses were planning to move to Walla Walla, where Linda still had family.

On April 21, 2000, Sheriff Sterk announced that DNA evidence linked Yates to nine murders, and that they expected more extensive DNA testing would connect him to three more. The nine connected victims were Jennifer Joseph, Darla Sue Scott, Melinda Mercer, Shawn Johnson, Laurie Wason, Shawn McClenahan, Sunny Oster, Linda Maybin, and Michelyn Derning. The three victims that had not yet been linked to Yates were Connie LaFontaine Ellis, Shannon Zielinski, and Heather Hernandez.

That meant the DNA on the nine connected victims was easily identifiable through preliminary DNA tests, a low-percentage DNA test that is cheaper, faster, and more accessible to local agencies and is used for preliminary identification. The DNA evidence for the other three victims probably needed more sensitive DNA testing, which required more time.

Immediately after the arrest, the Spokane PD reassigned

two detectives to the task force. Some thirty law enforcement agencies began investigating Yates for homicides in their jurisdictions. Federal police in Germany investigating the deaths of twenty-six prostitutes requested a DNA sample from Yates, who had been stationed on Army bases in Germany from 1990 to 1992. Local law enforcement agencies in Watertown, New York, and Dothan, Alabama, where Yates had also been stationed, contacted the task force in connection with several prostitute homicides.

Even if he had been responsible for all this carnage—dozens and dozens of murders—the more I learned about Robert Yates, the more ordinary he seemed, at least on the surface.

Yates had a religious upbringing in a small town. His family were Seventh-Day Adventists. He grew up hunting and fishing and playing ball.

Yates liked to work on cars, and owned several hot rods. Police surveilled Yates while he played catch with his son in the front yard. When arrested, he was driving a Honda Civic, with a bumper sticker that read, "Why must I be surrounded by frickin' idiots?"

I knew that over the following months, or even years, I would be hearing all sorts of explanations about why Robert Yates became a serial killer. A repressive upbringing. Stresses within his own family, particularly with his wife and four daughters. Guilt about his relations with prostitutes. Impotence and/or priapism. A head injury. Chemical imbalance. Whatever.

Maybe some of these theories will be at least partially accurate. But ultimately we will never know why a man would shoot a woman, have sex with her dead body, and dump her by the side of the road.

Robert Yates himself doesn't know.

We feel that if we could understand a serial killer, or at

least be able to explain him, somehow he won't be so threatening. He won't be so much like us.

Evil is a force of nature. Try as we might to understand, control, correct, eliminate, or ignore it, evil will always be with us. It's like the weather. Maybe you understand the elemental composition of a thunderhead. Maybe you don't. Either way, when it passes overhead, you better get inside before the lightning strikes.

We're not any closer to understanding the mind of a sexual psychopath than we were thirty years ago, when very little was known about them. In fact, the more we know about serial killers, the more there are.

Tony Bamonte has documented a serial killer who murdered some twenty victims in Coeur d'Alene, Idaho, at the turn of the last century. A fifteenth-century French nobleman who fought alongside Joan of Arc was one of the most prolific serial killers in recorded history, snatching hundreds of young girls and boys from his village, then torturing, molesting, and killing them.

In the 1960s and 1970s, the concept of serial killing came into being. The more attention serial killers like the Boston Strangler, Son of Sam, and Ted Bundy received in the media, the more serial killers there seemed to be. Now there are serial killer groupies and fan clubs. The Internet has sites devoted to the worship of serial killers, where you can buy one of John Gacy's paintings or get a tape of Charles Manson playing guitar in a prison hospital.

Serial killers are made, not born. And society helps create them. We have built a stage for these misfits to play on, and given them a persona for them to adopt. Then we are surprised when they don't fit the role we've developed for them.

Hollywood has created a caricature of the serial killer, most notably Hannibal Lecter in *Silence of the Lambs* and the killer played by Kevin Spacey in *Seven*. Hannibal Lecter is a psychiatrist who speaks several languages, paints Florentine landscapes, and listens to Bach's *Goldberg Variations* while he's killing his victims. He's so efficient that he can take the clip from a ballpoint pen and use it to break out of a maximum security prison, proceed to kill several people, and end up eating someone's liver in Haiti.

The serial killer has become a mythic figure—our modern-day Frankenstein or Dracula, a monster created by society's own fears projected onto a single, grotesque creature. And when we discover that the monster is just a man, we're disappointed.

Why are we so fascinated by serial murder? For me it was a puzzle, the ultimate challenge to a homicide detective, whether I wore a badge and a gun, or had a microphone and a laptop computer. I found myself falling into the same trap that everyone else did.

When the Spokane suspect did not have a face, and he was just a specter killing women and dumping their bodies and through his actions taunting the police, I wanted him to be the most evil, cunning, and intelligent killer there ever was. I wanted him to live among rotting body parts of his victims, his walls full of press clippings and drawers filled with mementos. I wanted him to shock and disgust me. I wanted to be awestruck by his crimes.

When the task force released no information concerning these cases, Mike and I were left to speculate, and our speculations had a tendency toward the more bizarre, the more pathological, the more cunning.

Listening to those early radio shows again, I was struck by my own tunnel vision.

Darla Sue Scott was found partially buried near a golf course. A little more than a month later, Shawn Johnson was dumped about a mile away. I approached these two cases thinking that nothing could be just as it seemed, there were no simple or obvious answers. So I began thinking that the killer cherished Scott and simply threw Johnson away. I had read about many other serial killers who had relationships with their victims after death, revisiting their graves, keeping trophies, even exhuming them and having sex with their rotting bodies.

As it turns out, the best reason I can find for his dumping Shawn Johnson was that he had already killed at least five women, and nobody was giving him any credit. A newspaper article appeared on December 17, stating that Shawn Johnson was still missing. The police did not seem very active on the case. No one wanted to link the recent prostitute murders to a single suspect. So Yates exhumed Shawn Johnson from wherever she had been buried and dumped her where he knew she would be found, with a plastic bag on her head, just like Scott and Palmer. He was tired of being ignored. He wanted the media, the police, and the public to be part of his game.

And we played along with him.

As I speculated about the case on the radio, I often found myself spinning out a theory that only the killer would be able to contradict. And if he ever was caught, why would he want to be less interesting?

I imagined that he was keeping his victims alive for days or weeks before finally killing them. That he had two or more of them alive together. That he killed one while he made the other watch. That he was using heroin as a lure, but also as a way to keep them incapacitated. Maybe he was even using withdrawal as a form of torture.

We all wanted the serial killer to have supernatural powers. The police wanted him to be a genius, so they wouldn't be humiliated if they didn't catch him. The public and the press wanted him to rank high on the ghoul meter, so we would have something interesting to talk about.

When the bodies started turning up, I wanted everything the killer did to be a message. I wanted every piece of evidence to be a window into his mind, every detail a riddle for me to unravel. Instead of seeing him clearly as a disorganized psychopath, I wanted his every movement to fit into some smooth master plan. Mike and I spent hours trying to figure out if the plastic bags were signature or MO. We wanted to think that the bags gave him some perverse sexual thrill, that he was dehumanizing his victims, or that perhaps he was using the bags to partially asphyxiate them. In the end, the truth was that he didn't want them to bleed inside his vehicle.

The victims he killed were in various stages of undress (some clothed, some nude, some partially disrobed, others with their clothing strewn around them). But most of them were barefoot. At first I thought that the shoes were a fetish item, kept and cherished by the killer as mementos. Then I wondered if he was keeping them captive somewhere they could not escape without shoes—in a room with broken glass scattered around their beds, or somewhere deep in the wilderness where they wouldn't be able to walk far or fast in bare feet.

After the arrest of Robert Yates, I realized the more mundane but also most probable explanation. He was having sex with these women. In order to take their clothes off, they would first have to remove their shoes. Once they were naked and whatever sex act was consummated (or not, as we discovered that part of Yates's anger toward women was related to his periodic impotence), he would kill them. Then he would either keep the shoes, throw them onto the dump site, or dispose of them elsewhere.

As this book goes to press, the task force is still looking for many of the victims' shoes and clothing. They haven't found a satellite location where he kept them captive or stored his trophies. Maybe he didn't have one. Maybe Yates's MO was, as one senior police official described it, simply: "Rape 'em. Shoot 'em. Dump 'em. Or shoot 'em. Rape 'em. Dump 'em. Depending on how he felt."

Yates fit only the most generic of profiles. He was a white male, age forty-seven, a little bit older than most serial killers—but then he had been working for some time.

He didn't look like Ted Bundy. He wasn't educated like Hannibal Lecter. He didn't have body parts in his refrigerator, like Jeffrey Dahmer. He didn't have his mother's skeleton propped up in a rocking chair in the basement, like Norman Bates.

Yates was anything but special. In fact, he was so ordinary that nobody suspected him—not the prostitutes who knew him as a regular, or the police who had him documented as a john.

Following Yates's arrest, several prostitutes came forward and described him as a regular customer. One woman who called herself "Mary" stated that she saw Yates cruising East Sprague on numerous occasions, both in his white Corvette and a blue Honda. Mary thought that Yates could have been caught a lot sooner if detectives had shared information about a white Corvette possibly being involved in the Joseph homicide.

"It was the only white Corvette I've ever seen out there," Mary, who had worked East Sprague for ten years, told the *Spokesman-Review.* "He would stand right out on the street in front of everybody. The police officers would drive by and wave at me while I was talking to him."

Profiler John Douglas says, "Your greatest partner in solving any crime of violence is the public. Somebody has seen something. Somebody knows something. Undoubtedly many people have seen this perpetrator and looked right through him."

That was true of even Yates's own family.

On the day her husband was arrested, Linda Yates told detectives that sometime in the fall of 1996, her husband drove her daughter to work at Certified Security Systems, located at Sprague and Napa. They left around 11:00 P.M. At 2:30 A.M. her husband still hadn't returned home, so she locked the door. At 6:30 A.M., Linda woke up to hear Robert banging on the front door. When she opened the door, he was dressed in coveralls. He retrieved cleaning supplies from the house and started cleaning the fold-down bed in the back of his black Chevy Sport van.

He told his wife that he had been driving down the road and accidentally hit a dog. He said he loaded the dog in the back of the van and took it to a veterinarian—that's why the cushion was covered with blood. He later told his daughter a slightly different story. Shortly after that incident, Linda Yates sold her husband's van.

Could that be the murder of JoAnn Flores? She was found on November 7, 1996, dead from a gunshot wound to the head. The police won't discuss the Flores case. They won't even release her cause of death, even though it's public record.

On August 1, 1998, Spokane prostitute Christine Smith filed a police report for assault and robbery. She had been picked up by a john in a 1970s-era black van with an exterior yellow-orange stripe, bucket seats, interior wood paneling, and a raised bed in the back. She got in the van and they drove to an empty parking lot. They both went to the back of the van. She began performing oral sex on him, but he couldn't maintain an erection. Suddenly, Smith felt a blow to the head. She thought the man had hit her. "What are we doing here, Christine?" the man asked, surprised to see her crawling toward the door. She escaped from the van and went to Sacred Heart Hospital, where she was treated for head trauma. In her police report, Smith described her assailant as a man about fifty years old, five feet ten, 175 pounds, with sandy blond hair. Before she got in the van, Smith asked, "You're not the psycho killer, are you?"

"I wouldn't do that," he replied. "I've got five kids."

He also said he was a National Guard helicopter pilot.

I remember hearing about this attempted robbery and assault, and figuring that the task force had investigated it and found it to be unrelated. The task force had investigated a South Hill doctor in April 1999 for kidnapping, assault, and robbery of another prostitute. The doctor was subsequently cleared of suspicion in the serial killings, but that led me to believe the task force routinely investigated assaults on prostitutes.

In March 2000, Christine Smith was involved in a car accident. During treatment at a hospital, doctors found bullet fragments embedded in her scalp. Apparently, Christine Smith had been shot with a small-caliber handgun. An empty .25-caliber shell casing, several bloodstains, and a spent bullet were found during the search of a van owned by Robert Yates that matched the description Smith had given police.

BOB KEPPEL: The suspect can be invisible, but the information might be already in the police's hands. They have so much data in serial cases. In the cases I've been around and looked at and analyzed, it's amazing how they have the data on this guy in the very beginning of the case.

Once they caught him, Sheriff Sterk said that he wanted to know what made Yates stop killing.

Between August and December 1997, the Spokane serial killer was in a highly active phase. Joseph, Hernandez, Scott, Johnson, Wason, McClenahan, Oster, and Maybin were probably all killed before Christmas 1997.

In June 1998, Yates was laid off from his job at Pantrol, located at 2214 East Riverside in Spokane. Soon after that, Derning's body was found near the Pantrol offices. Task force detectives speculated that the Derning kill was a statement by the killer to his former employers. In one detective's words, "It was a fuck-you kill."

In August, Christine Smith was shot in the head and escaped from his van. Sometime after that, Connie LaFontaine Ellis was abducted and killed. But Ellis carried a .380 automatic. And she apparently got a shot off at her attacker. A .380 bullet was recovered at the crime scene. Ellis was shot with a .25-caliber bullet.

On November 12, Yates was charged with domestic violence against his daughter Amber. The fight was ongoing when police arrived at their home. "He hits me all the time," Amber told police. Yates was arrested, but not booked, and the charge was reduced to fourth-degree misdemeanor assault.

Things were getting hot for Yates, and he might have decided to cool off. Even after all this, he was still patronizing prostitutes in Spokane as late as March 1999, when Cheryl Siekerman's boyfriend took down his license plate number after Siekerman got into Yates's Honda.

We will probably never know why he stopped killing. Or if he ever did. Jennifer Joseph and Heather Hernandez had just come into town when he picked them up and killed them. How do we know that Yates didn't cruise Sprague looking for recent arrivals? He could have killed only women he knew wouldn't be missed, and dumped their bodies somewhere they would never be found.

And there are still at least five other body finds that the Spokane authorities have never identified, classified, or accounted for. The skeleton at Seventh and Sherman. The corpse floating by the Carousel. The skeleton at Quincy Lakes. Jennifer Justus in Snoqualmie. The decomposed body found at Mount Spokane. And who knows how many others? How many missing women? How many dead ones?

Robert Yates will probably never tell us. Will Sheriff Sterk?

When Yates made his first court appearance, I did a call-in from home onto Mike's show. KXLY had a live audio feed from the courtroom, so I could hear the proceedings in the background, and recognized the familiar drone of court business—the mumblings of the bailiff, the shuffling of papers, the sound of footsteps. There was an audible reaction when Yates walked in, and I heard the judge address Yates directly. He responded in a calm, emotionless voice. The sound of him talking was like a wet, cold wind.

The next day, the newspaper photographs showed Robert Lee Yates Jr. standing in front of the judge, wearing eyeglasses and an old sweatshirt over his bulletproof vest, looking weary and middle-aged and pathetic. I was glad the police had caught him. The fact that he was so ordinary only made me wonder why they hadn't caught him a long time ago.

CHAPTER 21

Second Thoughts

When I heard that Robert Yates had initially been arrested for the murder of Jennifer Joseph, I was surprised. Mike and I had always thought she was linked to the other victims, but the case didn't seem to have the obvious connections, or as much evidence as the later victims. Even though Joseph was always included in lists of possible victims, the task force had never officially connected her to the other victims. This indicated that there was no DNA evidence, and perhaps the ballistics were different.

If that were the case, then the task force would need to make another connection between Joseph and the other homicides. Perhaps that connection would be the suspect himself.

As soon as Mike got the arrest affidavit, he faxed it over. While my fax machine started spewing the affidavit, I read each page as it came out. The affidavit showed that the Joseph case hinged on a couple of important clues that, once connected, identified Robert Yates as the suspect. On August 16, 1997, at 11:35 P.M., Jennifer Joseph was seen by Yolanda Carey, another prostitute, getting into a white Corvette driven by a white male aged thirty to forty. On September 24, 1997, Robert Yates had been pulled over on

East Sprague driving a white Corvette. On November 10, 1998, he had been pulled over again in the area, with a known prostitute in his car. On September 15, 1999, Yates was brought in for questioning by task force detectives. He was noted to have the same hair color as was found on evidence retrieved from the Joseph case. He didn't have a good alibi for a couple of key dates on the time line. He refused to give a blood sample. The task force detectives found his Corvette, which now belonged to a different owner. Under a voluntary search, they took fibers from the carpet in that car, which turned out to match fibers found on Jennifer Joseph's clothing. Using this as probable cause, they executed a search warrant on the Corvette, which produced a cuff button that matched one on Joseph's jacket and blood that showed a close, though not conclusive, match to Joseph's.

This looked like good police work. The clues were pretty thin, but the task force worked them hard and made a connection between Joseph and the suspect. They put Joseph in his car just prior to her death, and they found evidence of at least an altercation with her in that same car. Since they had DNA evidence on nine of the other victims, but not Joseph, they could use the Joseph case to connect Yates to at least her murder. Then they could use the Joseph arrest as probable cause to obtain a blood sample for comparison to the DNA found on the other nine victims.

On the air, Mike was in his element, a veteran newsman working one of the biggest stories of his life.

I heard the click that signaled I was on the air:

FITZSIMMONS: Mark Fuhrman has agreed to join me again to talk about the arrest and the affidavit of probable cause. Mark, what is your read of the arrest warrant?

FUHRMAN: Well, I have to say that I'm impressed. It looks like some pretty good police work. They connected

fibers from the Joseph case to a car owned by Yates and
then through blood recovered from the car connected
Joseph to the car.

FITZSIMMONS: Everybody knows we have had our problems with the task force, and we had been at times critical of their work, or what we knew of it, but it looks like
they were doing a lot we didn't know about.

FUHRMAN: Absolutely. They were really working this case,
and I expect they'll connect Yates up to the other homicides and clear about a dozen cases.

After my appearance on Mike's show, I had planned to
go back out and finish repairing the fences in the front pasture, but I wanted to take another look at the affidavit, so I
would have it fresh in my mind as I worked, and I could
think about it some more.

I began to read the affidavit again. The facts remained
the same but this time something caught my attention. The
first two paragraphs began with dates: "On 08/26/97 . . ."
"On 08/28/97 . . ." But the next few paragraphs didn't. As I
read those subsequent paragraphs again, I realized that the
author of this document neglected to mention the dates
associated with these events. It was odd, because the affidavit seemed to be a very carefully written document.

On the next page, every paragraph had dates. I shrugged
off my earlier questions. If it had been a big deal, the prosecutor or judge would have noticed the omissions and
asked the affiant to include this information. It was probably not anything worth thinking about.

I went back out to the pasture and finished repairing the
fences. As I was working, the questions kept gnawing at
me. This was probably the most important affidavit the affiant ever wrote. Certainly other detectives and administrators from the task force had read and reread the document.
Then the prosecutor. Then the judge. I figured I was just

being obsessive, overly critical. The task force had done their job. They had identified the suspect and arrested him. That was all that mattered.

Prior to going on the radio for my own show, I called Sheriff Sterk. I wanted to congratulate him on a job well done and clear the air between us. It had been several months since we had last talked, and I had been very critical of him and the task force since our discussions over the summer. I also wanted to get him on the radio show, and hopefully be able to interview him in depth for the final chapter of the book.

A secretary answered the phone. I asked to speak with the sheriff. She politely informed me that he was in a meeting and asked if she could take a message. I gave her my name and was about to hang up when she asked me to wait. In a few seconds Sterk's voice came on the line.

"Congratulations, your guys did a great job," I said, right off the bat. I don't think Sterk was expecting me to be so positive, but I meant it. "Listen, I haven't finished my book yet, and now I've got a happy ending. You're going to look like a real hero, and you'll probably be sheriff for a long time."

"Thanks," Sterk replied, a little cautiously.

I assumed that now that the killer was caught, the information would be less sensitive to confirm. I could sense tension, uneasy gaps between sentences, language that seemed too thought out, or maybe labored upon too long.

"Before we can do anything for you," Sterk said, "you owe my task force an apology. You were pretty hard on them last year."

I couldn't disagree with him.

"Listen to the show," I said.

Nobody wants to be wrong, but this was different. It had nothing to do with being right or wrong. I couldn't argue with the results. They had caught the killer, and that was all that mattered. I wanted to repair our relations with Sterk and the task force. Also, I genuinely felt that they had done a good job and deserved praise.

When I went on the air that afternoon, the first thing I did was apologize for second-guessing their investigation. In fact, I went on for so long that Mike started making faces at me. I sincerely believed what I was saying. But there were certain things I wouldn't apologize for. I was a journalist, and it was my job to seek information that the public had a right to know. I was supposed to ask tough questions, and without any answers it was difficult for me to come to conclusions other than the ones I had expressed on the air.

After I was finished eating crow, several listeners called in to say that there was no reason for me to apologize. They said that Mike and I helped keep the case alive, and probably spurred the task force into doing a better job.

I knew what it was like to be criticized by the media. Although I tried to keep my questions about the task force professional and pertinent to the case, I couldn't help remembering how it felt to be on the other side.

After the radio show, I drove back to Idaho, hoping I would get to Sandpoint in time to catch the end of my son's soccer practice. I stopped at a gas station in Elk, Washington. While I was at the station, I filled up my travel mug with coffee and sat in the truck for a minute. I was tired and still had a long drive ahead of me. I found myself thinking about the affidavit. I had a copy with me, so I started reading it again. Then I read it again. And again. And again.

The more I read the affidavit, the more the same question came back to me. What problem did they have with these dates? When did the witness who saw Joseph get into the white Corvette come forward? When did the police get blood samples from Joseph's parents? Why did Yates's name come up? When did they match him up to the white Corvette?

I looked at my watch and realized I had just spent thirty-five minutes sitting in a gas station parking lot with my engine running. If I didn't hurry, I would miss soccer practice entirely. I drove off, but the questions didn't go away.

Later that night, I read the affidavit again, this time looking at it with the eyes of a detective, not a journalist. I examined each paragraph in isolation. Some of them were crisp and clean and detailed. Others were suspiciously evasive. I didn't put anything to paper, just read and reread the document and tried to think like its author. Why did he use this word instead of that one? Why did he reveal certain facts and details and not others? Why did he state these events in this particular order?

The more I scrutinized this document, the more questions I had. If the affidavit was flawed, then what did that say about the case itself? Part of me didn't want to find anything wrong with this case. The book was almost done, and it would be easy enough just to write the happy ending and send it off to the publishers. The last thing I wanted to do was take on another police department, but I had to follow the evidence, wherever it led.

I needed some kind of corroboration, so I called Steve Weeks. Without giving him any indication of my opinion, I asked him what he thought of the affidavit. He said the same thing I had been thinking, that the dates were squishy. Why would they mention some dates and not others? We started talking, and immediately I knew that we couldn't leave this alone. I had seen it happen before. The Simpson case went sideways because the Robbery-Homicide detectives and the prosecutors were unwilling to admit mistakes. The Moxley murder was unsolved for twenty-three years for many of the same reasons. Sure, the

Spokane Task Force had found their man. Then why did they act as though they were hiding something? I didn't know what it was, but I had to find out.

Before dawn, I got out of bed and made my first pot of coffee. I intentionally did not read the affidavit again until I had done all the morning chores. When I got back in the house, I saw the document sitting there on the kitchen table. Before picking it up, I stared out the window. Watching the sun rise over the Cabinet Mountains, I could feel one question looming above all the others.

When did the white Corvette clue come in?

I needed to answer this question before I could go any further. I could read the affidavit until I went cross-eyed, but that document didn't tell me what I really needed to know. If the witness who saw Jennifer Joseph get into that white Corvette didn't come forward until late 1999 or early 2000, then it wasn't that much of a problem; but if the clue had come in immediately following the discovery of Joseph's body on August 26, 1997, then something was seriously wrong, and that might be what that document was trying to hide.

On April 27, Mike and I met with Sheriff Sterk at the radio station. Sterk had already gotten the apology from me, and he would probably not give us any more information than anyone else who was following the case. That didn't matter. I was sick of asking questions that I knew would never get answered. So this time I walked into the meeting with just one question. It was the only question I cared about, and I would not let Sterk leave that room until he gave me an answer. I needed to know when the Yolanda Carey clue came into the task force.

We all went into the conference room at KXLY. Sterk began the meeting by telling Mike and me that cooperating on the book would be a delicate issue, since at least two other people had plans to write their own books, and he would have to balance all our demands equally. He was also very concerned about compromising the anticipated trial, and said that any information would have to first be cleared through Steve Tucker, the Spokane County prosecutor who was in charge of the Yates case.

At this point, I didn't care what Sterk would or would not give us. It didn't matter that two other people were writing books. I was concerned only with the affidavit and, specifically, the Yolanda Carey clue.

Sterk's mouth kept moving, and sounds were coming out of it, but I paid no attention to him. I could tell he was uncomfortable, and trying hard to maintain a professional demeanor, but he was obviously afraid of something.

I told Sterk that I understood the difficulty of releasing information, and then, almost like an afterthought, I mentioned the Carey clue.

"Hey, good thing Yolanda Carey came forward in 1997, that was a great clue."

"Yeah," Sterk said. "It was a great clue."

"It made your case, once you connected it to Yates's traffic stop."

Sterk's body language became even more visibly nervous. He shifted in his seat and wouldn't look me in the eyes.

"So you guys got the Carey clue in 1997 and the Yates field interview was in the task force clues," I said, trying to look him right in the eyes, but he kept staring at the top of the conference table. "It was just a matter of getting through the hundreds of clues, right?"

"Yeah, basically," Sterk said, hesitantly.

I looked at Mike, who gave me a quick, sly smile. We had just committed the task force to the date that they wouldn't mention in the affidavit—because it had taken them two years to follow up on the clue.

Sterk must have had some glimmer of what was going

on, because he kept talking, just like a suspect who knows he's caught dead to rights and now tries to implicate someone else.

"Cal Walker prioritized the clues as they came in and they went into a stack. When we finally got to the Yates field interview, it all came together."

That was all I needed, but I figured I'd ask about Carey to make Sterk think that I was more interested in her than in the investigative time line.

"How is Carey?" I asked. "Will she be a good witness? Can you even find her?"

Sterk responded positively to both questions, and then I mentally checked out. The meeting went on for several minutes, but I have no idea what else was said. Sterk and Mike went back and forth about the trial, but Mike was just playing decoy. Sterk left a little less nervous than he had been.

What Sterk had revealed was that the task force had sat on a couple of clues for two years. During that time, at least nine women had died. Whether it was laziness, incompetence, or just simple human error, the task force could have caught Yates back in September 1997.

Around this time, I had a phone conversation with John Douglas about Spokane. John was the FBI profiler in the 1990 homicides, which my sources in the task force were now saying were not serial killings, but drug related. This seemed like more retroactive history from the task force, and I wanted to talk to someone who could give me a straight answer. And John did, telling me that there was no indication that the three 1990 homicides were anything but the work of a serial killer.

This wasn't a formal interview, just two cops talking. I gave him a detailed briefing on what I had discovered in the Spokane case. We talked more about Yates, the task force investigation, and the book I was writing. I asked him

what the task force should have done with the Yolanda
Carey clue.

"The clue should have been given to the public almost
immediately," John said. "That's a great lead."

I wasn't looking for confirmation or corroboration.
Maybe I just wanted to be certain that my perspective
hadn't been slanted by the events of the past couple of
years. Hearing John Douglas say exactly what I had been
thinking made me feel a lot better about what I was going
to do.

I was about to lay open another police department that
was afraid of the truth and, instead of facing up to it, was
trying to dodge and weave around it. So, after reading the
affidavit I don't know how many times, I finally started
putting down on paper everything I found wrong with it.

CHAPTER 22

The Affidavit

While I was still convinced that Yates was the right suspect, the case against him was very problematic. After closely considering the affidavit in detail, I came away convinced that the task force had made some serious blunders that could possibly jeopardize the case if and when it went to court. The task force detectives were aware of these blunders and tried to conceal them by the use of language in this very carefully worded document.

The most obvious problems with the affidavit were the dates. While most dates were cited, some were conspicuously absent, or buried, or unclear. Considering the amount of time and work that obviously went into the drafting of this affidavit, I became convinced that these omissions or imprecisions had to be intentional. This was not a haphazard, hastily thrown together indictment. Every word was carefully chosen, and yet so many of them were unclear or possibly misleading.

This document shows not only the mistakes made by the task force, but their awareness of them. If Yates did not cop a plea, the arrest affidavit would be a significant part of his trial defense. Since almost all the evidence accumulated against him came subsequent to, and as a result of, his arrest on April 18, 2000, the affidavit was the basis of the prosecution's case against Robert Yates. Any flaws and weaknesses revealed by this affidavit could be exploited by his defense counsel, with potentially disastrous results.

Here is the six-page document in its entirety.

SUMMARY OF FACTS

State of Washington)

　　　　　　　) ss. ROBERT LEE YATES
　　　　　　　　　 JR.,W/M, 05/27/52

County of Spokane)

The undersigned, being competent to testify and sworn on oath, deposes and testifies that he believes a crime was committed by the defendant/defendants in the County of Spokane, State of Washington, because:

On 08/26/97 a badly decomposed body was discovered at approximately 9800 Forker Road, Spokane County, Washington by witness KEVIN KAELIN. Detectives Ruetsch and Grabenstein, as well as Ident. Officers, processed the scene, and in addition to the body and clothing worn by the victim, also recovered at the scene were the victim's shoes and a brownish-gray towel, as well as other items. The victim was identified through fingerprints as JENNIFER A. JOSEPH, an Asian female, born 10/06/80. Crime scene investigation strongly suggested that JOSEPH was transported to the rural area she was found in by a vehicle of some sort.

On 08/28/97 an autopsy was performed on JOSEPH's body by Dr. George Lindholm and P.A. Randy Shaber. Cause of death was determined to be multiple gunshots. It was noted that the blouse worn by the victim still had a right wrist cuff button but that the left wrist cuff button was missing.

Witnesses JOHN JOSEPH and MI HAE JOSEPH are the parents of JENNIFER A. JOSEPH and provided investigators samples of their blood in the event that it ever became necessary to establish a biological link between themselves and their daughter.

Subsequent investigation revealed that JOSEPH was last seen alive by witness YOLANDA CAREY, traveling eastbound on Sprague Avenue at approximately Thor in the City of Spokane, in a white-colored vehicle described as looking like a 1975 Corvette. This vehicle was being driven by a white male, 30 to 40 years of age. This was observed by CAREY on Saturday, 08/16/97, at approximately 23:35 hours, and just prior to this CAREY observed JOSEPH to be working in that area as a prostitute.

During the course of the investigation, information was obtained about ROBERT LEE YATES JR., W/M, date of birth 05/27/52. YATES was identified by SPD Officer Turman, #407, as the driver of a white 1977 Corvette, Washington license KIH442, that Turman stopped in the vicinity of Sprague and Ralph in Spokane, Washington on 09/24/97 for a traffic violation. Turman did a complete field contact of this stop. This was within a few blocks of where JOSEPH was last seen alive and is an area known to be frequented by both working prostitutes and their customers.

YATES was again contacted by SPD Officer Reynolds, #558, on 11/10/98 at 1:25 A.M. after he was observed picking up JENNIFER ROBINSON, a known prostitute at 1st and Crestline in Spokane, Washington. This is another area known to be frequented by working prostitutes and their customers. YATES told Officer Reynolds that he had picked up the woman to give her a ride home at her father's request. At the time of this contact, YATES was driving Washington license 918AJH, a 1985 Honda Civic, registered to him.

On 09/15/99 YATES was interviewed at the Public Safety Building by Detectives Bentley and Grabenstein. It was noted by both investigators upon initial contact that YATES seemed to be sweating profusely. It was also noted by investigators that YATES' hair color was light brown. YATES was initially questioned about the contact with police on 11/10/98, and he repeated the same story that he had related to the officer at that time. YATES had trouble recalling the female's name, but thought that it was JENNIFER. He was asked the female's father's name but could not remember it. He was asked how he knew her father, and he stated that they had worked together for a short time. Also during this interview YATES was asked about his contact with police on 09/24/97. He recalled the incident and stated that he was driving a Corvette at the time, which he had since sold to a friend of his named RITA JONES. YATES was asked about any contacts that he may have had with prostitutes, and he stated there was one occasion during the fall of 1998 when he picked up a female hitchhiker because it was cold, and that when she propositioned him, he dropped her off about a mile from where he had picked her up. He denied having patronized this female or any other prostitute in Spokane.

On 09/16/99 witness JENNIFER ROBINSON told investigators she remembered the contact between police and YATES on 11/10/98, that she did make an agreement between herself and YATES for oral sex

for $20.00, and that when YATES was stopped by po-
lice she instructed him to tell police the story about
her father. At this time she said that story was not
true.

On 11/28/97 Trooper Nick Gerard, #985, stopped
YATES northbound on Hwy. 195 at MP 91, in
Spokane County, Washington, for speeding. At the
time of the stop, YATES was driving the 1977
Corvette, Washington license KIH442. YATES was is-
sued a citation for speeding.

On 01/12/00 witness SARAH MARSH was contacted by an investigator and indicated that she sold
the 1977 Corvette to ROBERT YATES in September,
1994.

On 01/07/00 witness RITA JONES was contacted
by Detective Grabenstein and she indicated that she
purchased the 1977 Corvette from ROBERT YATES
in May, 1998. At the same time she allowed Detective
Grabenstein to remove several samples of carpet
fibers from the interior of the Corvette.

On 04/05/00 Forensic Scientist Kevin Jenkins of
the Washington State Patrol Crime Laboratory informed investigators that fibers obtained from the
Corvette quite closely matched fibers recovered during the investigation of the JOSEPH homicide, from
JOSEPH's shoes and the brownish-gray towel. One
group of fibers was identical visually and microscopically in regard to color, texture and shape. They are
both nylon and they also appear to be the same, as
closely as can be determined, by measurement of the
absorbance spectra. A second group of fibers, described as somewhat lighter and slightly different
colored from the first fibers, are also similar to one
fiber retrieved during the investigation. These fibers
are similar visually and microscopically and as to

color, shape and texture. The samples are smaller and more extensive testing could not be done at this time. This information indicates there are two different-colored fibers, both in the car and recovered from the body of the victim, that exhibit respectively high levels of similarity.

WSP Crime Lab personnel also located several light-brown Caucasian head hairs on the brownish-gray towel recovered with JOSEPH's body on 08/27/97.

Investigators have obtained certified copies of paperwork from Washington State Department of Licensing concerning the titling and registration of the 1977 Corvette, Washington license KIH442. This paperwork contains a hand-written receipt signed by SARAH MARSH showing she sold the Corvette to ROBERT YATES on 09/08/94. Registration paperwork shows YATES as the registered and legal owner of the Corvette as of March of 1995. Vehicle title application/registration certificate shows that RITA JONES applied for title on 05/29/98. The aforementioned paperwork establishes ROBERT LEE YATES as the owner of the 1977 Corvette from 09/08/94 through 05/29/98.

On 04/10/00 a search warrant was prepared for the 1977 Corvette by Detective Grabenstein and presented to be reviewed and signed by Superior Court Judge Donohue. It was executed the same day, and numerous items of potential evidence were seized from the vehicle including the following:

From the area of the passenger side floorboards, a white button with two holes was collected.

The passenger-side seat belt buckle and attachment were noted to be stained with what appeared to be blood. Several areas of the driver's seat were swabbed and tested with a presumptive chemical test for blood which reacted positively, and this seat was collected.

WSP Lab personnel further examined the passenger seat and passenger seat belt buckle and noted numerous areas with bloodlike stains. The majority of the stains appear to have soaked through the seams of the seat. Human DNA was recovered from the two stains off the seat and one stain off the seat belt buckle. A DNA profile was generated for these three samples and they appear to be from a common donor. Based on this profile and the profile of JOHN JOSEPH and MI HAE JOSEPH, the human DNA recovered from the passenger seat and the passenger-side belt buckle is approximately 850 times more likely to have come from an offspring of JOHN and MI HAE JOSEPH than if the DNA was from a randomly-selected individual from the Caucasian population. In other words, JOHN and MI HAE JOSEPH cannot be eliminated as the parents of the donor of this human blood.

WSP Lab personnel further examined and compared the questioned button recovered from the Corvette and the known button from the right sleeve of JENNIFER JOSEPH's jacket. This examination revealed them to be the same size and design, and both buttons are made of the natural material known as "mother of pearl." The button recovered from the Corvette either came from JENNIFER JOSEPH's jacket or an article of clothing with identical buttons.

On 3/22/00, Detective Hammer came into possession of a list of license plates which was kept by Joe Lockridge. Joe Lockridge was the boyfriend of known prostitute Cheryl Siekerman, and told Detective Hammer that Cheryl dated the driver of Washington license 507JKN on 3/7/99. Joe further stated this date picked Cheryl up at 1st and Scott in Spokane, Washington for the purposes of oral sex. Washington license 507JKN is a 1985 Honda Accord registered to Robert Yates at 2220 E. 49th, Spokane, Washington.

On 4/18/00, at approximately 0630 hours, Detective Grabenstein and other members of the Spokane County Sheriff's office contacted Robert Lee Yates, white male, 5/27/52, on North Market in Spokane County, Washington and took him into custody for 1st Degree Murder based on the aforementioned probable cause.

On 04/19/00 Detective Ruetsch prepared this affidavit charging ROBERT LEE YATES, JR., W/M, 05/27/52, with the crime of Murder in the First Degree based on his having Premeditated Intent to Cause the Death of Another Person and did cause the death of JENNIFER A. JOSEPH.

I HEREBY CERTIFY (OR DECLARE) UNDER PENALTY OF PERJURY UNDER THE LAWS OF THE STATE OF WASHINGTON THAT THE FOREGOING IS TRUE AND CORRECT. 9A.72.085

DATE_____PLACE_____SIGNATURE_____

Whether this is the first arrest warrant you have read, or the five hundredth, you may well be impressed at the case against Robert Yates. But the closer you look at this document, the more problematic it becomes. Before you think that I'm being overly critical of the affidavit, keep in mind that the writers of this document are also quite aware of the problems in this case, and doing their best to try to camouflage them.

The task force was afraid of mistakes that they made during the course of their investigation. I asked myself, What was the task force afraid of? Rereading the affidavit, my question was answered.

As I began to dissect the affidavit, I was struck by its unevenness in tone. In certain areas, it was incredibly precise. In others, it was sketchy, even intentionally evasive. It almost seemed as if two different people had written the document independent of each other, as if a veteran detective and a young policeman were put in separate rooms with the same facts.

Of course, this document had been gone over, not just by the signatory Fred Ruetsch, but also the DA, several other attorneys, detectives, and Sheriff Sterk himself.

The first two paragraphs begin with dates. Such documentation is standard and necessary for a police investigation. The first dates mentioned record the discovery of Joseph's body and the autopsy. The third paragraph describes how John and Mi Hae Joseph, the victim's parents, gave blood samples to investigators "in the event that it ever became necessary to establish a biological link between themselves and their daughter." No date is mentioned.

Why would investigators need to establish a biological link between Jennifer Joseph and her parents?

I went back to the official death certificate and saw that Jennifer Joseph had been cremated at the Cremation Society of Washington on East Sprague in Spokane. The police had contacted John Joseph (he and his wife were divorced; he was living near Tacoma, she was living in Hawaii) and told him that his daughter was dead.

The task force knew that John and Mi Hae Joseph were Jennifer's parents. That's why they were notifying them of her death. So the task force didn't collect blood from them in order to establish a biological link. In the early days of the Joseph investigation, John Joseph submitted a blood sample, because he was being considered as a possible suspect. Why did they need a blood sample from Mi Hae Joseph? And when did they take it?

During the autopsy, a long bone was taken from Jennifer Joseph's body and saved as a source for DNA. For some reason, when the task force needed DNA to compare to the blood found in the Corvette, they used samples from Jennifer's parents. Apparently, marrow from the long bone had not yet been processed, and the task force didn't have the victim's DNA. So they went to the next closest source— her parents.

This indicated that the Joseph homicide was not very high up on the task force's priority list. When the connection was finally made between Yates, the white Corvette, and the Yolanda Carey clue, the Joseph homicide became the most important case of them all. Unfortunately, the detectives and the crime lab weren't ready for it.

Which leads to the million-dollar question: When did the task force detectives actually make the connection between Yates, his Corvette, and the Yolanda Carey clue?

Yolanda Carey reported seeing Joseph on August 16, 1997, at East Sprague, getting into a 1975 white Corvette. Yates was pulled over for a traffic violation while driving a white 1977 Corvette on September 24, 1997. Carey didn't know the difference between a '75 and a '77 Corvette because there is no obvious difference.

So why did it take the task force three years to make the connection between the Carey clue and the Yates traffic stop?

The paragraph describing the Corvette clue begins: "Subsequent investigation revealed . . ." This is a phrase common to police investigations, often used when a date is undetermined or unspecific. When I first read the phrase, I thought it was just another overused connective description in a police report—a paperwork cliché. That is the innocent explanation for beginning a paragraph in this manner. Another explanation is not so innocent. I believe that Fred Ruetsch used such vague wording because the task force was not willing to admit when they developed the information that followed.

The affidavit never states when the Yolanda Carey clue was first reported to the police. When I began looking closely at the document, I assumed that due to the precision of the time, location, and description Carey provided the police that she must have come forward shortly after Joseph went missing or was discovered dead. After even a few days, the memory begins to fade and descriptions become more imprecise. The time alone, stated to the fifth minute, made me certain that police had this clue soon after Joseph's body was found.

I had already confirmed through Sterk that Yolanda Carey came forward with the clue shortly after Joseph's murder. Several news agencies had reported that the clue was given to patrol officers in roll call. I was able to confirm that report through my sources. I also learned that the task force officer who went to roll call was none other than Cal Walker. No one I spoke to seemed to remember exactly when he did alert patrol officers about this very important clue.

The next paragraph describes the September 24, 1997, traffic stop. Yates was pulled over on East Sprague, within a few blocks of where Joseph was last seen alive. Officer Turman did not cite him for the traffic violation; instead, he simply filled out a field contact report and sent Yates on his way.

Once again, the timing of the affidavit's language is

vague and confusing. We know when the traffic stop occurred, but the first sentence of that paragraph reads, "During the course of the investigation, information was obtained about ROBERT LEE YATES JR., W/M, date of birth 05/27/52."

In other words, the field contact report that Turman filed subsequent to his stopping Yates on East Sprague somehow did not immediately reach the attention of the detectives working the Joseph case, or those working on the task force after it was formed.

The writer of the affidavit either knows or could easily find out exactly when this information about Yates was obtained. Instead we read yet another civil service literary device: "During the course of the investigation . . ." This paragraph, like so many others in the affidavit, should begin with a date. But in this instance, the date is embarrassing. The serial killer was stopped for a traffic violation on September 24, 1997, a little less than a month after Joseph's and Hernandez's bodies were found and certainly after the Yolanda Carey clue had come in. Officer Turman knew the task force was looking for a white Corvette when he pulled Yates over.

Turman could have solved the case right there. Imagine the scenario. Officer Turman questions Yates, finds probable cause to search the car, finds a small-caliber handgun, brings Yates in for questioning, gets a search warrant for the Corvette, the search reveals blood and other evidence connected to Jennifer Joseph, Yates is arrested for her murder, the killings stop. There's no serial killer and no task force. Turman gets a commendation and probably makes detective in a couple years.

Unfortunately, it didn't happen that way.

Turman told the *Seattle Post-Intelligencer* that he knew the task force was looking for a suspect driving a white Corvette. He said that patrol officers had been told a serial killer task force was seeking information on white Corvettes. Turman also told the newspaper that the Corvette stood out, and that he did not recall ever stopping a similar car.

> Yates was very cooperative and calm when pulled over, Turman said. He gathered as much information as he could without tipping Yates that he was a suspect in a serial killing investigation, then sent him on his way, he said.

Turman stated that a serial killer task force was looking for a suspect driving a white Corvette as early as September 24, 1997. But the city-county task force hadn't been established until December 22, 1997.

Exactly what information did Turman get from Yates, aside from the routine field interview (FI) data? If he thought that Yates was a serial killer suspect, why did he let him go? Why was he worried about tipping Yates off? Why didn't he let detectives know that he had pulled over this suspect vehicle? Why didn't he arrest Yates? Why didn't he search the car? Or at least give Yates a ticket?

Once Turman sent Yates on his way, Yates killed at least nine more women.

By September 25, 1997, the police had all the information they needed to catch the killer. Ruetsch and Grabenstein should have read Turman's FI over their morning coffee. Running a DMV report would have given them more precise and detailed information. Within a few weeks, or even days, they could have arrested Yates for the murder of Jennifer Joseph.

But that wasn't the only opportunity they missed.

On November 10, 1998, at 1:25 A.M., Yates was stopped by Officer Reynolds of the Spokane Police Department. Reynolds had seen Yates stop to pick up Jennifer Robinson, a known prostitute, at First and Crestline, an area fre-quented by prostitutes. Yates was driving a 1985 Honda Civic, Washington license 918AJH, registered to himself. When questioned by Officer Reynolds, Yates claimed that the woman was the daughter of a friend, and he had been sent to find her at her father's request. The officer released Yates and apparently also wrote a field contact report.

Once again, a patrol officer pulled over the suspect in the neighborhood frequented by prostitutes. Yates could have intended to kill Jennifer Robinson. Most probably he was armed. There was a very good chance that the car he was driving had physical evidence from one or more of his previous victims. The patrol officer let him go with a field contact report.

Even though Yates was driving a Honda when Reynolds pulled him over, Reynolds didn't also know that Yates was the driver of the white Corvette, because the DMV records had not been checked on the 1977 Corvette after Yates was initially pulled over by Turman.

When Officer Reynolds stopped Yates, he had already killed eight more women after Jennifer Joseph. Reynolds at least can be satisfied that he possibly saved the life of Jennifer Robinson. But he, too, let the arrest of a lifetime slip through his fingers.

From the beginning of their investigation, task force de-tectives were aware that the serial killer might be driving a white Corvette. They often spoke about the Carey clue among themselves, considering it one of their best vehicle clues. The Washington State Patrol had run all Corvettes (both white and "other") for the task force's database. So they knew the Corvette clue was important, but they never seemed to work it. After collecting a list of Corvette own-ers, and narrowing it down by color, they didn't focus on this line of inquiry until after they had already identified Yates as a suspect following his interrogation.

Even though the white Corvette clue was common knowledge in the windowless offices of task force headquarters, they apparently hadn't notified the WSP. On November 28, 1997, Washington State Patrol trooper Nick Gerard stopped Yates going northbound on Highway 195 in Spokane County. At this time, Yates was driving the white 1977 Corvette. He was issued a citation for speeding, but nothing else. Apparently, the WSP did not know that a white Corvette had been connected to the Jennifer Joseph murder, or that Yates had been pulled over previously in the neighborhood where she and several other prostitutes had last been seen.

We already know that the Spokane police never ran a DMV check on Yates during their two traffic stops. We can assume, or at least hope, that Trooper Gerard did run Yates's driver's license for wants or warrants and his car license for DMV. Gerard is, after all, a traffic cop, and should do this as a matter of routine. He should have known that the Spokane police were looking for a white Corvette in possible connection to the prostitute homicides. Unless the task force didn't tell the WSP about the clue. There was no reason for the task force not to give the Yolanda Carey clue to the WSP. In fact, the WSP should have had that clue hours after it came in.

After three traffic stops, two of them in neighborhoods frequented by prostitutes and one of those with a prostitute in the car with him, Yates was finally brought in for questioning on September 15, 1999. Detectives Bentley and Grabenstein interviewed Yates at the Public Safety Building. The detectives reportedly noticed that Yates had light-brown hair and he was sweating profusely upon their first contact. Were these observations further examples of retroactive memory enhancement? The weather on September 15 was sunny and warm, eighty-five degrees. It's not surprising that he was sweating.

When did the task force know that their suspect had light-brown hair? If they collected a light-brown hair from the Joseph evidence shortly after her body was found, then they should have known the suspect might have had that color hair before Yates was pulled over by Officer Turman on September 24, 1997.

And on two separate occasions in 1999, the task force pursued suspects with reddish blond hair. The first was the suspect in the composite drawing from the Barnes case. The second was Brad Jackson. I never thought they were identifying the suspect from hair, since street prostitutes could possibly have several different foreign hairs on their bodies and clothes. So why were Bentley and Grabenstein interested in Yates's light-brown hair? Or, I should ask, when were they interested in it—after he refused to give a blood sample? The way the affidavit is written makes it look as if Bentley and Grabenstein knew they were looking for a suspect with light-brown hair. I don't believe they knew the suspect's hair color until after they had already determined it was Yates. Then they remembered his hair was light brown.

The first line of questioning that the detectives followed concerned the November 10, 1998, traffic stop by Officer Reynolds. Yates gave the detectives the same story he told Reynolds, that he was picking the girl up at her father's request.

The detectives obviously did not know that Yates owned a white Corvette, because they referred to his driving a Camaro during the September 24, 1997, traffic stop. He corrected them, saying that he was driving a Corvette, and not a Camaro. This meant that Detectives Bentley and Grabenstein did not have Yates's DMV report in front of them, probably because it had never been run, or, once it had been run, for some reason this information wasn't given to the task force.

How did Yates's Corvette get mistaken for a Camaro? Subsequent affidavits stated that the FI form described the car as a Camaro. Officer Turman does not look like the kind of guy who can't tell a Corvette from a Camaro. Sheriff Sterk referred to the discrepancy as "a penmanship error." In other words, Bentley and/or Grabenstein (or whoever recorded the information onto the tip sheet) misread the field interview form, and they blamed Turman, the city patrol officer. The error, whoever was to blame, was compounded by the fact that the task force detectives didn't have Yates's DMV information in front of them when they brought him in for an interview as one possible suspect among literally thousands in the serial killer case.

Even without the Corvette connection, Yates was looking like a pretty good suspect. He was unable to account for his whereabouts during the period when victims Melinda Mercer and Connie LaFontaine Ellis were killed in Tacoma. And he continued to lie about his contacts with prostitutes, admitting only to have patronized them while serving in the Army in Germany.

This raised another red flag for Bentley and Grabenstein. Shortly after interviewing Yates, they contacted the FBI to find out when Yates was in Germany, and whether he was available for some of the earlier murders in Spokane.

When questioned further about his contact with prostitutes, Yates stated that in the fall of 1998 he picked up a girl hitchhiker because it was cold. When she propositioned him, Yates said that he let her out about a mile from where he picked her up, because he wasn't interested. Here Yates was either establishing a lame alibi to put him in Spokane around the time Connie LaFontaine Ellis was killed in Tacoma, or else he thought he was seen picking up a prostitute in the fall of 1998 and wanted to account for it.

One day after interviewing Yates, the detectives talked to

Jennifer Robinson, the prostitute Yates had picked up on November 10, 1998. She admitted that she and Yates came to an agreement that she would perform oral sex on him for $20.

If the detectives were interested in catching Yates in this comparatively harmless lie, why didn't they interview Jennifer Robinson first? And if Yates's lie about his contacts with prostitutes was significant enough for them to seek out Robinson to contradict it, why didn't they follow up with a subsequent interview of Yates?

During the interview, the detectives apparently didn't ask Yates about his November 28, 1997, speeding citation, probably because they didn't have the DMV information.

On November 12, 1998, Yates had been arrested on a domestic violence charge stemming from a physical altercation with his adult daughter. The fight was still going on when police arrived at the Yates house. The charges were later reduced to misdemeanor assault, and Yates was never formally booked, but the arrest was still on record. If the detectives had run a complete criminal record and background on Yates before the interview, they would have at least brought the incident up.

Detectives Bentley and Grabenstein were obviously not prepared to interrogate a real suspect. They simply brought Yates in and asked him a few ill-prepared questions. Then they asked him to submit a blood sample. Yates said that he would have to discuss the matter with his wife. Three days later, he left a message with the detectives saying that he would not voluntarily provide a blood sample.

Right then, it would appear that Yates is a pretty good suspect. Even without the Corvette clue, he has been linked to prostitutes and refused to give a blood sample. Instead of following up on Yates, the task force apparently ignored him until the beginning of the next year.

The affidavit jumps ahead to January 12, 2000, when

Sarah Marsh is contacted and tells an unnamed investigator that she sold a 1977 Corvette to Yates in September 1994.

The next paragraph jumps back to January 7, when Rita Jones tells Detective Grabenstein that she purchased the 1977 Corvette from Yates in May 1998. During the September 15, 1999, interview, Yates had told the detectives that he sold the Corvette to Jones. Why did it take them three months to follow up on the Corvette?

During the January 7 interview with Rita Jones, Detective Grabenstein was allowed to remove several samples of carpet fibers from the interior of her Corvette.

In a subsequent television interview, Rita Jones said that detectives told her that the Corvette had been owned by a suspect in a serial killer case. What happened between September 15, 1999, when there seemed to be little suspicion surrounding Yates, and January 7, 2000, when detectives were telling Rita Jones that he was a suspect?

Did Detectives Bentley and Grabenstein just come up with a theory over the holidays? Or did the Yolanda Carey clue finally surface? Or did the task force detectives have political and career motives to sit on Yates as a suspect until the beginning of the following year? Remember, I-695 had passed in November 1999. The Spokane PD dropped out of the task force on Christmas Eve. If the sheriff's department waited to make their move on Yates until after the city dropped out, and after the town hall meeting and Sterk's steely-eyed promise to catch the killer, then they would all look like heroes.

But I'm getting ahead of myself.

Paragraph thirteen stands out like a pimple on your nose: "WSP Crime Lab personnel also located several light-brown Caucasian head hairs on the brownish-gray towel recovered with JOSEPH's body on 08/27/97."

When exactly were those head hairs recovered? The only

date offered is when Joseph's body was found, and it doesn't specifically refer to the recovery of those hairs. The writer of the affidavit put that date in because he couldn't state the actual date when that evidence was in fact recovered, because it was probably more than two years after her body was found.

I don't believe the Joseph evidence was processed until sometime in early 2000, when the evidence bag containing her clothes was probably examined forensically for the first time. There would be no reason for fibers or hairs to be processed until the task force had something to compare them to. Paragraph thirteen wants the reader to assume that the light-brown hairs were recovered in 1997, but the previous paragraph recounts how a WSP forensic scientist matched fibers from the Corvette with fibers found on Joseph's shoes and the brownish gray towel. I find it hard to believe that a forensic scientist would collect carpet fibers from the shoes and towel and miss head hairs.

The affidavit describes when the fiber evidence was tested, not when it was found. Not only does this document not describe when the hair was found, but there was no test described to determine, at the very least, the blood type of the donor. Why?

Because, I believe, when the hairs were recovered, the detectives already knew who they were looking for. Yates was in the military for eighteen years, which means that his blood type could be easily accessed by law enforcement (it was even on his dog tags). Blood type is easily tested from a hair sample. Prior to the advent of DNA evidence, blood type was considered very powerful physical evidence, often the basis of criminal convictions. Now blood type is at least powerful probable cause evidence for arrest or further search warrants. By the time they had the blood type on the hairs, they probably didn't need it.

Based on the fiber match, a search warrant was issued

on April 10, 2000, for the 1977 Corvette. Rita Jones was contacted and the car was seized pursuant to that warrant.

The search yielded evidence of blood on the passenger seat and the seat belt buckle. These blood samples were tested and found to originate from a common DNA donor. The blood samples taken from John and Mi Hae Joseph were used to determine if the donor of the blood in the Corvette was their offspring.

The testing resulted in a finding that the DNA sample from the Corvette was 850 times more likely to have come from the combined DNA of the parents than a randomly selected individual.

In terms of DNA evidence, this is pretty thin, but at least it's something.

The Joseph case had always been a weak link. There was no plastic bag, no DNA, and as Mike and I were to learn later, the ballistics didn't match those of the later victims.

If there was any other evidence linking Yates to any of the other victims, whose cases weren't as problematic as the Joseph homicide, you can be certain that the task force would have pursued those avenues of investigation and used them for the basis of an arrest. Perhaps that is what they were doing for three months, trying to make another case against Yates. And that could be one of the reasons for the town hall meeting, to stimulate tips that would lead them to Yates from another direction, so they wouldn't have to answer embarrassing questions about the way the Joseph case was handled.

Paragraph twenty recounts how Detective Hammer came into possession of a list of license plates kept by Joe Lockridge, the boyfriend of Cheryl Siekerman, a known prostitute. This occurred on March 22, 2000. Lockridge told Hammer that Cheryl had dated the driver of Washington license 507JKN on March 7, 1999. That plate belonged to a 1985 Honda Accord registered to Robert Yates.

This shows that Yates was still soliciting prostitutes as late as March 1999. Why didn't Bentley or Grabenstein refer to the Lockridge clue during their first interrogation of Yates, back when they were trying to catch him in a lie about soliciting prostitutes? Did they even have the Lockridge clue?

Detective Ruetsch wrote and signed the affidavit. He is the same detective who handled the Joseph homicide in 1997, and then stayed on as part of the task force.

Detective Ruetsch must know that he messed up. Otherwise, he wouldn't have written the affidavit so carefully, conveniently forgetting to mention several embarrassing facts, which, if he had the courage to admit to them in the beginning, would not be as problematic as his attempts to camouflage them. The arrest affidavit was not written in good faith. Scattered among the salient facts are a series of small yet important deceptions and half-truths. Read carefully, it's like a window into the windowless offices of the task force headquarters, revealing what was wrong with the rest of their investigation.

CHAPTER 23

The Simple Art of Murder Investigation

The task force failed to catch Robert Yates for two years because they relied on DNA and computer technology instead of old-fashioned detective work. Finding DNA evidence on most of the victims and creating a massive computer database actually took them further from a solution, and gave Robert Yates ample time to destroy evidence and possibly kill more women.

A serial killer case can be very difficult, even overwhelming. But it's still just a series of singular homicide cases that happen to be connected. In the Spokane case, there were eighteen victims, which means eighteen times more evidence, and that many more chances the suspect might be observed by a witness or make a mistake.

The Spokane Task Force didn't see it that way. They were too busy compiling a database to analyze or even understand the clues they had in front of them. Instead of recognizing the value of individual clues, and working them as they came in, they inputted everything into the computer database, hoping that the machine would find their killer for them. They believed that the more information they had, no matter what its value, the better. They saw eighteen connected homicides as being exponentially more difficult than eighteen separate cases that all had a common suspect.

In short, the task force couldn't see the trees for the forest. Overwhelmed by the responsibility of solving a serial killer case, they ignored a suspect who was killing and dumping bodies right under their noses. Blinded by the science of DNA and computer technology, they forgot any commonsense detective skills they ever had, and relied on blood tests and databases to do their work for them.

The task force was supposed to be chasing a killer. Instead, they became file clerks.

"The task force sounds so glamorous. It's not glamorous," Chuck Bown told the *Spokesman-Review* when the task force was first established. "It's basically just database management software. Instead of the information going into the database being about manufacturing or what have you, it's about case management."

I thought the task force was supposed to be about solving murders. This sounded more like working for Microsoft.

"Basically, what we had was thousands of bits of information," Cal Walker said. "There is no bad-guy button you can push that makes one person stick out."

Cal Walker is missing the essence of the crime by labeling, categorizing, and filing evidence into bits of information. The essence of the crime is its human element.

The task force created one database, then they outgrew that. So they got a database from the FBI and outgrew that as well. Finally, they built another database. None of three databases were compatible with each other. All the information had to be reentered by hand. This was done by Captain Doug Silver, when he wasn't acting as the official spokesperson for the task force. Silver inputted field interviews, tips, vehicle descriptions, and the names of possible suspects and known criminals into the growing database.

The task force compiled all this information hoping that their computer would find common denominators of one individual that would implicate him in the homicides. This is how the *Spokesman-Review* described the process: "The Task Force methodically contacted the potential suspects spit out from computer queries." In September 1999, the computer spit out the name of Robert Yates. That's the only reason he was called in.

When Yates came to the Public Safety Building to speak with Detectives Grabenstein and Bentley, it was just another routine interview. They were going to ask Yates a few questions and then request a blood sample. They hadn't properly prepared for the interview. They hadn't run a DMV check on him. They hadn't spoken to the prostitute he was seen with. They didn't know he drove a white Corvette. They didn't know he was in Tacoma on National Guard duty during the periods when Melinda Mercer and Connie LaFontaine Ellis were killed. They didn't know about his November 1998 domestic violence arrest. They didn't know that Christine Smith had reported being assaulted by a man fitting Yates's description, a father of five and National Guard helicopter pilot who drove a distinctive black van.

They hadn't prepared for the interview because they couldn't imagine Yates was the suspect. These detectives had grown so accustomed to interviewing names given to them by the computer, asking them for blood samples, and filing the subsequent reports that they lost faith in their own abilities as detectives. They didn't think they could catch the killer without a computer or a lab technician.

And they didn't consider Yates a suspect until he refused to give a blood sample. Even then, they waited four months to retrieve fibers from the Corvette. And then they waited another three months before actually getting a search warrant on the Corvette and recovering the blood and other evidence that linked Yates to the murder of Jennifer Joseph.

Why did it take the task force so long to make a case against Yates? Was the sheriff's department playing politics, and waiting for the city to drop out of the investigation, so they could get all the credit for arresting Yates? Were they trying to link Yates to one of the other homicides because they knew the Joseph case was problematic, since they had neglected the Corvette clue and other evidence for two years? Were they busy chasing other suspects? Just what was going on?

As curious as I am to find out what the task force was doing for those seven months, it really doesn't matter. They had already wasted two years, and watched ten women die.

During those seven months, at least one person knew that Yates was the suspect. And that was Robert Yates himself. No doubt he systematically cleaned up, destroyed, or hid any evidence that he knew might connect him to the murders. At least three vehicles he had used in the commission of the crimes were no longer under his control. But he had plenty of time, even if he couldn't have known this, to dispose of the rest of the evidence—any trophies or articles of clothing belonging to the victims, the weapons he used, clothes he had been wearing during the commission of the murders.

After the September interview, the task force should have been working Yates as a suspect. Instead, they relied on technology to make their judgments for them. The crime lab would tell them whether Yates was a suspect. Or not.

That's the way they had conducted their entire investigation. The task force amassed hundreds of blood samples, creating a massive backlog at the Washington State Patrol Crime Lab. The lab had so many DNA tests to perform that they didn't have time to process other evidence from the serial killings, or from other cases.

It's difficult to pin down exactly how many blood samples the task force obtained. Cal Walker told the *Spokesman-Review* that he didn't know for certain, but he thought it was less than a thousand. At the town meeting, Walker said that the task force had eliminated two thousand suspects through DNA comparison (many of these were no doubt from DNA databases and did not require blood samples). Walker also stated that there were $200,000 worth of DNA tests remaining to be done. If Robert Yates had voluntarily submitted a blood sample during his September 15, 1999, interview, there's a very good chance that sample would still be sitting at the crime lab, waiting to be processed.

The larger question is not how many blood samples the task force took, or how long it took them to be processed, but why they relied on DNA testing and computer technology almost to the exclusion of all other investigative methods in the first place.

If the task force was collecting as many as six blood samples a day, when did they have time to do any actual detective work? They seemed to be conducting a blood drive, instead of investigating murders. They leaned so much on technology that they forgot how to be cops.

Technology has made a lot of things possible. The technological advances of the last century, even the last ten years, have changed the world we live in. For good and for bad.

Sure, it's much easier to write a book using a laptop computer. But there haven't been more reliable guns made than a Colt single-action revolver or a lever-action Winchester. And when it comes to detective work, not much has changed. Even with all the advances in high-tech criminalistics, there's a homicide textbook written in 1948 that I still find very useful. Given the tools available to him in the 1940s, a hardworking gumshoe like Philip Marlowe could have solved this case in a matter of weeks.

The more we rely on high tech, the less we tend to use the finest piece of technology ever constructed—the human brain. Detectives may welcome the speed and accuracy of computers. But computers will always be one tool among many available to a resourceful detective. He still needs his brains, his imagination, his experience, his gut, his feet, and sometimes his fists.

Detectives are in the business of catching criminals, the most irrational and unpredictable of humans. This is one career that demands the human element, because it involves the world of human weakness, error, and sin. Executing a search warrant, processing a crime scene, interrogating a suspect—there is no technology that will ever be able to do these jobs.

Machines can do only what humans tell them to. They can't think for us. They don't have analytical skills, they can't make connections that they haven't been programmed to make, they don't have imaginations. All these skills are essential to good detective work.

Though we rely on scientific methods, scientific evidence, and scientific truth, solving homicides is an art. Yes, it's a simple art, although it's a very difficult job. The Spokane Serial Killer case is a good example of just how simple a murder investigation can be—if only it's done right.

Let's start from the beginning. On August 26, 1997, Detectives Ruetsch and Grabenstein got a Jane Doe homicide.

The victim had been dead for several days. Her body had lain in a hayfield during the hottest month of the summer. Near her body was a brownish gray towel, a used condom, and a broken radio antenna. She was so severely decomposed that anal and vaginal swabs were impossible. Her identity had to be established through dental records, and a biological sample preserved by saving one of her long bones.

Ruetsch didn't have much homicide experience, but

Grabenstein was due for retirement and didn't want the case hanging over him. So Ruetsch took lead detective. Whether they thought at the time that Jennifer Joseph was connected to any of the other unsolved homicides, she was their case and they had only a handful of clues.

By September 2, the Spokane Sheriff's Department identified the victim and released her name—Jennifer Joseph. Her photo ran in the newspaper. Yolanda Carey saw it and contacted police, saying that she last saw Jennifer Joseph on August 16, 1997, at 11:35 P.M., traveling eastbound on Sprague in a white 1975 Corvette driven by a white male approximately thirty to forty years old.

This is the kind of clue that a detective prays for. The witness didn't see Joseph get into a pickup truck or compact import. Corvettes are unique vehicles, as recognizable as Volkswagen Bugs. The witness was no doubt confident of her description.

From 1974 until 1977 Corvettes maintained a certain body style—rubber bumpers front and rear, a straight notched rear window—and with the exception of wheel and engine options, and emblem variations, they were identical. The production runs were limited. In 1975 only 38,465 Corvettes were made, 8,000 of which were white.

The detectives took the clue seriously. Reportedly, Cal Walker went to the Spokane PD roll call and told patrol officers to be on the lookout for it. Ruetsch and Grabenstein obtained Washington and Idaho State DMV records for all Corvettes (white and others) within certain years bracketing 1975. The printout listed hundreds of cars.

On September 24, 1997, Spokane PD Officer Corey Turman stopped Robert Yates in a white 1977 Corvette and completed a field interview card. This FI card went into the task force's stack of tips. Someone couldn't read Turman's handwriting on the FI card and thought it said that Yates was driving a Camaro. No one ran a DMV check on Yates at the time. Not Turman, not the task force. No DMV check was run on Yates until two years later.

Ruetsch and Grabenstein had two significant piles of information. One was the list of a few hundred Corvette owners. The other was the FI cards on johns stopped by patrol officers on East Sprague. Let's say there were a few hundred of these, too.

This is not information that needs to be turned over to civilian crime analysts or computer technicians. It needs to be investigated by the detectives themselves.

As a detective you have to place people in a specific area where they at least have the opportunity to commit a crime. That is the first step toward including them as possible suspects. Ruetsch and Grabenstein should have spent just one weekend in their office alone—no supervisors, no phones ringing—and broken down and cross-referenced these two piles of information in search of a connection.

The process is simple. First, alphabetize all the FI cards. Now you have twenty-six different stacks, at the most. One detective holds the DMV records and reads out loud the last name of each registered owner. The other detective picks up the stack that begins with the first letter of the last name of the registered owner and searches that pile for a hit. Had the detectives done this "old-school," labor-intensive detective work, Yates's name would have come up. His name was on the Corvette list. His name was on the FI that Turman filled out. Even if they misread Turman's FI as having stopped a Camaro, they would have known that Yates owned a Corvette, because he was on the DMV list. And that mistake would have been meaningless, because the license plate on the FI card and the license plate on the list from the DMV would be the same.

Even with the hit on Yates they would have to continue going through this process. Maybe they would have gotten another hit. Maybe not. After Yates's arrest, prostitutes on

Sprague said his was the only white Corvette they ever saw.

Now they would have Yates connected to East Sprague in a vehicle described by a witness as possibly connected to a crime. Next, Ruetsch and Grabenstein could have obtained a driver's license photo of Yates and placed him in a photo lineup with five other similar-appearing white males, and showed this to Yolanda Carey. They could have driven out to Yates's house, taken a photo of his Corvette, and shown that picture to Carey.

With a positive ID, Ruetsch and Grabenstein could have gotten a search warrant for the Corvette. They would have found all the evidence found during the execution of the April 2000 search warrant, and probably much more.

Case closed. Yates is arrested for the murder of Jennifer Joseph. Unless he confesses to any other murders, at least six homicides go unsolved (Sapp, Lowe, Brisbois, Palmer, Zielinski, Hernandez). And Spokane doesn't even have a serial killer. Ten women—Darla Sue Scott, Shawn Johnson, Melinda Mercer, Laurie Wason, Shawn McClenahan, Sunny Oster, Linda Maybin, Melody Murfin, Michelyn Derning, and Connie LaFontaine Ellis—are not murdered.

In this scenario, a computer helped generate the list of Corvette owners. But the rest was old-fashioned detective work.

Does that seem too easy? Okay, let's complicate things a little. For some reason, Yolanda Carey doesn't identify Yates or his vehicle. That doesn't necessarily eliminate him as a suspect. Direct surveillance, either of Yates or the East Sprague strip, could be very effective.

If Ruetsch and Grabenstein had surveilled Yates, or even just sat on East Sprague waiting for him, they probably would have seen him pick up a prostitute. They might have seen him pick up Darla Sue Scott or Shawn Johnson, or some other victim who was never reported missing and whose body hasn't turned up yet.

Here's another way they could have caught him. Forget about the Carey clue. Even without it, Ruetsch and Grabenstein still could have caught Yates months before they finally did.

At the September 15, 1999, interview, Yates told Grabenstein and Bentley that he had been in the Army, stationed in Germany. He had been pulled over twice by patrol officers in prostitute districts, once with a known prostitute in his car. He did not have an alibi for the two periods of time when Mercer and Ellis had been murdered in Tacoma. Yates was a good suspect.

And the detectives had a piece of evidence that could pin the murders on him. A fingerprint had been recovered from one of the plastic bags wrapped around Shawn Mc-Clenahan's head.

A fingerprint is either visible or latent. A visible print is the result of the suspect's contact with a foreign substance such as dirt, blood, or grease. A latent fingerprint is invisible to the naked eye, left by natural skin oils and/or perspiration. Latent prints can be seen and lifted using fingerprint powders or chemicals.

Whether the plastic bag print was visible or latent, within a very short period, the task force had a print of a possible suspect that could be compared to others. If this print had the sufficient amount of points to input it into the automated fingerprint identification system (AFIS) computer, then the task force probably entered the print, but didn't find a match.

AFIS technology is great if the suspect's print is in your available databases. But what if it isn't? What if the print doesn't have enough points of identification for the computer? You have a print of several points. Now you need someone to compare it to. Back to real police work.

Robert Yates didn't have a criminal record, but his fingerprints were registered with the Department of Defense.

Yates had told the detectives that he served in the military. They should have run the McClenahan fingerprint against the Department of Defense database. Actually, they could have done that as soon as the fingerprint was processed, if they were working the fingerprint as a clue. But that doesn't seem to have happened. The task force didn't match Yates's fingerprints to the print found on the plastic bag until April 25, 2000.

Then there's Christine Smith. This was an easy case—a robbery and assault with a deadly weapon with a victim who met the profile of the serial killer's victims and offered a very detailed description of the suspect, down to his occupation and the number of children he had. Why didn't the task force investigate this case? Did they even know about it?

In the end, and in the beginning, the Joseph case had the best evidence. If Ruetsch and Grabenstein had worked that case like a singular homicide, they had a real good chance of solving it. But they were immediately overwhelmed, not just by the amount of evidence and information generated by a serial case, but by the mystique of the serial killer.

This is not uncommon in serial killer cases. Police departments approach a serial killer case differently from any other. After several victims are discovered and apparently linked, the police form a task force. Subsequent publicity and political pressure create the demand for new and different methods of detection, which often just confuses and overburdens investigators, leading them further from a possible solution. Soon they're so buried in minutiae that they can't even imagine solving the case.

In the process, police lose sight of solving any one case individually, and instead try to solve all of them at once. As a result, they are overwhelmed by information, much of it meaningless or distracting, when the very clue they need is sitting right there in front of their nose.

It's happened before, most notably during the "Ted" killings in Seattle in the mid-1970s. Bob Keppel's task force compiled a massive database, hoping that new computer technology would give them the suspect's name. Meanwhile, a woman had contacted the police on several occasions with very strong circumstantial evidence against a suspect named Ted Bundy. But those clues were never followed up until Bundy was arrested in Utah on kidnapping charges.

Bob Keppel was working at a time when people didn't really know what computers could or couldn't do in law enforcement. And at least he made the suspect and vehicle descriptions public, probably saving many lives in the process.

If the police didn't work the Yolanda Carey clue, why couldn't they at least make it public? Throughout this investigation, I have tried to get into the mind of the killer. Now let's try looking through the eyes of a prostitute standing on a street corner waiting for a trick to pull to the curb.

The white Corvette slows down as it passes. She knows he'll circle back and probably stop. She remembers that the cops had just been on the street, warning her and the other working girls about a car that looked just like that one.

Here he comes again. . . . Shit, he pulled over. Be cool, she thinks to herself. Make up a reason not to get into the car, get his license plate.

She smiles with the confidence of a streetwise hooker as she talks to him. He tries to convince her to come with him. She listens, but a sickening knot forms in her stomach. She's been on the street a long time and has learned to be careful, to trust her gut. She's seen him before, but now she's suspicious. This could be the guy who killed Jennifer. She finally just turns away from him. After a few choice words, the john in the white Corvette drives away, disappointed. He goes off looking for another girl.

She goes to the pay phone in front of Kmart. She picks up the receiver and dials the number on the card the detective gave her. "Hello, yes, I'm calling to report that I saw the car you told me about. . . . The white Corvette . . . He's cruising Sprague right now. . . . My name? Darla Sue Scott."

Darla Sue Scott, Shawn Johnson, Melinda Mercer, Laurie Wason, Shawn McClenahan, Sunny Oster, Linda Maybin, Melody Murfin, Michelyn Derning, and Connie LaFontaine Ellis all died after the Corvette clue came in. Some of these women got into Robert Yates's white Corvette. If they had known that Jennifer Joseph was last seen getting into a white Corvette, would they have gone with him?

If the rest of Spokane didn't seem to care, these women on Sprague wanted the serial killer caught. I know, because I talked to them. I could see the fear in their faces, and hear it in their voices. Prostitutes might often find themselves on the other side of the law, but when their lives are threatened, they can be very cooperative. These women at least had a right to know the dangers they faced.

But the Spokane Task Force didn't release the Carey clue, or anything else. Throughout the course of the investigation, the task force never shared any useful information with the public—until the town meeting, when they already had Yates in their sights. They withheld information from the public for the same reason they leaned so heavily on technology. They didn't trust their own detective skills.

"You can't replace gumshoe detective work with technology," John Douglas told me. "Being a detective is an art; not everyone can do it, not just anyone should."

Murder investigation is a simple art. That doesn't mean it's easy. There used to be a breed of men and women who welcomed the challenge of answering for the dead. It was their job, their duty, and their passion to search out the truth no matter what the cost, or whom it hurt, even if it was themselves. That detective is being replaced by DNA strips and computer databases.

A computer can't think beyond its own programming. It can't remember things it is not told to store. It cannot analyze facts or make connections between disparate pieces of information. It can't make intuitive leaps. It doesn't have hunches. It doesn't have the experience of years on the street.

Detective work cannot be reduced to a software program or database management. It is an endeavor of men and women to challenge evil and answer for the dead.

At the beginning of this book, I said that you never forget what a dead body smells like. Cops work long and hard to get that detective badge. Then they find themselves looking down at a decomposing corpse. Some realize they don't have the stomach for it. Others barely tolerate it and start dreaming of retirement. And there are a few who thrive in this dark and ugly work. They overcome the disgust and revulsion of death and somewhere along the way learn to deal with their own mortality. They see the ease with which humans come and go in this world. I don't think it offers any real answers about what happens after we die, but someone who is surrounded by death in his or her professional life at least can make peace with the fact that it will happen. A homicide detective lives in the constant shadow of loss. There is the loss that the murder victim and his or her family members experience, of course. But the detectives lose something, too. Outside work, they try to live a normal life, putting behind them all the violence and perversity they see on the job. Their professional world is a place that people do not want to be reminded of—except within the very controlled environment of a

TV show, a movie, or even a true crime book. That world is an ugly place where children are raped and murdered, women are tortured and dismembered.

Someone must try to find answers, to take what remains and paint a methodical yet imprecise picture, a mosaic of human lust, vengeance, greed, envy, and every other reason that people find to kill. With each piece of evidence and every word that is spoken, the picture slowly takes shape. If the detective is lucky, that picture will be the portrait of a killer, but that picture won't tell the whole story. Though it might close the homicide case, it doesn't solve anything else.

This picture tells two different stories, each tragic in its own way. Robert Yates killed at least eighteen women, for reasons that will forever escape human comprehension. And ten of those women didn't have to die.

EPILOGUE

On October 19, 2000, Robert Yates pleaded guilty to thirteen counts of first-degree murder and one count of attempted first-degree murder.

As part of a plea bargain negotiated between Yates's public defender, Richard Fasy, and Spokane County prosecutor Steve Tucker, Yates agreed to confess to fourteen murders, plead guilty to thirteen of them, make a public apology in court, and reveal where the body of one of his victims was still buried.

Fasy and his associates led a small caravan of Spokane officials back to the former Yates residence, where, following a map Yates drew in jail, they discovered and dug up the remains of Melody Murfin. She had been buried six to eight inches deep in a flower bed outside Yates's bedroom. The bark and foliage from the flower bed matched samples found with other bodies. During the two months when the task force searched the house, they never thought to dig up the flower bed.

Later, Yates confessed to the following murders:

Susan Savage and Patrick Oliver, a young couple from Walla Walla who were shot to death while picnicking in 1975

Stacy Hawn, a Seattle prostitute found shot to death in
    rural Skagit County in 1998
Shannon Zielinski
Jennifer Joseph
Heather Hernandez
Darla Sue Scott
Shawn Johnson
Laurie Ann Wason
Shawn McClenahan
Sunny Oster
Linda Maybin
Michelyn Derning
Melody Murfin

He also confessed to the attempted murder of Christine
Smith.

Although Yates confessed to the murder of Shawn Mc-
Clenahan, he was not charged in that case. Prosecutors decided to hold the McClenahan murder back in case Yates
tries to recant his confessions or appeal his plea. The Mc-
Clenahan case was considered the strongest in terms of evidence, with a fingerprint, DNA, and other forensics
linking Yates to the murder.

On October 26, 2000, Yates was sentenced to 408 years
in prison and ordered to pay $620,000 in restitution.

Yates still faces charges in the murders of Melinda Mercer and Connie LaFontaine Ellis. Pierce County prosecutors have said that they will ask for the death penalty. Fasy
has already dropped hints that his client has more to tell
officials, in return for a reduction in charges.

In addition to several pending investigations in jurisdictions where Yates once resided, the following murders remain officially unsolved:

Yolanda Sapp
Nickie Lowe
Kathy Brisbois
Sherry Palmer
Patricia Barnes
JoAnn Flores

Yates has reportedly passed a polygraph test in which he was asked about his involvement in other murders, specifically the 1990 cases. Cal Walker has publicly stated that Yates is still a suspect in these murders—even though my source on the task force told me shortly after Yates's arrest that Walker and other investigators thought the 1990 cases were "drug related." Either way, Cal Walker is still on the job, and will probably be promoted to lieutenant.

Meanwhile, Washington State attorney general Christine Gregoire said of the Yates case: "We're not convinced we have all the victims."

And we probably never will. Over the next few months, and even years, Robert Yates may give us glimpses into the depth and extent of his pathology, but he will never give us the full picture. At one time there was evidence that could have led a dedicated and experienced homicide detective to solve each one of Yates's murders. Now it is too late. The trail is cold, the evidence either gone or compromised. Only Robert Yates knows exactly what he did. And when he dies, whether by execution or natural causes in prison, his secrets will die with him.

December 8, 2000

TIME LINE

February 22, 1990

Body of Yolanda Sapp found along the Spokane River near 4100 East Upriver Drive. Cause of death: gunshot wounds to chest.

March 25, 1990

Body of Nickie Lowe found draped over a guardrail under the Greene Street Bridge on 3100 East Upriver Drive near Spokane River. Cause of death: gunshot wound to lower chest.

May 15, 1990

Body of Kathy Brisbois found near the Spokane River south of the East 12300 block of Trent Avenue. Cause of death: multiple gunshot wounds to head and chest. Plastic bag with blood from victim found nearby.

Sometime in 1990

Task force assembled in Spokane to investigate murders. Worked for more than a year without producing an arrest.

May 12, 1992
   Body of Sherry Palmer found near Bill Gulch Road and Mount Spokane Drive. Cause of death: multiple gunshot wounds. Plastic bag on head.

August 25, 1995
   Body of Patricia Barnes found in 15900 block of Peacock Hill Road, Kitsap County, Washington. Cause of death: gunshot wounds. Plastic bag with hair curlers and blood from the victim found nearby.

April 1996
   Robert Yates leaves Army two years before retirement. Yates and family move to Spokane.

June 14, 1996
   Body of Shannon Zielinski found near Holcomb Road and Mount Spokane Drive. Body was badly decomposed. Could have been killed up to four weeks before discovery. Cause of death: gunshot wound to head.

November 7, 1996
   Body of JoAnn Flores found in an alley in the 200 block of West Riverside. Cause of death: gunshot wound to head.

August 16, 1997
   Jennifer Joseph last seen by Yolanda Carey at 11:35 P.M. Joseph was traveling eastbound on Sprague in a white Corvette driven by a white male between the ages of thirty and forty. Sometime after Joseph's death, Carey goes to police with this information.

August 26, 1997
   Body of Jennifer Joseph found near Forker and Judkins Roads. Cause of death: gunshot wound to chest.

Body of Heather Hernandez discovered in an overgrown lot behind the 1800 block of East Springfield. Cause of death: gunshot wound to head.

September 24, 1997
Robert Yates pulled over for committing traffic violation in vicinity of Sprague and Ralph, driving a white Corvette, at approximately 12:45 P.M. Officer Turman does not issue ticket, writes field interview form.

October 17, 1997
Body of Teresa-Lyn Asmussen found floating in the Spokane River near the Post Street Dam. Cause of death: cerebral contusions as a consequence of blunt impact injury to head. Classified as a homicide after an autopsy was performed.

October 29, 1997
Shawn Johnson reported missing.

November 3, 1997
Laurie Ann Wason reported missing.

November 5, 1997
Body of Darla Sue Scott found partially buried near the Hangman Valley Golf Course. Cause of death: gunshot wound to head. White plastic bag on head.

November 28, 1997
Robert Yates stopped in white Corvette by Washington State Patrol driving northbound on Highway 195. Issued a citation for speeding.

November 29, 1997
Linda Maybin reported missing.

December 7, 1997
Body of Melinda Mercer found by a transient in a weed-covered field near railroad tracks in south Tacoma. Cause of death: gunshot wounds to head. White plastic bag over head.

December 15, 1997
Last time Shawn McClenahan seen by her family.

December 18, 1997
Body of Shawn Johnson found in the 11400 block of South Hangman Valley Road near sewage treatment station, approximately one mile away from where Darla Sue Scott was found. Cause of death: gunshot wound to head. Plastic bag over head.

December 22, 1997
Police and sheriff's department administrators meet to establish a task force.

December 26, 1997
Body of Laurie Ann Wason found buried on top of body of Shawn McClenahan in a vacant gravel pit near Fourteenth Avenue and Carnahan Road in southeast Spokane. Cause of death: gunshot wound to head. Body in severe state of decomposition. Fully clothed with no shoes or socks. Plastic bag over head.

Body of Shawn McClenahan found in state of advanced decomposition, fully clothed with no shoes. Plastic bag over head. Cause of death: gunshot wound to head.

February 8, 1998
Body of Sunny Oster found on Graham Road 8/10 of a mile south of the intersection of Salnave Road in

Spokane County. Cause of death: gunshot wound to head. Clothed in green undergarment, dark blue sweater, gray pants. White plastic bag over head.

February 19–20, 1998
Area of Fourteenth Avenue and Carnahan Road searched by ground crews and helicopters. Other possible dump sites searched by helicopter.

April 1, 1998
Body of Linda Maybin found loosely buried in a ditch along Fourteenth and Carnahan. Cause of death: gunshot wound to head. Body clothed and partially decomposed. Evidence of animal predators. Plastic bag on head.

April 19, 1998
Human skeletal remains found by woman walking dog at northwest corner of Seventh and Sherman.

April 28, 1998
Doug Silver announces that deputies discovered two T-shirts and evidence of sexual activity near Fourteenth and Carnahan a week prior.

April 29, 1998
Pornographic video boxes found by local television reporter near Fourteenth and Carnahan.

May 20, 1998
Melody Ann Murfin last reported seen alive.

June 6, 1998
Murfin reported missing to authorities.

June 9, 1998
Body of woman found on Mount Spokane at Elliot and Wallis Roads. (At least one report of suspicious vehicle driving in the area—description not released by police.)

June 15, 1998
Decomposed body found in Spokane River near the Carousel, trapped beneath a floating catwalk just west of the Howard Street Bridge.

July 7, 1998
Body of Michelyn Derning found concealed under grass, a piece of styrofoam, and two hot tub covers in an overgrown field in the 200 block of North Crestline in east Spokane. Cause of death: gunshot wound to head. Derning was naked, and her bottom denture was missing. Authorities believe the body was dumped less than a week before it was found.

July 17, 1998
Spokane police "redouble efforts" to find Melody Murfin.

August 1, 1998
Spokane prostitute Christine Smith files police report for assault and robbery. Her assailant is described as a man about fifty years old, five feet ten, 175 pounds, with sandy blond hair. Smith tells police that she was struck in the head during a sex act. The assault occurred in a 1970s-era black van with an exterior yellow-orange stripe, bucket seats, interior wood paneling, and a raised bed. The suspect described himself as a National Guard helicopter pilot and father of five.

August 21, 1998

Body of twenty-one-year-old woman found in Tacoma. Gunshot to the head. Not linked to Spokane serial killings.

October 13, 1998

Body of Connie LaFontaine Ellis found in ditch along 108th Street in Parkland, near Tacoma. Cause of death: gunshot wound to head. Body fully clothed and barefoot, and in advanced state of decomposition. A .380 bullet was recovered at the scene. Ellis had been shot with a .25-caliber weapon.

October 23, 1998

Three hunters find skeletal remains of a sixteen-to-twenty-three-year-old black woman in Quincy Lakes Wildlife Refuge. Cause of death: gunshot wound to head. Time of death estimated sometime between April and date of discovery.

November 10, 1998

Robert Yates observed by police picking up prostitute Jennifer Robinson at First and Crestline. Officer Reynolds pulls over Yates's vehicle. Yates says that he was asked to give Robinson a drive home by her father. The contact is recorded on field interview form.

November 30, 1998

Spokane authorities unveil a billboard and bus advertisements showing the faces of sixteen female murder victims under the headline, "Help us find our killer!"

January 8, 1999

Connie LaFontaine Ellis officially declared a victim of Spokane Serial Killer.

March 7, 1999

Robert Yates observed patronizing a prostitute at First and Scott in Spokane. His license plate number is noted and given to police.

April 14, 1999

Spokane Task Force searches home and vehicle of a doctor, calling him a "person of interest" in the serial killer case because of his possible involvement in the assault and robbery of a Spokane prostitute.

April 27, 1999

Badly decomposed body of Jennifer Diane Justus, twenty-six, found by dog near Snoqualmie.

May 4, 1999

Doug Silver says "there's nothing obvious" linking Justus to serial killer, even though Justus fits the profile, with arrests for prostitution, drugs, and theft in Seattle area.

May 7, 1999

Body of Lilla Faye Moler found in Portland's Forest Park. Cause of death: strangulation. Had been in park for up to two months.

While searching the park, police find the body of Stephanie Lynn Russell. Cause of death: strangulation. Russell was likely killed within a week of being found.

May 12, 1999

Spokane Task Force asks Alabama investigators to question a "person of interest" there.

June 2, 1999

Body of Alexandra Nicole Ison found in Portland's Forest Park. Cause of death: strangulation. Portland police

chief announces task force of twelve detectives assigned
to solve three murders. A little more than a month later,
the Portland Task Force arrests a suspect. The killings
are unconnected to the Spokane homicides.

June 10, 1999

Sheriff Mark Sterk tells Mark Fuhrman and Stephen
Weeks that the task force is "sitting around, waiting for
another body." According to Sterk, the task force will be
dismantled in the fall if they don't get a break in the
case.

September 15, 1999

Robert Yates is interviewed by task force detectives
Grabenstein and Bentley at Public Safety Building. They
ask him for a blood sample. Yates says he has to talk to
his wife.

September 18, 1999

Robert Yates leaves a message for Grabenstein on his
phone-mail system, saying that he will not voluntarily
provide a sample of his blood.

December 24, 1999

Spokane PD pulls its five detectives from the task force.

January 7, 2000

Rita Jones, new owner of Yates's white Corvette, is contacted by Detective Grabenstein. She is told that her car
once belonged to a suspect in the serial killings. She al-
lows Grabenstein to remove samples of carpet fiber
from the interior of the Corvette.

February 28, 2000

The task force holds a town meeting. Sheriff Sterk
promises they will find the killer.

March 2000

Christine Smith is involved in car accident. Doctors find bullet fragments embedded in her scalp.

April 5, 2000

Washington State Patrol Crime Lab discovers match between fibers found with Jennifer Joseph's body and those in Corvette once owned by Robert Yates.

April 10, 2000

Detective Grabenstein prepares a search warrant for the Corvette. The search is executed and several items of potential evidence are secured.

April 18, 2000

Robert Yates arrested on one count of first-degree murder, charged with the homicide of Jennifer Joseph.

Christine Smith sees photograph of Yates in newspaper and identifies him as her assailant in August 1998.

April 25, 2000

A fingerprint found on the plastic bag covering Shawn McClenahan's head is matched to Robert Yates.

May 10, 2000

Police search Yates's black 1979 Ford van, which has bucket seats, wood paneling, and a raised bed. An exterior yellow-orange stripe had been covered with black paint. Numerous bloodstains are found inside, as well as a .25-caliber bullet casing and a spent bullet in the van's roof.

May 18, 2000

Prosecutors file seven additional counts of first-degree murder against Yates, citing robbery as an aggravating circumstance that warrants the death penalty. They also file one count of first-degree attempted murder and attempted first-degree theft in the Christine Smith incident.

May 31, 2000
Robert Yates arraigned on eight counts of murder and one count of robbery and attempted murder. He pleads not guilty.

October 19, 2000
Robert Yates pleads guilty to thirteen counts of murder to avoid the death penalty. In the agreement with prosecutors, Yates has to disclose the location of Melody Murfin's body. Murfin's body is found buried in a shallow grave next to Yates's home.

October 26, 2000
Robert Yates sentenced to 408 years in jail.

INDEX